DRAWING NEAR
A DAILY EXPEDITION

Mark,

Maximize every moment God gives you to know Him more intimately!

Stephen
Heb. 4:16

DR. STEPHEN TRAMMELL

DRAWING NEAR
A DAILY EXPEDITION

DR. STEPHEN TRAMMELL

Copyright © 2012 Stephen Trammell

All Rights Reserved

Published in the United States by Champion Forest Baptist Church, Houston, TX
www.championforest.org

Scripture taken from the Holy Bible, New International Version®, NIV®

Copyright© 1973, 1978, 1984 by Biblica, Inc.™

Used by permission of Zondervan. All rights reserved worldwide.
WWW.ZONDERVAN.COM

The "NIV" and "New International Version" are trademarks registered in the United States Patent and Trademark Offices by Biblica, Inc.

Book design by Jacque Sellers

Cataloging-in-Publication Data

Trammell, Stephen.

    Drawing Near : a daily expedition/by Stephen Trammell.

        384 p. 22 cm.

    Summary: 365-day devotional designed to enhance the reader's daily walk with God.

    ISBN 978-0-982-6630-4-2 (pbk.)

    1. Devotional Calendars. 2. Devotions, Daily.
    3. Devotional Literature. 4. Spiritual Growth. 5. Meditations.
    6. God-Meditations. 7. Discipleship. 8. Prayer Books and Devotions.
    I. Title.

242.2 –dc22

DEDICATION

*To my precious Champion Forest Baptist Church family,
an irresistible influence for God's glory.*

FOREWORD

A daily "quiet time" is a precious gift from our Heavenly Father. A friend once said to me, "It's difficult to find time for a quiet time every day." The book you now hold in your hand is the "perfect tool" to help you have a daily time with God. The author is well qualified to assist you in such a daily time, because he maintains a quiet time of his own. This book will help you develop your own daily time with the Heavenly Father, and you will find it to be your own "precious gift" from God.

Stephen is a warm, sincere minister whose heart and life is dedicated to serving God and sharing His Word. Often I have seen him at the restaurant leave a tip on the table along with a tract presenting the plan of salvation… he is genuine.

In using this book you will find steps that will draw you closer to the Father. It will also be helpful as you make your daily journey a closer walk. I am sure that is Stephen's objective in writing this devotional guide. I believe it will do just that, draw you closer to God.

My prayer for you is this: As you read these Bible verses and devotional thoughts, your days will be sweeter and more secure.

Rev. Wallace B. Cobb
Pastor of Pastoral Ministries (Ret.)
Champion Forest Baptist Church
Houston, Texas

ACKNOWLEDGMENTS

I recently celebrated my five-year anniversary serving on the amazing team at Champion Forest Baptist Church. It is such a joy to wake up each day and head to the office to serve alongside such servants of God. My best friend and our Senior Pastor, Dr. David Fleming, embodies a passion for preaching God's Word and keeping us on mission to fulfill the Great Commission. I appreciate his unyielding support of my writing ministry and for allowing me to maximize my gifts and abilities for God's glory.

A vibrant commitment to Christ is a common denominator among our staff, deacons, and church members. I am thankful for their commitment to help all kinds of people make sense out of life through Christ-centered living.

God fashioned a dream team to make this project a reality: Chris Todd, Lee Harn, Joey Mouton, and Jacque Sellers. Jacque designed the cover and the interior layout. She is truly gifted by God and constantly amazes us by her creativity.

I want to say a special thank you to my administrative assistant, Mary Shemroske. She has the unique gifting of being extremely organized and creative. I appreciate Mary's vibrant work ethic and her passion for excellence. She is a delight and ensures our office efficiency. Thank you for investing in this project.

The Lord blessed with me a godly mother, Judy Trammell, who consistently models the value of serving God through the local church. Her commitment to the Lord has inspired me for over four decades.

Now to the love of my life for over twenty-one years, I want to express my appreciation to Tonya. Thank you for the countless sacrifices you have made to allow me to lead our family to be in the center of God's will. You have always demonstrated a deep abiding commitment to Christ and our marriage. Thank you for making room in our marriage and family for my writing ministry. I am grateful to God for you and your unconditional love. To my children, Tori and Austin, you lavish the landscape of life with your love. I am so proud to be your daddy. Continue to walk with God and make wise decisions.

DRAWING NEAR
INTRODUCTION

My parents divorced when I was seven years old. That interruption generated the opportunity to search for a father who would never let me down. The pain of my parents' divorce produced in me the desire to find security, meaning, and purpose in life. After being exposed to the Good News of Jesus in my home, through my church, Horseshoe Drive Baptist Church, and through interactions with other Christians, the divine transaction took place on March 28, 1979. I made the decision to turn from my sin and to trust in Christ alone for salvation. That was my conversion experience that changed my eternal destiny. I was instantly adopted into God's family, forgiven of my sin, and filled with the Holy Spirit. I became a child of God.

Since my day of salvation, God has placed me on a journey of growing in my love relationship with Jesus. Day-by-day over the past thirty-three years, I have had the privilege of walking with God. The most prominent spiritual discipline has been that of having a daily quiet time. Spending time alone each day with the Lord through unhurried and unbroken fellowship has transformed my life. Reading and feeding on God's Word intentionally and consistently has conformed me into the image of Christ.

Can you fathom the privilege you have to commune with the Creator of the universe? God invites you into this journey by trusting in Jesus alone for salvation and then growing in your relationship with Him through daily communion. You determine the level of intimacy with God. "Come near to God and he will come near to you" (James 4:8 NIV). Will you maximize the opportunity God gives you each day to know Him personally and intimately?

If you are a morning person, wake up earlier than usual and carve out some precious uninterrupted time to spend time with the Lord reading His Word and praying. If you are a night owl, consider staying up later to spend time alone with God. Make room in your life and in your schedule for the spiritual discipline of a daily quiet time.

Be proactive. Prepare for your daily time alone with God. As you draw near to God, select a specific place where you can enjoy unhurried time alone with Him. Let this become your place of prayer. Develop and implement a plan for your daily quite time. You may want to choose to read a devotional entry for the specific date from this devotional book each day, then open God's Word and read through a book of the Bible. You can read one chapter per day or step up to the challenge of reading four chapters each day so that you can read through the Bible in one year.

The key is to feed on God's Word. Don't rush your reading time. Let God speak to you through His abiding Word. God wants to reveal Himself to you. Make room for the encounter.

As you pray, you can pray aloud, pray silently, or write your prayers. It is a healthy discipline to occasionally write down your prayers. It will help to keep your mind focused and will allow for meaningful dialogue with God.

You may want to incorporate the spiritual discipline of journaling. You can journal your journey with God by writing down the verses God uses to speak to you. Write down some general observations about those verses and then write a specific application related to what you sense God is saying to you. Having a journal is a wonderful tool use in order to review God's activity in your life. Get personal by writing down your questions, your struggles, your victories, and your spiritual markers.

Drawing near to God is the most important decision you will make each day. Your vertical relationship with God will determine your horizontal interactions and influence. Keep your love relationship with the Lord your top priority. Guard your daily intimacy with God. Enjoy the journey!

Drawing Near,
Stephen

January 1
SPIRIT-FILLED FAITH

"And without faith it is impossible to please God, because anyone who comes to him must believe that he exists and that he rewards those who earnestly seek him." Heb 11:6 (NIV)

This is your fresh start. You have a clean canvas for God to apply the paint of His plan for you this year. Let go of last year and latch onto this new year of untapped potential. God has doors for you to walk through, bridges for you to cross, and experiences for you to embrace.

Faith is the key that unlocks God's plan for your life. Without faith, you cannot please God. Make His smile your goal as you exhibit Spirit-filled faith. The great adventure of the life God has for you is right in front of you. Do you believe that God exists? Do you have a personal relationship with God through Christ? Then you have the faith that unleashes God's power and the faith that illuminates the path God has for you.

Earnestly seek the Lord. Passionately pursue Him daily through your Spirit-filled faith. You can look in the rear view mirror of life to trace God's faithfulness in your past. Revisit the spiritual markers that remind you of God's abundant provision. Recall all that God has done to bring you this far. Celebrate each victory!

Now look to the future through the eyes of faith to see where God wants you to join Him in His activity. Leave room for mystery. God wants you to walk with Him daily and to trust Him completely. God may take you places you have never been.

Stay close and clean. Keep your love relationship with the Lord your top priority. Enlarge your Spirit-filled faith through daily intimacy with God. Draw near to Him each day and enjoy His abiding Presence. Seize God's invitation to join Him in His activity. God loves you!

January 2
SINCERE INTEGRITY

"And David shepherded them with integrity of heart; with skillful hands he led them." Psalm 78:72 (NIV)

Does the tongue in your mouth line up with the tongue in your shoe? Is your talk in alignment with your walk? If so, that's integrity! Honesty and truthfulness are garments that every child of God should feature. To be a person of integrity is to be honest about who you are and truthful in your conversation and your conduct.

Perhaps you know of people who are loaded with talent, but lack integrity. In many cases, their talent took them farther than their character could sustain them. We have watched countless talented men and women fall into grave immorality due to the lack of integrity.

In God's economy, talent and skill are insufficient without integrity. God wants us to use the gifts and abilities He has blessed us with through the avenue of integrity. The level of our integrity determines the veracity of our testimony. Purity, honesty, and authenticity are vital components for the person God uses. Sincere integrity is crucial for being on mission with God in a corrupt world.

King David was not perfect. He made some poor choices and leveraged his position to indulge his sinful appetite. Yet, in brokenness and humility, he confessed his sin and received God's forgiveness. David shepherded the people with integrity. He led the people with skillful hands. God's grace was more than sufficient for the race. David learned to depend upon God and to trust in His daily provision.

If God can make someone like King David into a man after God's own heart, then there's hope for us. We can walk in integrity through our daily dependence upon God. Without His ample supply of grace, we have no chance of living a life of integrity. Let's surrender completely to the Lord's control and allow Him to live His life of integrity through us.

January 3
Unrelenting Pursuit

"I want to know Christ and the power of his resurrection and the fellowship of sharing in his sufferings, becoming like him in his death, and so, somehow, to attain to the resurrection from the dead." Phil 3:10-11 (NIV)

What makes you come alive? What are you passionate about? What gets your focus, attention, and energy? Paul was clear about the pursuit of his life. God had radically transformed his life on the road to Damascus and called him to a life of dangerous surrender.

In his letter to the church at Philippi, Paul gave insight to his unrelenting pursuit of knowing Christ. His passion was to know Christ more. Paul desired to take his love relationship with Christ to a deeper level. He wanted to personally know the power of Christ's resurrection and the fellowship of sharing in Christ's sufferings. Paul was not satisfied with religion and routine. He passionately desired the real, authentic, and vibrant love relationship with Christ that no other relationship could offer. Assess your pursuit. Are there fragments of apathy and lethargy? Have you been distracted by worldliness or worry? Living in a fallen world can dilute your passion for the things of God. Recognize those things in your life that have stifled your spiritual appetite. Remove those things that have usurped your hunger and thirst for God.

You determine the level of your pursuit of knowing Jesus more. Be unrelenting in your pursuit of a vibrant and growing love relationship with Christ. Emulate Paul's passion to know Christ and the power of His resurrection and the fellowship of sharing in His sufferings. Return to your first love. Guard your heart and passionately pursue Christ!

January 4
ASSESSING YOUR CURRENT REALITY

"Not that I have already obtained all this, or have already been made perfect, but I press on to take hold of that for which Christ Jesus took hold of me."
Phil 3:12 (NIV)

Do you know where you are spiritually? Have you identified your current reality? Paul knew where he was and where he was not. He understood that he was still in the process of becoming more like Christ. Paul had not arrived and was not ready to declare perfection.

One mark of maturity is recognizing your personal spiritual status. Being able to identify the reality of your spiritually is an important aspect of becoming like Christ. You are in the process of becoming who you are in Christ. You are still in motion. You have not crossed the finish line.

At the moment of your salvation, you received the Spirit of Christ (Rom. 8:9). You were adopted into God's forever family. You were justified (Rom. 5:1). Now you are on the path of sanctification. You are in the maturation marathon. Moment-by-moment as you recognize your current reality and your dependency upon the Holy Spirit, you have the opportunity for the character of Christ to be formed in you. You participate with God in working out what He has worked in (Php. 2:12).

Assess your current reality. Are you becoming more like Christ each day? Are you on a path to spiritual maturity? Is the character of Christ being formed in you? God does not want you to be spiritually stagnant or lethargic. God does not want you to settle for mediocrity or to be at ease in Zion (Amos 6:1). Reject passivity and take responsibility for your spiritual maturity. Employ daily spiritual disciplines, engage in weekly small group Bible study, and experience weekly corporate worship with other believers.

January 5
FINDING THAT ONE THING

"Brothers, I do not consider myself yet to have taken hold of it. But one thing I do: Forgetting what is behind and straining toward what is ahead, I press on toward the goal to win the prize for which God has called me heavenward in Christ Jesus." Phil 3:13-14 (NIV)

Life is full of distractions. There are so many tugs on our lives coming from various directions. We daily combat the gravitational pull of the flesh, the world, and the devil. Countless opportunities to disobey God await our attention. Living the Christian life in a fallen world requires us to live on purpose and with intentionality.

Paul consolidated his energy to focus on one thing. He disciplined his life to release the past and to embrace the future God had for him. For Paul, his past was relegated to oblivion. He purposefully let go of the past and invested his life in the future God had ordained for him.

You have to decide how you will live each day. Being engulfed with past failures and past successes can keep you from seizing the life God has for you. Focus on this one thing: release the past and embrace the future God has in front of you. God will empower you to do this one thing. God will enable you to concentrate on His agenda. Tenacity, focus, and persistence are necessary to release the past and to march into your destiny.

God saved you and filled you with His Holy Spirit so that you can live for His global glory. God wants you to experience His daily provision and to encounter His abiding Presence. What is keeping you from letting go of your past? What is keeping you from walking in the forgiveness God has extended to you? Be forgiven and take possession of the land God is giving you.

January 6
Intentional Love

"But the chief priests stirred up the crowd to have Pilate release Barabbas instead." Mark 15:11 (NIV)

Have you ever encountered injustice? Have you ever been treated unfairly? I think we have all been there. It hurts! The scars serve as a constant reminder. In our verse today, we find a word that compels us to contemplate. It is the soothing word, "instead." Let me take this punishment instead of you. Allow me to receive this penalty instead of you.

Jesus will be flogged and crucified instead of Barabbas. The innocent man dies in his place. The guilty man goes free. Jesus receives what He doesn't deserve while Barabbas receives what he doesn't deserve. Jesus receives death! Barabbas receives life! Is that justice? Should the guilty go free?

God's intentional love was clearly displayed. God took the initiative to come to our rescue. "But God demonstrates his own love for us in this: While we were still sinners, Christ died for us" (Romans 5:8 NIV). Christ died instead of us! Yes, while we were still sinners! How can you demonstrate that kind of love? Who in your sphere of influence needs to know what instead looks like?

Forgive instead of holding a grudge. Show acceptance instead of forging a gap. Offer help instead of ignoring the need. Appreciate Jesus instead of taking Him for granted. It's your move!

January 7
BE TENACIOUS

"Josiah removed all the detestable idols from all the territory belonging to the Israelites, and he had all who were present in Israel serve the LORD their God. As long as he lived, they did not fail to follow the LORD, the God of their fathers."
2 Chron 34:33 (NIV)

Be tenacious.

God used Josiah to bring forth a reformation in Israel. Here are a few of the reformation verbs found in II Kings 22-23 and II Chronicles 34-35: removed, burned, did away with, took, ground it to powder, scattered, tore, desecrated, pulled down, smashed, cut down, covered, defiled, slaughtered, got rid of, purged, cut to pieces, broke to pieces, tore down, and crushed. Josiah was willing to tenaciously follow God's lead and remove all the detestable idols.

Like his great-grandfather, Hezekiah, Josiah cleansed the nation of idolatry, repaired the temple, restored the worship, and celebrated a great nationwide Passover. Josiah tenaciously renewed the Covenant and reformed the culture.

What is keeping you from reaching your God-given potential? What are you giving your life to? Where does your life give evidence of tenaciously following God's lead?

God placed you right where you are so that you could be an irresistible influence for His glory. God allowed you to wake up this morning so that you could spread the aroma of Christ through your conversation and your conduct. God did not call you to reflect the environment, but to set the environment. God did not save you so that you would embrace the way of the world. God saved you so that you would tenaciously follow the way of Christ.

January 8
BE TEACHABLE

"Josiah was eight years old when he became king, and he reigned in Jerusalem thirty-one years. He did what was right in the eyes of the LORD and walked in the ways of his father David, not turning aside to the right or to the left." 2 Chron 34:1-2 (NIV)

Be Teachable.

Can you imagine an eight-year-old child becoming the President of the United States of America? That's hard to fathom. Yet, in the sovereignty of God, Josiah became the king of Judah when he was the tender age of eight. God enabled Josiah to reign for thirty-one years.

How does an eight-year-old rule his kingdom? He doesn't by himself. Josiah surrounds himself with people who can help. He willingly brings people around him who can do what he can't and who can exercise gifts that he may not personally have. Josiah becomes an effective king by being teachable. Josiah allows others to speak into his life.

You need four people in your life to help you reach your God-given potential. You need a "Paul" who will mentor you. You need a "Timothy" to invest your life in. You need a "Barnabas" to encourage you and to bring out the best in you. And you need a "Nathan" to speak the truth in love to you.

Are you teachable? Do you allow God to stretch you and mold you and grow you? Are you willing to allow others to get close enough to you in order to learn from them?

Ask God to bring a Paul, a Timothy, a Barnabas, and a Nathan into your life. Be willing to be a Paul, to be a Timothy, to be a Barnabas, and to be a Nathan in someone's life. Seek to add value to others as you allow the life of Christ to be expressed through you.

January 9
BE THIRSTY

"In the eighth year of his reign, while he was still young, he began to seek the God of his father David." 2 Chron 34:3 (NIV)

Be thirsty.

What caused Josiah, at the age of sixteen, to begin to seek God? When you look at his family tree, you find that both his father, Amon, and his grandfather, Manasseh, did evil in the eyes of the Lord. It is obvious that Josiah did not receive his spiritual heritage from them. When you look into the life of his great-grandfather, Hezekiah, you find a much different portrait.

- *"Hezekiah was twenty-five years old when he became king, and he reigned in Jerusalem twenty-nine years. His mother's name was Abijah daughter of Zechariah. He did what was right in the eyes of the LORD, just as his father David had done."* 2 Chron 29:1-2 (NIV)

I wonder if Josiah was influenced by the godly life that his great-grandfather, Hezekiah, lived. Another possibility is that Josiah began to seek God when he became a daddy, at the age of sixteen, to Jehoahaz. For me personally, when I became a daddy my understanding of God's love and my pursuit of God intensified. There's something about seeing your own flesh and blood and embracing the awesome responsibility of parenthood that draws you to God. You recognize your dependency upon God.

Regardless of your age or life stage, assess your level of thirst for God? Are you passionately seeking God daily and allowing Him to have full access to your mind, emotions, and will? Is there anything or anyone you desire more than you desire God? Make Jesus your top priority. Draw near to Him.

January 10
BE TENDER

"Tell the king of Judah, who sent you to inquire of the LORD, 'This is what the LORD, the God of Israel, says concerning the words you heard: Because your heart was responsive and you humbled yourself before the LORD when you heard what I have spoken against this place and its people, that they would become accursed and laid waste, and because you tore your robes and wept in my presence, I have heard you, declares the LORD.'" 2 Kings 22:18-19 (NIV)

Be tender.

At the age of twenty-six, Josiah encountered the reading of the Book of the Law. Though he was a king, Josiah allowed the Word of the Lord to impact his life. Instead of seeking to get God's Word to conform to his life, Josiah conformed his life to the Word of God.

- *"But the one who received the seed that fell on good soil is the man who hears the word and understands it. He produces a crop, yielding a hundred, sixty or thirty times what was sown."* Matt 12:23 (NIV)
- *"All Scripture is God-breathed and is useful for teaching, rebuking, correcting and training in righteousness, so that the man of God may be thoroughly equipped for every good work."* 2 Tim 3:16-17 (NIV)

Do you read the Bible? When you read the Bible, are you allowing God's Word to take root in your life? Are you tender towards God and sensitive to what He speaks into your life? Jesus wants us to move from being hearers of the Word only, to being doers of the Word.

Is your heart responsive to God's Word? How do you respond? Have you allowed God's Word to affect you emotionally and intellectually? Strive to have a consistent daily intake of God's Word. A healthy daily discipline is to read four chapters of the Bible each day. In one year, you will have read through the entire Bible.

January 11
START YOUR DAY WITH GOD

"But you are a chosen people, a royal priesthood, a holy nation, a people belonging to God, that you may declare the praises of him who called you out of darkness into his wonderful light." 1 Peter 2:9 (NIV)

If you have become a child of God through faith in Jesus alone, then you are a priest before God. Your new identity in Christ has given you direct access to God. You do not need to go through a human mediator. The priesthood of every believer is the reality for those adopted into God's forever family.

As a priest before God, start your day with God. Make it your daily spiritual discipline to start your day with the One who saved you. Do as Jesus did during His earthly ministry. "Very early in the morning, while it was still dark, Jesus got up, left the house and went off to a solitary place, where he prayed" (Mark 1:35 NIV). Carve out time to start your day with your Creator. No one knows you as intimately as God does. No one loves you as intensely as God does. You are His treasure.

Start your day with God by feeding on His Word, communing with Him in prayer, and receiving His daily provision. Guard your daily intimacy with the Lord. You will have to strive to protect this most important daily spiritual discipline. Many other things will tug at your time, energy, and attention.

What needs to change in your daily routine in order to start your day with God? Have you found a place to have your time alone with God without interruption? Prepare for this daily spiritual discipline. Develop a plan for reading through the Bible. Try to read at least one chapter from the Bible each morning. Remember, if you choose to read four chapters each day, you will read through the entire Bible in one year.

January 12
MAKE ROOM FOR MARRIAGE

"However, each one of you also must love his wife as he loves himself, and the wife must respect her husband." Eph 5:33 (NIV)

Being selfish requires no effort. Selfishness comes naturally to us. If we aren't careful, we will operate our lives on the assumption that life revolves around us. Being self-centered and self-absorbed is the antithesis of marriage. In the marriage relationship, the husband and wife must release selfishness and embrace selflessness.

The husband is to love his wife as he loves himself. The wife is to respect her husband. In his book, Love and Respect, Dr. Emerson Eggerichs identifies what he calls the Crazy Cycle: "When a husband feels disrespected, he has a natural tendency to react in ways that feel unloving to his wife. When a wife feels unloved, she has a natural tendency to react in ways that feel disrespectful to her husband."

Our culture is not marriage-friendly. The pace of life and the demands on our time can strain a marriage relationship. As a partner, you have to make room for marriage. You have to conscientiously and intentionally make room for the one you love. In order to have a healthy, vibrant, and growing marriage, you have to create space for the relationship. It takes time to nurture a meaningful relationship with your spouse.

Busyness is the prominent enemy to intimacy. We divert our energy to parenting, to our career, to recreation, and to other things to the neglect of our marriage relationship. It is so easy to neglect the sacred union God calls us to with our spouse. We can give our best to others and give our spouse the crumbs. That's a recipe for an unhealthy marriage. Remember, you will make room for what you value!

January 13
Model What You Want to Multiply

"Be imitators of God, therefore, as dearly loved children and live a life of love, just as Christ loved us and gave himself up for us as a fragrant offering and sacrifice to God." Eph 5:1-2 (NIV)

Did you know that you will multiply what you model? Now that is convicting! That means that it truly does matter how you live your life. It truly matters how you conduct your daily living. Your beliefs and your behavior both matter to God and impact others. So how do you live a life of love? Imitate God!

Maybe you have heard parents remark that they want you to do as they say and not as they do. Of course, you would define that behavior as hypocrisy. God wants us to live in such a way that we encourage others to do as we say and as we do. We are to strive to live in such a way that the way we live lines up with what we say.

What kind of love does God want you to model? God wants you to model sincere love. God wants you to set an example for others to follow. In other words, be a model to follow. Model the kind of life that draws others to Christ. Live the kind of life that models the fruit of the Spirit: love, joy, peace, patience, kindness, goodness, faithfulness, gentleness, and self-control.

What are you multiplying? You know the answer: whatever you are modeling. Model what you want to multiply. May your children and those in your sphere of influence become fully devoted followers of Christ as a result of the sincere faith and love that you are modeling before them!

January 14
LIVE TO BENEFIT OTHERS

"Do nothing out of selfish ambition or vain conceit, but in humility consider others better than yourselves. Each of you should look not only to your own interests, but also to the interests of others." Phil 2:3-4 (NIV)

Have you ever written a mission statement for your own life? Let me share a few personal mission statements I have seen. I exist to love God and to love others. I exist to know Jesus and to make Jesus known. I exist to leave the world a better place than I found it. I exist to take as many people with me to heaven as possible.

God re-created you in Christ to reorient your life from selfish ambition to selfless ambition. Instead of living to benefit yourself, God empowers you to live to benefit others. When pride seeps in, your ability to serve others erodes. In humility, you consider others better than yourself. In humility, you esteem others above yourself.

Are you looking to the interests of others? Have you considered how you can invest in others? God has blessed you in Christ to be a blessing to others. You have been planted right where you are by God so that you can bloom for His glory and for the benefit of those in your sphere of influence. In humility, serve them. In humility, love them the way Jesus loves you.

What if you adopted the following mission statement? I exist to bring glory to God by living to benefit others. How would that impact your relationships? How would that affect your attitude about waking up each day? You would be living on purpose and on mission with God. You would begin to see your home, your neighborhood, your campus, your place of employment, and your sphere of influence as your mission field.

Start today! Bring glory to God by living to benefit others!

January 15
NURTURE PHYSICAL HEALTH

"Do you not know that your body is a temple of the Holy Spirit, who is in you, whom you have received from God? You are not your own; you were bought at a price. Therefore honor God with your body." 1 Cor 6:19-20 (NIV)

You are the walking tabernacle of the Presence of God. God has chosen to take up residence in your body by the indwelling of the Holy Spirit. Everywhere you go, the Holy Spirit goes with you because He is living inside of you. Your body is His temple.

As the temple of the Holy Spirit, how should you live? Your lifestyle should be consistent with the Person living inside of you. You are to embrace a lifestyle of holiness, righteousness, and godliness.

As the temple of the Holy Spirit, you should also nurture physical health. Take care of your physical body. Eat properly, exercise regularly, and rest thoroughly. When it comes to eating properly, there are so many options and opportunities to satisfy your appetite in an unhealthy manner. It takes discipline to make wise choices when it comes to deciding what kind of food to eat.

God has designed the human body to respond to physical exertion. When you exercise regularly, your body is strengthened and your energy level elevates. Honoring God with your body includes executing an intentional plan for physical fitness. God created your body to move. As you move, you benefit your physical health.

You also nurture physical health through resting thoroughly. It is possible to sleep and not rest. Your body needs a daily pit stop. You honor God with your body as you allow time for your body to rest, recharge, and rejuvenate. God replenishes your mind, your emotions, and your muscles as you rest. What adjustments do you need to make to nurture physical health?

January 16
NURTURE A CREATIVE SOUL

"Dear friend, I pray that you may enjoy good health and that all may go well with you, even as your soul is getting along well." 3 John 1:2 (NIV)

How's the condition of your soul? Are you at peace? Are you living a life of balance? In order to nurture a creative soul, you have to provide space in your schedule and you have to provide pause in your pace. The Christian life is not a sprint; it is a marathon. To finish strong you must consistently nurture a creative soul.

Create margin in your life. You need space to allow God to put you back together. Margin is the space between your load and your limit. Designate time in your schedule to participate in life-giving activities that replenish your soul. If you like reading, then allocate time for reading. If you enjoy walking outdoors, then carve out time for that life-giving experience. You must find what makes you come alive. You must insert those activities into your schedule that enable you to get your fire back and your passion rekindled.

- "Find rest, O my soul, in God alone; my hope comes from him." Psalm 62:5 (NIV)
- "When anxiety was great within me, your consolation brought joy to my soul." Psalm 94:19 (NIV)

Sometimes the most spiritual activity you can employ is rest. When you rest, you allow your soul to catch up with your body. Strategically insert a pause in your pace. Stop periodically to be still before the Lord and allow Him to restore your soul and to restore the joy of His salvation.

Assess your current reality to identify where you are overextended and overcommitted. If you are feeling overwhelmed and burnout in life, then something is out of order. Take the initiative to nurture a creative soul.

January 17
God's Restoration Plan

"And I heard a loud voice from the throne saying, 'Now the dwelling of God is with men, and he will live with them. They will be his people, and God himself will be with them and be their God. He will wipe every tear from their eyes. There will be no more death or mourning or crying or pain, for the old order of things has passed away.'" Rev 21:3-4 (NIV)

You are not a robot. God created you with the capacity to accept His plan or to reject His plan. He made you to be relational. You can respond to God's offer of restoration or you can choose to go your own way.

God grants the freedom to accept Him or reject Him. By the power of His Holy Spirit, He comforts and convicts. He guides and He provides. However, God will allow you the freedom to choose a selfish path or a selfless path. He will alert you when you are taking a path that is not His best for you. Yet, God will allow you to maneuver in the direction of your choice.

The prodigal son made a poor decision when he selfishly requested his share of the estate so that he could carelessly spend it. Yet, God allowed him to get to the pigpen level of living. It was there that the prodigal son came to his senses and made the life-giving decision to get up and go back to his father (Luke 15:17-20).

Restoration awaits! How will you respond to God's offer?

January 18
Taking the Next Step

"The LORD had said to Abram, 'Leave your country, your people and your father's household and go to the land I will show you.'" Gen 12:1 (NIV)

What is keeping you from obeying God? Do you fear the unknown? Are you uncomfortable making a move without having more information? Maybe God has chosen to limit His revelation to match your obedience. Once you obey what He has already said, then He will show you the next step.

- *"So Abram left, as the LORD had told him; and Lot went with him. Abram was seventy-five years old when he set out from Haran."* Gen 12:4 (NIV)

Abram took God at His word! He simply obeyed God. God told Abram to leave and go to a land that He would show him. Guess what? Abram left, as the Lord told him. He obeyed.

You can never go wrong obeying God. His way is always the best way. Even when it doesn't make sense or seem remotely logical, God's way is the right way. If you are confused about your next step, just obey what He has already said. Start there!

Identify what you are wrestling with right now? What is keeping you from taking the next step? Place that fear or frustration before the Lord in prayer and see how He helps you take the next step. You can trust God with your present circumstances and your future hopes and dreams.

January 19
SEEING THE UNSEEN

"Then the word of the LORD came to him: 'This man will not be your heir, but a son coming from your own body will be your heir.' He took him outside and said, 'Look up at the heavens and count the stars--if indeed you can count them.' Then he said to him, 'So shall your offspring be.'" Gen 15:4-5 (NIV)

Sometimes life can be foggy. You try to make sense out of what you don't know and out of what you can't see. You look back to review where you have been and identify the spiritual markers in your past. Being confident of God's faithfulness, you look into the fog knowing that God is up to something.

Abraham was in one of those foggy seasons where his current reality just didn't make sense. He was past age and Sarah was barren, yet God promised to make Abraham into a great nation. In God's perfect timing, the fog began to lift as He took Abraham outside to look up at the heavens and count the stars. Then God promised that Abraham's offspring would be as numerous as the stars.

As you walk with God, you will go through seasons of uncertainty and seasons of silence. When that happens, recapture that last thing God said to you and obey Him. Walk in the light God gives you until He shows you the next step He has for you. In God's perfect timing, the fog will lift and you will be able to see clearly.

Trust God to build the bridges that He wants you to cross and to open the doors that He wants you to walk through. Don't be so preoccupied with the destination that you bypass the beauty of experiencing God in the journey. Discover the joy of the journey.

January 20
BEING GOD'S CONDUIT OF BLESSING

"The Scripture foresaw that God would justify the Gentiles by faith, and announced the gospel in advance to Abraham: 'All nations will be blessed through you.' So those who have faith are blessed along with Abraham, the man of faith." Gal 3:8-9 (NIV)

The gospel begins with God. God is the Creator of life and the initiator of reconciliation. The grace of God has been poured out on us. God is the lover who persistently and consistently seeks to restore those who have fallen. God's love is unconditional and His mercy is unleashed to redeem us.

God chose to announce the gospel in advance to Abraham. God enabled Abraham to become a conduit of the blessing God has for all nations. Abraham was blessed by God to be a blessing to all people groups. As a man of faith, Abraham believed God.

God blesses you with salvation so that you can be a blessing to all nations. God redeemed you so that you can join Him in bringing redemption to all people groups on our planet. God's abundant love and forgiveness is available to all. Will you be a conduit of God's blessing?

You can pray. You can give. You can go. You can radiate God's love through your conversation and your conduct. You can join God in His redemptive activity by seizing every opportunity God gives you to make Jesus known. Begin viewing people through the lens of the gospel. As a recipient of the gospel blessing, commit to share your salvation story with others. Let the light of God's love shine through your life. Be willing to go wherever God wants you to go. Be willing to do whatever God wants you to do. Place your "yes" on the altar and say, "Lord, I'm yours!"

January 21
Journey of Faith

"By faith Abraham, when called to go to a place he would later receive as his inheritance, obeyed and went, even though he did not know where he was going." Heb 11:8 (NIV)

Is it possible to obey God and not know where you are going? God told Abraham to leave and go to a place that God would show him and Abraham went (Gen. 12:1-4). Even though he didn't know where he was going, by faith Abraham obeyed God. He was willing to take God at His word and launch into the unknown and the unfamiliar.

Sometimes God will unveil the details of your journey and at other times God will simply ask you to step out and trust Him with the details. You may not be able to see very far into the future God has for you. But, you can trust God every step of the way. Will you obey what God has already revealed to you? Obey and go based on what you know, then God will show you what's next. Live from faith to faith.

Walking with God is like walking down a trail in the woods at night with a flashlight. You can only see a few feet in front of you, but as you move forward the light illuminates a portion of the path that was not visible to you. As you walk with God, He illuminates the path He wants you to take. God will not mislead you. Walk closely to Him and listen for the echo of His whisper. Spend time in His Word and in prayer. Seek godly counsel from a person who walks in the Spirit and who cares about you and your future. God will speak through His word, through circumstances, and through other believers as you seek His next step for your life.

January 22
Faith that Works

"We continually remember before our God and Father your work produced by faith, your labor prompted by love, and your endurance inspired by hope in our Lord Jesus Christ." 1 Thess 1:3 (NIV)

You cannot work for your salvation. Once you experience salvation, you will want to work. The faith operative in your life will motivate you to do the work of God. Your faith will want to be expressed by your good deeds. Paul prayed for the church of Thessalonica and praised God for their work produced by faith. They gave evidence to genuine saving faith as they engaged in good deeds to bless others. Their work did not save them, but their salvation caused them to work consistently putting feet to their faith.

- *"And without faith it is impossible to please God, because anyone who comes to him must believe that he exists and that he rewards those who earnestly seek him." Heb 11:6 (NIV)*
- *"As the body without the spirit is dead, so faith without deeds is dead." James 2:26 (NIV)*

God wants your good deeds to be produced by faith. As you grow in your daily love relationship with the Lord, you will have a heightened sensitivity to the activity of God. Each time you join God in His activity, you will be giving outward evidence of your inward faith in Christ. Being on mission with God requires a faith that works.

Does your faith work? Is there fruit resulting from your faith? Deepen your faith by obeying what God says. Obedience is an indicator of genuine faith. As you obey, your good deeds will be fueled by faith.

January 23
LOVE THAT LABORS

"We continually remember before our God and Father your work produced by faith, your labor prompted by love, and your endurance inspired by hope in our Lord Jesus Christ." 1 Thess 1:3 (NIV)

What prompted Jesus to leave the glory of Heaven in order to come to earth and be mistreated, misunderstood, and crucified? Why would Jesus leave an environment where He was worshipped and come to earth to be rejected by His creation? There's one word to answer both questions: Love! The same sacrificial love Jesus exhibited on the cross is the kind of love that Paul affirmed in the believers in Thessalonica. This unconditional love prompted their labor in the Lord.

Jesus demonstrated this labor of love on the cross between two thieves. One thief repented of his sin and received the forgiveness Jesus provided. Jesus announced to him that he would be with Him in paradise (Luke 23:43). The other thief ridiculed and rejected Jesus. However, Jesus loved both thieves unconditionally.

What motivates you in your service to the Lord? Why do you do what you do? Allow the love of Jesus to be operative in your life. Find a need and meet it. Seek to demonstrate the love of Jesus through random acts of kindness. Remember the love Jesus has shown you and allow that reality to unleash unconditional love toward others.

Do what Jesus did by loving the way Jesus loved. Continue the ministry of Jesus by loving people unconditionally and leading them to experience the love of Jesus eternally. You can make an everlasting impact on a person's life by sharing the love story of God's redemptive plan.

January 24
LISTENING AND OBEYING

"Then a cloud appeared and enveloped them, and a voice came from the cloud: 'This is my Son, whom I love. Listen to him!'" Mark 9:7 (NIV)

Peter, James, and John had a mountaintop experience with Jesus on Mount Transfiguration. They were privileged to hear the voice of God affirming His Son and our Savior, Jesus. God's direct word to them was an imperative for them to listen to Jesus. Listening is equivalent to obeying. Thus, to listen to Jesus is to obey Him.

Are you listening? We have the ability to engage in selective listening. We hear what we want to hear. We choose to tune in or to tune out. God is a God who speaks. He has revealed Himself to us through His Son and through Scripture. To know Jesus is to know God. To grow in your knowledge of Jesus is to grow in your understanding of His Word. Revelation demands a response. God expects instant obedience.

- *"We know that we have come to know him if we obey his commands." John 2:3 (NIV)*
- *"'Be still, and know that I am God; I will be exalted among the nations, I will be exalted in the earth.'" Psalm 46:10 (NIV)*

How do you know if you are really listening to God? Is your life marked by obedience to God's Word? Obedience to God's Word is a clear indicator of your level of listening to God.

Is your life too noisy to hear from God? Is your schedule too busy to hear from God? The men and women who have been greatly used of God have ensured unhurried time alone with God each day. They intentionally carved out time to be still and simply listen for God's voice.

January 25
FINDING YOUR SHEPHERD

"The LORD is my shepherd, I shall not be in want." Psalm 23:1 (NIV)

God never intended for you to walk through adversity alone. Maybe you have heard someone say that God will never put more on you than you can handle. That's not true. God will not put more on you than you can handle with His help. When you come to know Christ as your personal Savior and Lord, you find the Shepherd and Overseer of your soul (1 Pt. 2:25).

The Christian life is not a solo flight. God does not launch you into the world and expect you to live the Christian life on your own. God provides refuge when you need to retreat, strength when you need to endure, and help when you need relief. Your Heavenly Father knows exactly what you need and the exact moment you need it.

- *"And I will ask the Father, and he will give you another Counselor to be with you forever--the Spirit of truth. The world cannot accept him, because it neither sees him nor knows him. But you know him, for he lives with you and will be in you." John 14:16-17 (NIV)*

God gives you His Holy Spirit at the moment of your conversion. You are inhabited by the Counselor who is the Spirit of truth. You are the walking tabernacle of God's Presence. Your body is His temple. The Holy Spirit is your Comforter.

Are you in need of help? Are you hurting, lonely, or discouraged? Share your heart with God in prayer and anticipate His response. No need to count sheep, just talk to your Shepherd.

January 26
RESTORING YOUR SOUL

"He makes me lie down in green pastures, he leads me beside quiet waters, he restores my soul. He guides me in paths of righteousness for his name's sake." Psalm 23:2-3 (NIV)

The Shepherd will restore your soul. Living in a fallen world can erode your enthusiasm and erase your energy. The constant friction of the world, the flesh, and the devil can drain your reserves. There are times in your weekly schedule when your greatest need becomes a pit stop whereby God renews your mind and recharges your strength.

God will provide you with opportunities to disconnect from the demands of life in order to replenish your soul in the green pastures of His abiding presence. He will lead you beside quiet waters to allow you to catch your breath and to enable your soul to catch up to your body. Slow down and allow God to put you back together.

Your loving Shepherd will guide you in paths of righteousness to bring glory to His name. God's path is always the best option. You must choose to walk in unbroken fellowship with the Lord and to be sensitive to His prompting. Give the Lord your undivided attention. Seek Him first each morning and align your life with His agenda.

God's restoration may come at the expense of your unrealistic pace. Allow God to interrupt the flow of your routine and to help you make necessary adjustments to give Him room to work. Busyness is one of Satan's most effective tools to keep you from focusing your energy on that which brings God the most glory. Weariness is a symptom of a life that is out of order. Learn to say "no" to good things so that you can say "yes" to the best that God has for you.

January 27
PRACTICING GOD'S PRESENCE

"Even though I walk through the valley of the shadow of death, I will fear no evil, for you are with me; your rod and your staff, they comfort me." Psalm 23:4 (NIV)

In the Seventeenth Century, a monk named, Brother Lawrence, worked in the kitchen of the Carmelite Monastery in Paris, France. He is remembered for his daily intimacy with God in the midst of menial tasks within the confines of the monastery. Brother Lawrence learned to practice the presence of God. In one of his letters he wrote, "I turn the cake that is frying on the pan for love of him, and that done, if there is nothing else to call me, I prostrate myself in worship before him, who has given me grace to work; afterwards I rise happier than a king. It is enough for me to pick up but a straw from the ground for the love of God."

Whether you are occupying the kitchen of grief or delighting at the table of abundance, God is with you. His abiding presence will sustain you and comfort you as you walk through the valley of the shadow of death. God will shepherd you through the adversity and bring you to the place of peace. You will never walk alone. God is with you. While you were sleeping, God was working.

Will you choose to practice the presence of God today? Regardless of your physical location or your emotional reality, you can practice God's presence throughout the day by acknowledging His perpetual love, faithfulness, and grace. Elevate your awareness of God's abiding presence by praying without ceasing (1 Thess. 5:17). Enjoy uninterrupted communion with God.

Where you go this day, God is with you. Whatever comes your way, God is with you. Practice God's presence and feast on His continuous provision of comfort and assurance.

January 28
OVERFLOWING WITH GOD'S PROVISION

"You prepare a table before me in the presence of my enemies. You anoint my head with oil; my cup overflows." Psalm 23:5 (NIV)

God is not limited by your limitations. Your overwhelming circumstances do not overwhelm God. The challenges in your environment are not impossible for God. God can see that which you cannot see. God knows that which you do not know.

God will provide nourishment and strength in the midst of your obstacles. God will provide manna when you experience the desert of the daily grind. His protective care will sustain you in battle. His grace will match the need of each moment. God will anoint your head with the oil of gladness and the oil of security. God's power is made perfect in your weakness (2 Cor. 12:9).

Your desperation for God and your dependency upon God releases His provision. As you place your faith in God's ability to meet your needs, His provision will cause your cup to overflow. The depth of your need will never surpass the endless supply of God's storehouse.

Honor the Lord with what He has given you. Be a good steward with everything God has entrusted to you. Give thanks for His daily bread. Praise Him for bringing you this far. Acknowledge His sufficiency.

Trust Him to meet your every need (Php. 4:19). Find comfort in the fact that God knows what you need before you ask Him (Matt 6:8). Allow the Lord to shepherd you through the life He has for you.

Take a moment to write down the specific items that have weighed heavily upon your heart. What has been bothering you? What has been consuming your thoughts and your energy? Submit each item to your faithful Shepherd in prayer.

January 29
LOOKING TO YOUR ETERNAL HOME

"Surely goodness and love will follow me all the days of my life, and I will dwell in the house of the LORD forever." Psalm 23:6 (NIV)

You are not home, yet! God has a mission for you to fulfill before He calls you home. Don't get so focused on your destination that you neglect the daily ministry God wants you to extend and the daily provision God wants you to experience. You were placed here by God to accomplish His will.

God's goodness will shadow you every step of the way. There isn't a moment that goes by in which the goodness of God is not functioning in your life. His goodness follows you because God is good.

God's love will be your companion every moment for the remainder of your life on earth. There is never a love deficit when God is near. His love will inspire you and sustain you through the various terrains of life.

You will dwell in God's house for eternity. You will have a mansion in glory and enjoy unending fellowship with the Master of the universe. Heaven is your destiny. Eternity with Jesus is your reality.

As you look forward to your eternal home, how many people will be there because of your influence? How many people will experience the joy of eternal life in heaven as a result of your witness on the earth? Share your salvation story with people that God brings into your sphere of influence. Be active in sharing your faith. Pray for the lost. Give financially to support missions. Go on a short-term mission trip to sow the gospel seed. Walk across the room to serve others and to show them the love of Jesus. Continue the ministry of Jesus!

January 30
GOD'S COMPASSION IN ACTION

"During that long period, the king of Egypt died. The Israelites groaned in their slavery and cried out, and their cry for help because of their slavery went up to God. God heard their groaning and he remembered his covenant with Abraham, with Isaac and with Jacob. So God looked on the Israelites and was concerned about them." Ex 2:23-25 (NIV)

God is passionate about His creation. His passion is consistently evidenced by His compassion in action. God saw the Israelites in their desperation and seized the opportunity to reveal Himself to them and to respond to their need.

People matter to God. You can trace God's redemptive activity throughout the entire Bible from cover to cover. He passionately pursues fallen humanity in order to bring reconciliation and restoration. God's endless love is portrayed intimately in His patience with us and in His passion for us. We matter to Him!

We experience God's compassion in action through the salvation of our souls. The redemptive act of God in Christ on the cross is the ultimate demonstration of God's compassion. "But God demonstrates his own love for us in this: While we were still sinners, Christ died for us" (Romans 5:8 NIV). We are the recipients of the bountiful compassion of God.

How will we relay God's compassion on earth? Now that we have been perpetually and eternally blessed by God's compassion, what should our response entail? We have received God's compassion so that we can extend God's compassion to others. God invites us to participate with Him in His redemptive activity.

Whenever you have difficulty putting compassion into action, consider the depth of compassion God has extended to you. God is not asking you to do anything He has not already done for you.

January 31
MOVING WITH GOD

"In all the travels of the Israelites, whenever the cloud lifted from above the tabernacle, they would set out; but if the cloud did not lift, they did not set out-- until the day it lifted. So the cloud of the LORD was over the tabernacle by day, and fire was in the cloud by night, in the sight of all the house of Israel during all their travels." Ex 40:36-38 (NIV)

God makes His Presence known. For the children of Israel, God revealed His Presence through the glory cloud. God would guide the Israelites by the visible manifestation of the cloud during the day and fire by night. When the cloud lifted and shifted, the Israelites moved. The Tabernacle was constructed in a way that emphasized ease of mobility. This enabled the Israelites to move when God moved.

As God's workmanship, where did Moses learn that kind of sensitivity to God's movement? Did he learn it in the palace during his first forty years on the earth or perhaps during the second forty years of his life as a shepherd in the desert? The burning bush experience obviously made an abiding difference in his sensitivity to God's Presence.

God is always at work. Are you sensitive to His activity? You can experience God's presence moment-by-moment as you commune with Him through prayer and feed on His Word. You can experience God's presence as you maintain a posture of expectation and anticipation. You always find what you are looking for. If you are looking for the activity of God, you will find it.

Recognition of God's activity is proportionate to your sensitivity.

February 1
SHARE THE GOSPEL INTENTIONALLY

"For we know, brothers loved by God, that he has chosen you, because our gospel came to you not simply with words, but also with power, with the Holy Spirit and with deep conviction. You know how we lived among you for your sake."
1 Thess 1:4-5 (NIV)

Be intentional in sharing the gospel. Paul, Silas, and Timothy brought the gospel to the Thessalonians (Acts 17:1-4). The gospel came with a demonstration of the Spirit's power (I Cor 2:4-5). Many of the Thessalonians responded by turning to God from idols to serve the living and true God (1 Thess 1:9). The gospel transformed their lives and influenced their culture.

In Christ, we have the cure to the cancer of sin. We have been entrusted with the gospel of light that delivers people from the kingdom of darkness. God has armed us with the Good News of Jesus Christ and empowered us with the Holy Spirit to be the salt of the earth and the light of the world. God still uses human instrumentality in the redemptive process.

Will you be faithful to share the gospel intentionally? Paul, Silas, and Timothy lived among the Thessalonians to benefit them, to bless them, and to bring Christ to them. Instead of allowing the pagan culture to influence them, Paul, Silas, and Timothy intentionally influenced the culture by continuing the ministry of Jesus.

Be a thermostat, not a thermometer. A thermostat sets the environment while a thermometer reflects the environment. God has not called us to be absorbed by the culture, but to influence the culture with the gospel. Be a spiritual thermostat for the Lord by sharing the gospel intentionally.

February 2
BEING IMITATED BY OTHERS

"You became imitators of us and of the Lord; in spite of severe suffering, you welcomed the message with the joy given by the Holy Spirit." 1 Thess 1:6 (NIV)

Paul, Silas, and Timothy modeled Christ before the new believers in Thessalonica to the extent that they were motivated to imitate them. The new believers imitated Paul, Silas, Timothy, and the Lord.

If people imitated you, would they be imitating the Lord? Are you living in such close communion with Jesus and doing what He did, that others would notice that you are imitating Christ? As you bring others to a saving knowledge of Jesus Christ, you become their spiritual parent. They look to you to see what the Christian life is supposed to look like. They imitate you as you imitate Christ. What kind of example are you portraying for others to follow?

As followers of Christ, we are to live the gospel missionally by presenting living proof of a loving God to a watching world. God wants us to be an irresistible influence for His glory. Will others come to know Christ as a result of our love relationship with Him? Does our conversation and conduct demonstrate a consistent loyalty and devotion to Christ?

Be fully yielded and fully surrendered to the Lordship of Christ and allow Him to live His life through you to touch lost souls. May others welcome the message of Christ into their lives as you faithfully sow the seed of the gospel. Imitate Christ by loving people and showing them how they can have heaven and eternal life.

If others are imitating you, will they become fully devoted followers of Christ? Will their daily walk with God be infused with passion and enthusiasm?

February 3
Being a Model to Follow

"And so you became a model to all the believers in Macedonia and Achaia."
1 Thess 1:7 (NIV)

Are you a model to follow? Are you reproducing the life of Christ before a watching world? God has created you, redeemed you, and empowered you to continue the ministry of Jesus on the earth.

After Jesus took the towel and basin of water, He washed the disciples' feet. Then Jesus said to them, "I have set you an example that you should do as I have done for you" (John 13:15 NIV). Jesus is our model to follow. Do what Jesus did. Put the needs of others before your own. Focus your life on fulfilling God's agenda. Live to benefit others. Radiate Jesus' love and extend the compassion of Christ. Guard your daily intimacy with God. Extend personal touch ministry to those in need.

In his letter to his protégé, Paul reminded Timothy to "set an example for the believers in speech, in life, in love, in faith and in purity" (1 Tim 4:12 NIV). God wants you to set the pace for the gospel race. Model Christ in your home. Model Christ on your campus. Model Christ in your work environment and in your church. Be a godly example for others to see Christ in you.

The church at Thessalonica became a model to all the believers in Macedonia and Achaia. They consistently lived out the gospel before a watching world. They influenced their culture by continuing the ministry of Jesus. Instead of allowing the culture to determine their lifestyle, they allowed the life of Jesus to be unleashed through their lives.

Examine your life closely. What needs to change in your conversation and in your conduct in order to be a model to follow? How's your thought-life? What needs to change in your private world in order to model Christ personally? Exhibit the life of character and integrity that Jesus modeled for you to follow.

February 4
BEING A MEGAPHONE FOR THE MASTER

"The Lord's message rang out from you not only in Macedonia and Achaia--your faith in God has become known everywhere." 1 Thess 1:8 (NIV)

One of the features of a High School football game is the cheer squad. The cheerleaders seek to engage the fans in the stands in order to motivate them to cheer on the team. Regardless of the score, the cheerleaders seek to get the fans involved in the game in a positive manner. Often the cheerleaders utilize a megaphone to project their cheers and to amplify their message.

God has transformed your life by His grace so that you can become a megaphone to amplify the Good News of Jesus Christ. That's right! You are a megaphone for the Master! The message of Christ is to project from your life and from your lips. Are you encouraging people to get into the game? Are you sharing the Good News of Jesus Christ with those in your sphere of influence?

The church at Thessalonica became a megaphone for the Master. The Lord's message sounded forth like a blaring trumpet and like rolling thunder. The church boldly and continually trumpeted the gospel message. Their faith in God was not a secret to be concealed, but a glorious reality to be revealed.

God did not transform your life so that you could become a closet Christian. God did not deliver you from the kingdom of darkness and place you in the kingdom of light so that you could become a silent saint. You have been saved by the grace of God to become a megaphone for the Maker of heaven and earth. Your faith in God is to be projected for others to encounter the redeeming love of Christ.

Go public with your faith. Let others hear your personal testimony. Share your spiritual story and live out the gospel.

February 5
TRANSFORMATION AND ANTICIPATION

"They tell how you turned to God from idols to serve the living and true God, and to wait for his Son from heaven, whom he raised from the dead--Jesus, who rescues us from the coming wrath." 1 Thess 1:9-10 (NIV)

Before you were saved, you were running to sin and running from God. Now that you are saved, you run to God and run from sin. In Christ, you experience an authentic transformation whereby your sins are removed, you are reconciled to God, and you receive the imputed righteousness of Christ. Your appetite for sin is replaced with an appetite for righteousness. You hunger and thirst for God. There are no substitutes for a vibrant love relationship with the Lord. Nothing else will ever satisfy. The orientation of your life is centered on serving the living and true God.

The witness of the Thessalonian believers was widespread. Their authentic transformation reverberated throughout Macedonia and Achaia. Their contagious faith had become known everywhere. Turning to God from idols, they embodied the servitude of Christ and served the living and true God. They became an irresistible influence for the Lord.

When you experience the transformation Christ provides, you embrace a life of anticipation. You wait expectantly for the return of Christ from heaven. You live in light of His resurrection and His rescue. There is no one else who can rescue you from the coming wrath. God will judge sin. Those who have rejected God's plan of salvation will spend eternity separated from God. Rejoice! Your transformation in Christ changes your eternal destiny. Hell is not your destination. The transformation you experienced in Christ assures your ultimate destination in heaven.

Jesus will come for His church prior to the Tribulation. Jesus will come with His church after the Tribulation to establish His millennial reign upon the earth. Live in light of His return!

February 6
LIVING THE REDEEMED LIFE

"And now, O Israel, what does the LORD your God ask of you but to fear the LORD your God, to walk in all his ways, to love him, to serve the LORD your God with all your heart and with all your soul, and to observe the LORD's commands and decrees that I am giving you today for your own good?" Deut 10:12-13 (NIV)

What does the redeemed life look like in practical day-by-day living? Once a person becomes a follower of Jesus Christ, how does that new identity translate into daily living? God reveals His expectations for the redeemed life.

Revere supremely. When you experience God's redemption, your response to that redemption is a life of reverencing God. To revere God is to esteem Him and to give Him the rightful place He deserves in your life.

Live righteously. The redeemed life results in a righteous lifestyle. Godliness replaces worldliness. Selflessness replaces selfishness. Instead of allowing the world to influence your behavior, you influence the culture with the character of Christ in you.

Love completely. God loves you and demonstrated His love for you by allowing Jesus to die on the cross to pay the penalty of your sin. Love God completely by giving your heart to Him in full surrender. Express your love to Him in private and corporate worship.

Serve passionately. Now that you have been redeemed, serve God by continuing the ministry of Jesus. Serve God by spreading the fragrance of Christ through random acts of kindness. Find a need and meet it.

Obey instantly. Love what God loves and hate what God hates. "Anyone, then, who knows the good he ought to do and doesn't do it, sins" (James 4:17 NIV). Choose to obey God.

February 7
DEALING WITH DELAYS

"But Moses said to God, 'Who am I, that I should go to Pharaoh and bring the Israelites out of Egypt?'"
"And God said, 'I will be with you. And this will be the sign to you that it is I who have sent you: When you have brought the people out of Egypt, you will worship God on this mountain.'" Ex 3:11-12 (NIV)

What benefits were available to Moses in the desert that were unavailable to him in the palace? What could God teach Moses in the dusty desert that he could not learn in the palatial palace?

I remember going through a difficult season in ministry and felt led to call one of my mentors. I shared with him that perhaps God was preparing me for my next assignment. I'll never forget his response. He said, "Stephen, God is always preparing you for your next assignment. However, your next assignment may be right where you are."

Moses probably felt that way. He likely wondered what God could possibly be up to by allowing him to remain in the desert for forty years. God allowed Moses to experience forty years in the palace to prepare him for the forty years in the desert to prepare him for the forty years of leading the children of Israel to the Promised Land.

God does not waste our desert experiences. God uses those dry times in our lives to reveal Himself in a way that we would not comprehend otherwise. He is always preparing us for our next interaction, our next appointment, our next interruption, and our next assignment.

God will redeem the season you are in. Are you willing to trust God with your life? Are you willing to submit to His prompting?

February 8
OVERCOMING OBSTACLES

"So when the people broke camp to cross the Jordan, the priests carrying the ark of the covenant went ahead of them." Josh 3:14 (NIV)

Joshua came face to face with an obstacle that prevented entry into the Promised Land. He was in charge of mobilizing the children of Israel to inherit the land flowing with milk and honey. The Jordan River was the obstacle, which became an opportunity for God to do something great to reveal His glory.

We serve a great God who can take any obstacle and turn it into an opportunity for us to experience His power and for us to know His provision. Everyone has a Jordan. We all encounter obstacles along the path of life on this broken planet. Living in a fallen world ensures our confrontation with obstacles.

The challenge is not facing obstacles, but responding to the obstacles we face. Is it possible to turn an obstacle into an opportunity? Is it possible to navigate obstacles and be in the center of God's will? Some of the most meaningful experiences with God are those in which you feel like you are in the fourth quarter with only a few seconds left and God comes through for you.

The priests carrying the ark went ahead of the people in order to confront the obstacle. The Jordan River did not stand a chance on sabotaging God's agenda. God will make a way when there seems to be no way. God will give you just what you need in the moment of your need. God will not leave you hanging. God will not abandon you.

Identify your Jordan. What is keeping you from entering the land flowing with milk and honey? What is keeping you from operating in the center of God's will?

February 9
REMEMBERING GOD'S FAITHFULNESS

"So Joshua called together the twelve men he had appointed from the Israelites, one from each tribe, and said to them, 'Go over before the ark of the LORD your God into the middle of the Jordan. Each of you is to take up a stone on his shoulder, according to the number of the tribes of the Israelites, to serve as a sign among you. In the future, when your children ask you, "What do these stones mean?" tell them that the flow of the Jordan was cut off before the ark of the covenant of the LORD. When it crossed the Jordan, the waters of the Jordan were cut off. These stones are to be a memorial to the people of Israel forever.'"
Josh 4:4-7 (NIV)

Don't miss what God is up to in your life. Don't forget what God has done to bring you to the place where you are right now. Take note of all the difficulties God has brought you through. Recognize all the mountaintop experiences God has lavished on you in your lifetime.

Joshua wanted to solidify the crossing of the Jordan River as a spiritual marker for all of Israel. He wanted to ensure that future generations would know what God had done to bring about deliverance to the people of God. Joshua utilized the twelve stones, which were selected from the middle of the Jordan to serve as a memorial.

Solidify your spiritual markers. Think through the activity of God in your life. When did you come to a saving knowledge of Jesus Christ? When did you follow the Lord in believer's baptism? Where were you when God revealed Himself to you during a season of adversity? Identify some God-moments you have experienced in the journey of life. Slow down long enough to pray through those spiritual markers. You may want to list them out specifically so that you can thank God for each one.

Replace those toxic thoughts with healthy reminders of who you are in Christ. You belong to God. You are His treasure and His masterpiece (Eph. 2:10). You have everything you need for life and godliness (2 Peter 1:3).

February 10
AUTHENTICALLY SEALED

"And you also were included in Christ when you heard the word of truth, the gospel of your salvation. Having believed, you were marked in him with a seal, the promised Holy Spirit, who is a deposit guaranteeing our inheritance until the redemption of those who are God's possession--to the praise of his glory." Eph 1:13-14 (NIV)

If you believe, you will receive. At the moment of conversion, you receive the baptism of the Holy Spirit. It is an instantaneous experience, not a subsequent event. The indwelling presence of Christ, the Holy Spirit, comes to live inside of you. Having believed on the gospel of Jesus Christ, you were marked in Christ with the seal of the Holy Spirit.

The seal speaks of authenticity. The seal speaks of identification. You belong to God. You are His creation. You became His child and were adopted into His family when you placed your faith in Jesus alone for salvation. You were marked with a seal. That seal is the Person of the Holy Spirit.

Did you notice the Trinity in these two verses? God the Father, God the Son, and God the Holy Spirit are expressed in verses thirteen and fourteen. Look closely and you will see "Christ" and then "Holy Spirit" and then "God" which form the Trinity, which means three in one.

God created you. Jesus redeemed you. The Holy Spirit inhabits you. Your conversion is the real deal which has been sealed.

February 11
SPIRITUAL MATURITY

"It was he who gave some to be apostles, some to be prophets, some to be evangelists, and some to be pastors and teachers, to prepare God's people for works of service, so that the body of Christ may be built up until we all reach unity in the faith and in the knowledge of the Son of God and become mature, attaining to the whole measure of the fullness of Christ." Eph 4:11-13 (NIV)

Where do you fit in this picture? God has placed equippers in your life to help you develop into a fully devoted follower of Jesus Christ. God has placed a systematic process within the local church to promote spiritual maturity. Are you an intentional part of the process?

Take a close look at your level of participation in the life of the local church family. Are you being built up? Are you reaching unity in the faith and in the knowledge of Jesus and becoming mature? Are you attaining to the whole measure of the fullness of Christ? What is your level of teachability? Your spiritual maturity will be proportionate to your teachability. Are you teachable as you listen to your pastor's message? Are you teachable as you sit under the teaching of a godly small group leader? Are you teachable as you spend time alone with God in prayer and Bible reading?

Make the most of the opportunities God has given you to grow spiritually. Maximize the moments you sit under anointed teaching from God's Word. Move from hearing and reading God's Word to applying God's Word in daily living. Live out what God is depositing in you.

February 12
REJOICING IN TRIALS

"Consider it pure joy, my brothers, whenever you face trials of many kinds, because you know that the testing of your faith develops perseverance." James 1:2-3 (NIV)

Rejoice is a choice.

Living in a fallen world comes at a price. The consequences of sin have rippled throughout our family tree all the way back to Adam and Eve. When sin entered the human race, trials became the shadow. Trials are as much a part of life as the air we breathe. The question is not a matter of whether we will face trials or not in this life. The issue is how we choose to respond to the trials we face.

Trials are inevitable in a fallen world. We can choose to rejoice in the midst of the trials we navigate. We need not be surprised by the multifaceted trials that come our way. Instead, we need to live in the ready mode in order to anticipate trials and more specifically, plan our response to trials. Will you choose to rejoice? You cannot choose your trials, but you can choose your response to the trials.

- *"For it has been granted to you on behalf of Christ not only to believe on him, but also to suffer for him." Phil 1:29 (NIV)*
- *"Dear friends, do not be surprised at the painful trial you are suffering, as though something strange were happening to you. But rejoice that you participate in the sufferings of Christ, so that you may be overjoyed when his glory is revealed." 1 Peter 4:12-13 (NIV)*

Consider the trials that you are currently experiencing. How will you respond today? Will your choice be to rejoice?

February 13
OBTAINING GOD'S PERSPECTIVE

"If any of you lacks wisdom, he should ask God, who gives generously to all without finding fault, and it will be given to him." James 1:5 (NIV)

View your trials from God's perspective.

Knowledge is needed to take things apart. Wisdom is needed to put things back together. When your life is coming apart, you need God's wisdom to put your life in order. Trials tend to skew our vision and stifle our passion. It is so easy to lose perspective when facing trials. Our tendency is to be captured by the immediate and bypass the future that God has in store for us.

Why do we wait so long in the process to turn to God in prayer? We try to figure out circumstances on our own and frantically search for answers apart from God. Nothing comes into our lives without God's permission. If God permits trials, then God will use those trials for our good and for His glory. If only we can embrace that reality earlier in the process of our trials. God is both the Creator and Sustainer of our lives. He knows where we are and what we are facing and where we are heading.

- *"'Be still, and know that I am God; I will be exalted among the nations, I will be exalted in the earth.'" Psalm 46:10 (NIV)*
- *"Trust in the LORD with all your heart and lean not on your own understanding; in all your ways acknowledge him, and he will make your paths straight." Prov 3:5-6 (NIV)*

In faith, turn to God and ask for His wisdom. Seek to gain God's perspective on the trials you face.

February 14
BUILDING YOUR TESTIMONY

"Consider it pure joy, my brothers, whenever you face trials of many kinds, because you know that the testing of your faith develops perseverance." James 1:2-3 (NIV)

Without a test, there is no testimony.

God allows trials to come into our lives in order to prove the authenticity of our faith. We are like a tube of toothpaste, when squeezed whatever is on the inside comes out. Trials have a way of revealing character. When our faith is tested, we have the opportunity to demonstrate the character of Christ being developed in us. Our testimony is enriched as our faith increases. Learning how to trust God when trials ensue is part of our spiritual formation. God does not waste the trauma that comes into our lives. When difficult circumstances are in view, our faith is fortified.

- *"Therefore, since we are surrounded by such a great cloud of witnesses, let us throw off everything that hinders and the sin that so easily entangles, and let us run with perseverance the race marked out for us." Heb 12:1 (NIV)*
- *"Therefore, among God's churches we boast about your perseverance and faith in all the persecutions and trials you are enduring." 2 Thess 1:4 (NIV)*

Review your spiritual journey and identify those hard places in your life that proved your faith. You will find that some of your most meaningful moments with God were during those seasons of intensity and adversity.

February 15
ADVERSITY AND SPIRITUAL MATURITY

"Perseverance must finish its work so that you may be mature and complete, not lacking anything." James 1:4 (NIV)

Spiritual maturity may involve adversity.

The child of God is not exempt from adversity. Often, God will allow adversity to enter our journey in order to move us toward spiritual maturity. God expects us to grow spiritually. Mediocrity, lethargy, and apathy are foreign to the maturation process. God enables us to grow through seasons of uncertainty and through seasons of drought. We are reminded of our inadequacy and our total dependency upon God. God's desire is for us to not lack anything. Trials produce the canvas upon which the providence of God is painted for our personal engagement.

- *"...until we all reach unity in the faith and in the knowledge of the Son of God and become mature, attaining to the whole measure of the fullness of Christ." Eph 4:13 (NIV)*
- *"Epaphras, who is one of you and a servant of Christ Jesus, sends greetings. He is always wrestling in prayer for you, that you may stand firm in all the will of God, mature and fully assured." Col 4:12 (NIV)*

Our response to adversity demonstrates our level of spiritual maturity. Our response to difficult circumstances can also propel our spiritual maturity to the next level. Here's the bottom line: Are you becoming more like Jesus in the midst of the trials you face?

February 16
God's Purpose in Delays

"As she kept on praying to the LORD, Eli observed her mouth. Hannah was praying in her heart, and her lips were moving but her voice was not heard. Eli thought she was drunk and said to her, 'How long will you keep on getting drunk? Get rid of your wine.'" 1 Sam 1:12-14 (NIV)

Have you ever been misunderstood?

When you are hurting, your emotions will be expressed through anger, suppression, depression, or grief. At some point, your hurt will manifest. For Hannah, her pain was being expressed through heartfelt prayer. She was unveiling her broken heart before the Lord. Hannah was barren. Eli misinterpreted her pain as that of being drunk. That was far from the truth of Hannah's condition. She wasn't drunk. She was devastated with the reality of her circumstances. Can you relate?

- *"'Not so, my lord,' Hannah replied, 'I am a woman who is deeply troubled. I have not been drinking wine or beer; I was pouring out my soul to the LORD. Do not take your servant for a wicked woman; I have been praying here out of my great anguish and grief.'"* 1 Sam 1:15-16 (NIV)

God knows what you are feeling right now. God knows where you are and where you are headed. Nothing catches God by surprise. Maybe you are experiencing a delay that just doesn't make sense to you. Know that God has a purpose for every delay we endure. God understands our feelings and our frustrations even when others may not understand. God is all knowing. God has the final say!

February 17
TRUSTING JESUS IN YOUR STORM

"Looking at his disciples, he said: 'Blessed are you who are poor, for yours is the kingdom of God.'" Luke 6:20 (NIV)

Trials have a tendency to sneak up on us like weeds in a flowerbed. We can be living in the land of the familiar and enjoying our daily routine when all of the sudden, we get surprised by an unexpected interruption. Maybe we get an unwanted notice in the mail, or the check engine light in our car comes on, or the doctor walks in the room with a concerned look in his eyes. Life is filled with seasons of uncertainty.

Who do you turn to when trials come into your life? The disciples went to Jesus and woke Him and said, "Lord, save us! We're going to drown!" We must give them credit at this point. They knew to turn to Jesus. But, Jesus questioned them about their lack of faith and their pressing fear. Why would they be afraid of anything, knowing that Jesus was with them? Jesus seized the opportunity to demonstrate His power over nature. Jesus rebuked the winds and the waves and it was completely calm. The disciples experienced the demonstration of Jesus' power.

Whatever trials come our way, remember that Jesus is our sufficiency. The storms of this life can never catch Jesus by surprise.

Jesus is in the boat!

February 18
MAKING WISE DECISIONS

"When he came to his senses, he said, 'How many of my father's hired men have food to spare, and here I am starving to death!'" Luke 15:17 (NIV)

Do you have someone in your life who is currently suffering the consequences of their poor choices? Everything within you wants to shift into rescue mode. You want to pull them out of reaping what they have sown. Their trial has become your trial because of the love you have for them.

The prodigal son traveled down the road filled with the potholes of selfish choices. The consequences of his sinful lifestyle were in full bloom. The fast lane had not delivered what it promised. What I admire most about his father is that he allowed the natural consequences to flow. Instead of rescuing his son, the father gave God room to work and to produce deep conviction in his straying son's life.

Yes! It took a pigpen experience for the son to come to his senses. What if the father would have interrupted the process? What if the father would have chased the son down and prevented him from reaching the pigpen?

- *"No discipline seems pleasant at the time, but painful. Later on, however, it produces a harvest of righteousness and peace for those who have been trained by it." Heb 12:11 (NIV)*

Sometimes we just need to give God room to work to bring those He has created back to Himself. There are times when God wants to use us in the process of bringing a rebelling son or daughter back into alignment. Don't bypass God's disciplinary process.

February 19
HONORING GOD IN TEMPTATION

"No temptation has seized you except what is common to man. And God is faithful; he will not let you be tempted beyond what you can bear. But when you are tempted, he will also provide a way out so that you can stand up under it."
1 Cor 10:13 (NIV)

Temptation is an opportunity to honor God.

Our response to temptation will determine whether we honor God or dishonor God. As followers of Jesus Christ, we are not temptation exempt. Living in a fallen world and retaining our sin nature guarantee the presence of temptation. It is not a matter of if we will face temptation, but a matter of when we will face temptation. Even Jesus was tempted.

Temptation is a common feature in this life. Of course, temptation comes in different forms depending on where we are most susceptible. Satan knows what our weaknesses are and what will entice us toward sin.

We are not left alone to fend for ourselves. God is here! God is faithful! We can anchor our faith to the faithfulness of God. He will never leave us. He will not abandon us. In fact, God will not allow us to be tempted beyond what we can bear with Him. Temptation is a constant reminder of our dependency upon God. We need God!

God will also provide an exit strategy. When temptation knocks at our door, we don't have to submit to the temptation. God will always provide a way of escape so that we can stand up under the load and stress of the temptation.

How will you respond when temptation comes your way? Will you seize the opportunity to honor God?

February 20
TEMPTATION AND OPPORTUNITY

"When tempted, no one should say, 'God is tempting me.' For God cannot be tempted by evil, nor does he tempt anyone; but each one is tempted when, by his own evil desire, he is dragged away and enticed." James 1:13-14 (NIV)

God is holy and God is love.

The nature of God will not allow temptation to be an instrument of heaven. God cannot be tempted by evil because God is holy. As John MacArthur affirms, "God is aware of evil but untouched by it, like a sunbeam shining on a dump is untouched by the trash."

God is not the originator of temptation. God does not tempt anyone because God is love. In His love, God does not initiate temptation, but God will allow temptation to come into a person's life. The temptation provides the opportunity to choose the righteous path and to bring honor to God through the proper response.

When we choose to give in to temptation, we believe that it is the best option at that moment. Satan's goal is to get us to doubt God's Word and to doubt God's best.

- *"Now the serpent was more crafty than any of the wild animals the LORD God had made. He said to the woman, 'Did God really say, You must not eat from any tree in the garden?'" Gen 3:1 (NIV)*

God cannot be tempted by evil. God does not tempt anyone. How will you choose to respond to the temptation that God allows into your path? Will you take God at His Word and trust Him?

February 21
TEMPTATION AND PREDICTABILITY

"Then, after desire has conceived, it gives birth to sin; and sin, when it is full-grown, gives birth to death." James 1:15 (NIV)

Temptation has a predictable process.

James gives uses the metaphor of childbirth to capture the predictable process of temptation. In his letter to the Jews who were scattered outside of Palestine, James writes about the trials from without and the temptations from within.

We have God-given desires that are natural and are vital to life. For example, we have the desire for food. Without that desire we would die. We also have the desire for rest. Without that desire we would die. Yet, both desires can become sin when we take them beyond God's intended purpose. If we take our desire for food too far, we commit the sin of gluttony. In like manner, if we take our desire for rest too far, we commit the sin of laziness.

Arm yourself with the knowledge of the predictable process of temptation. We idolize something we desire. The next step is that we rationalize why we should have the desire fulfilled. In other words, we talked ourselves into compromising convictions. Then we strategize by coming up with a plan to obtain the object we are idolizing. Ultimately, we capitalize on the opportunity by seizing what we have desired. Remorse and guilt follow.

Look back over poor choices you have made in your lifetime. See if you can identify this predictable process. Here's the key to victory: The sooner in the process you avoid the sin, the more likely you will overcome the temptation.

February 22
MONITORING MEDIA INPUT

"Religion that God our Father accepts as pure and faultless is this: to look after orphans and widows in their distress and to keep oneself from being polluted by the world." James 1:27 (NIV)

God has called us to a lifestyle of moral purity. As followers of Jesus Christ, our constant assignment is to keep from being polluted by the world. Sin is rampant in our society and sin is present within our sin nature. As we battle temptation from within, we must establish guardrails to keep us on the straight and narrow path of holiness.

Let's consider using a MAP for walking in victory. The letter "M" will remind us to Monitor Media Input. In our age of technology, we have unprecedented access to images that dishonor God. High definition televisions, computers, and cell phones provide an array of images that pollute and contaminate the mind of the child of God. Filtering what we allow to come into our minds is a proactive step to walking in victory.

- *"Finally, brothers, whatever is true, whatever is noble, whatever is right, whatever is pure, whatever is lovely, whatever is admirable--if anything is excellent or praiseworthy--think about such things." Phil 4:8 (NIV)*
- *"Flee the evil desires of youth, and pursue righteousness, faith, love and peace, along with those who call on the Lord out of a pure heart." 2 Tim 2:22 (NIV)*

Take the initiative to monitor media input. When you put garbage in, you will get garbage out. When you put Christ in, you get Christ out. Fill your mind with that which brings honor to God.

February 23
AVOIDING SLIPPERY SLOPES

"Avoid every kind of evil." 1 Thess 5:22 (NIV)

Have you ever done something that compromised your convictions and broke the heart of God? When you look back on the experience, you still can't believe that you did such a thing. When you get too close to the edge, you slip down the slippery slope and immense guilt follows. Have you been there?

As we continue observing our MAP for walking in victory, let's use the letter "A" to remind us to Avoid Slippery Slopes. Because of our resident sin nature, we have a tendency to see how close we can get to the edge without slipping and falling. God's Word teaches us to guard our lives and to conduct our lives with caution. Slippery slopes abound. Opportunities to compromise our convictions are unlimited.

- *"It is God's will that you should be sanctified: that you should avoid sexual immorality; that each of you should learn to control his own body in a way that is holy and honorable, not in passionate lust like the heathen, who do not know God." 1 Thess 4:3-5 (NIV)*
- *"In your struggle against sin, you have not yet resisted to the point of shedding your blood." Heb 12:4 (NIV)*

God has called us to a lifestyle of self-control. Take the initiative to avoid slipper slopes. Ask God to give you wisdom to see the terrain as it is and to detect the slippery slopes awaiting your arrival. Living in a fallen world is a struggle. Resist sin at all costs.

February 24
PRACTICING BOUNCING EYES

"Let your eyes look straight ahead, fix your gaze directly before you." Prov 4:25 (NIV)

Eyesight is an amazing feature of the human body. God's creation throughout the earth is awesome to behold whether taking in the sight of the blue sky in the day or the star filled sky at night or observing a butterfly dancing from leaf to leaf. From gazing at the flowing wildflowers in the open field to examining the intricacies of a cell under a microscope, eyesight is a gift from God.

As we seek to walk in victory in this life on planet earth, let's use the letter "P" in our MAP to remind us to Practice Bouncing Eyes. There is so much to look at from day to day. To walk in victory, we must very selective in what we allow to come into our minds through the open window of our eyes.

- *"But I tell you that anyone who looks at a woman lustfully has already committed adultery with her in his heart." Matt 5:28 (NIV)*
- *"'I made a covenant with my eyes not to look lustfully at a girl.'" Job 31:1 (NIV)*

Take the initiative to practice bouncing eyes. Train your eyes to bounce off of anything that does not honor God. As Billy Graham has said, "The first look is natural; the second look is sin."

February 25
RESTING IN GOD'S TIMING

"God also said to Abraham, 'As for Sarai your wife, you are no longer to call her Sarai; her name will be Sarah. I will bless her and will surely give you a son by her. I will bless her so that she will be the mother of nations; kings of peoples will come from her.'" Gen 17:15-16 (NIV)

Can you imagine becoming a parent at age ninety or a hundred? That's difficult to fathom. However, the greater challenge would be to desire parenthood and having to wait until you were almost a century old to realize the dream.

Abraham and Sarah had to learn to live with delays. God had promised to bless them and to make them into a great nation. However, they had to walk in obedience to God and wait for His timing.

Have you noticed how our personal timetable doesn't always line up with God's timetable? We tend to want our blessing now. We don't usually "wait" very well.

God has a divine purpose in our delays. Sometimes delays are a result of poor choices we have made and sometimes a consequence of poor choices those around us have made. Either way, God can use delays to portray His grace.

God has the final say doesn't He? Nothing happens without God's permission. If God allows a delay in your life, He will utilize the delay. Now rest in God's timing. Entrust your life to Him.

February 26
CROSSING THE FINISH LINE

"In all my prayers for all of you, I always pray with joy because of your partnership in the gospel from the first day until now, being confident of this, that he who began a good work in you will carry it on to completion until the day of Christ Jesus." Phil 1:4-6 (NIV)

God is working. His purpose and plan will be accomplished. Satan cannot thwart God's will. Even when you experience doubts, delays, and distractions, God is still fulfilling His agenda. God is sovereign. He rules and He reigns. God factors in our sin. God factors in the reality of demonic opposition. God is not surprised by our surprises.

God's master plan includes you. It is God's will for you to be saved, to grow spiritually, and to join Him in His redemptive activity. Jesus took on the full wrath of God for your sin so that you could be set free to have a vibrant love relationship with God in Christ. You were filled with the Holy Spirit at the moment of your conversion so that you could continue the ministry of Jesus on this broken planet.

God will complete the good work He began in you. What God starts, He always finishes! God is not through with you. You are still in the process of becoming who God has made you to be. God is molding you and shaping you into the man or woman of God He created you to be.

Will you allow God to continue His work in you so that He can accomplish His work through you? Are you willing to trust God's timing? God knows where He wants you. God knows what the finished product of His character development in you looks like. God's timing is perfect. Entrust your life to His care.

February 27
FINDING SOUL REST

"Come to me, all you who are weary and burdened, and I will give you rest. Take my yoke upon you and learn from me, for I am gentle and humble in heart, and you will find rest for your souls. For my yoke is easy and my burden is light."
Matt 11:28-30 (NIV)

Jesus is always on time. He knows just what we need right when we need it. His invitation to join Him and to find rest in Him is the antidote to our fast pace lifestyle. As one person said, "If we don't learn to come apart, we will come apart!"

Why do we feel guilty when we slow down? Why do we gravitate toward the performance trap and end up equating productivity with spirituality? Sometimes the most spiritual move we can make is to slow down and experience the rest Jesus offers.

Be sure to notice in our verse for today that there is a prerequisite to encountering His rest. We must be willing to come to Him. We must be willing to take the initiative to respond to His invitation. That just doesn't fit our adrenaline-addicted society. We tend to long for the next high or the next rush. Maybe we can just capture a few more sips of caffeinated coffee. Will that deliver what we need most?

Perhaps the invitation is to come to the place of total reliance upon God. If I yoke up with Him, then I will have to be willing to go where He goes and embrace the pace He sets. Remember, His yoke is easy and His burden is light. Sounds refreshing!

February 28
UNVEILING THE REAL ZEAL

"Never be lacking in zeal, but keep your spiritual fervor, serving the Lord."
Romans 12:11 (NIV)

What are you passionate about? What are you giving your time, energy, and resources to? What gets the best of you? You answer unveils your zeal.

God placed zeal in you. Your passion is an expression of your spiritual DNA. God gives you the ability to be passionate in this life. However, it is possible to misdirect the passion God gives you. Your passion can be diverted to areas that are unhealthy or unfruitful. You can channel your passion to outlets that dishonor God or even to good things that rob God's best for you.

God's Word teaches us to keep our spiritual fervor. Our passion in action should be vertical in nature. We are to be passionate for God. Our zeal for God and His Kingdom should never experience a deficit. As we nurture our passion for God, we are to keep our passion channeled in the paths that God provides.

Are you passionate about the things of God? Does your life give evidence to the passion God desires from you? Take some time to assess your current reality. See if your passion is misdirected. Examine your life to the level of identifying the source of your passion and the expression of your passion in action.

March 1
DEMONSTRATING YOUR DEVOTION

"Do not let your heart envy sinners, but always be zealous for the fear of the LORD." Prov 23:17 (NIV)

The current of our culture is counter Christian. As you seek to live out your faith in a fallen world, you will quickly discover that walking in reverence to God and in full devotion to Jesus will place you in the minority. You may forfeit popularity in this sin-saturated culture, but you will not forfeit your position in Christ. You may not be affirmed by society for your faithfulness to God, but God will reward you because He is all knowing and takes care of His own.

Don't allow the prosperity of the wicked to distract you in this life. Don't allow the visible affluence of the disobedient to diminish your passion for the things of God. Always be zealous for the Lord. Guard your heart and fortify your passion for God.

Revere God as your Heavenly Father. Revere God as the One who created you, pursued you, rescued you, and empowers you for victorious living. Revere God for His holiness. Revere God for His nature and character. Demonstrate your devotion to God by your unwavering allegiance to His redemptive plan.

What if you had less than thirty days to live? How would your loyalty be adjusted? Would your allegiance to God's agenda expand? How differently would you channel your passion?

Let's live life for God with the intensity of our final days on the earth. God deserves our best! God deserves our reverence and our diligence!

March 2
ENLIGHTENED ZEAL

"I thank my God every time I remember you. In all my prayers for all of you, I always pray with joy because of your partnership in the gospel from the first day until now, being confident of this, that he who began a good work in you will carry it on to completion until the day of Christ Jesus." Phil 1:3-6 (NIV)

Paul identifies the possibility of being zealous for God and yet not being saved. Paul examined the fruit of the Israelites in his day and detected their zeal for God. He noticed that their zeal was not based on knowledge. As a result, their pursuit of righteousness was faulty. They were unwilling to submit to God's righteousness and as a result they failed to recognize Christ.

Don't allow your zeal to blind you from truth. Before you put your passion in action, make sure you are grounded in the truth of God's revelation. God has made His salvation plan known. Make certain of your personal born again experience. Revisit your conversion and trace your zeal from that moment to now.

What if you had less than one month to live? How would you inform your passion in order to properly unleash your passion for the things of God? Stay in the know. Invest time in securing a daily intake of God's Word. If you want to know the heart of God, read His Word. If you want to know the blessings of God, obey His Word.

God honors obedience! If you want to put your passion in action, be zealous to know and obey God's Word!

March 3
Contagious Passion?

"Now fear the LORD and serve him with all faithfulness. Throw away the gods your forefathers worshiped beyond the River and in Egypt, and serve the LORD. But if serving the LORD seems undesirable to you, then choose for yourselves this day whom you will serve, whether the gods your forefathers served beyond the River, or the gods of the Amorites, in whose land you are living. But as for me and my household, we will serve the LORD." Josh 24:14-15 (NIV)

Joshua's passion for God was contagious. He was willing to take responsibility for the spiritual condition of his home. Joshua made a bold proclamation that as for he and his household, they would serve the Lord. He did not apologize for his passion to obey God. His loyalty to God was expressed through his passion for God. Joshua's passion to lead his family spiritually impacted the nation.

- *"'Now then,' said Joshua, 'throw away the foreign gods that are among you and yield your hearts to the LORD, the God of Israel.'" Josh 24:23 (NIV)*
- *"And the people said to Joshua, 'We will serve the LORD our God and obey him.'" Josh 24:24 (NIV)*

It is interesting that Joshua did not ask the people to do anything he had not already done. Joshua put his passion in action by leading his family to revere and serve the Lord. Now the people could respond to his example and to his exhortation.

Are you putting your passion in action in such a way as to impact your family and those in your sphere of influence? Is your passion for God contagious or difficult to detect?

March 4
PASSIONATE INTERCESSION

"I thank my God every time I remember you. In all my prayers for all of you, I always pray with joy because of your partnership in the gospel from the first day until now, being confident of this, that he who began a good work in you will carry it on to completion until the day of Christ Jesus." Phil 1:3-6 (NIV)

The Apostle Paul demonstrated his love for the church at Philippi by his passionate intercession for them. He prayed with joy because of their partnership in the gospel. He prayed with confidence knowing that God began a good work in them and would bring it to completion. Paul's prayer life was energized by his love for the believers at Philippi. Paul was not alone. The Holy Spirit joined in the divine communication by interceding for the saints in Philippi. Jesus interceded for them from the right hand of God in heaven.

- *"In the same way, the Spirit helps us in our weakness. We do not know what we ought to pray for, but the Spirit himself intercedes for us with groans that words cannot express. And he who searches our hearts knows the mind of the Spirit, because the Spirit intercedes for the saints in accordance with God's will." Romans 8:26-27 (NIV)*
- *"Who is he that condemns? Christ Jesus, who died--more than that, who was raised to life--is at the right hand of God and is also interceding for us." Romans 8:34 (NIV)*

When you pray for others, you have the divine privilege of joining the Holy Spirit and Jesus in the ministry of intercession. Put your passion in action by embracing the ministry of intercessory prayer. Who will you begin to pray for today?

March 5
Running the Christian Race

"Do you not know that in a race all the runners run, but only one gets the prize? Run in such a way as to get the prize." 1 Cor 9:24 (NIV)

Life is not a sprint, but a marathon.

The Greeks had two athletic festivals: the Olympic games and the Isthmian games. Paul's audience would immediately connect this running imagery with the Isthmian games in their city of Corinth. Instead of receiving a gold, silver, or bronze medal like in our current day Olympics, only one prize was awarded in the Isthmian games. The winning runner would receive a wreath. Nothing was awarded to the runner who came in second or third. Only one person got the prize!

Paul is encouraging us as believers to run in such a way as to get that prize. We are to live the Christian life with passion. God desires our best and God deserves our best. So, how are you running the Christian race? Are you running with passion? Too often, we divert our passion to other venues. We rob God and we give our best to that which has no eternal value.

How you live is just as important as how much time you have left on this earth. The quality of your life is just as vital as the quantity of your remaining days. How will you live your life? If you had less than one month to live, would your passion in the race of life be vertical? Would your passion for God and His agenda be evident?

March 6
DYING TO LIVE

"I have been crucified with Christ and I no longer live, but Christ lives in me. The life I live in the body, I live by faith in the Son of God, who loved me and gave himself for me." Gal 2:20 (NIV)

Are you dying to live? You can spend your entire life trying to figure out how to really live. Your constant pursuit can be saturated with seeking to discover life. Meanwhile, life happens while you are trying to get a grasp on life.

Paul gives tremendous insight into the life God has for you. In order to live, you must die. The life God has for you is really not your life. As a follower of Jesus Christ, you have been crucified with Christ. You have already died to yourself so that Christ can live in you. Don't miss the parallel. You died so that Christ can live in you and through you. Yet, the life you now live in the body is lived by faith in Jesus, who loved you and gave Himself for you. You are dying to live.

- *"Then he said to them all: 'If anyone would come after me, he must deny himself and take up his cross daily and follow me. For whoever wants to save his life will lose it, but whoever loses his life for me will save it.'" Luke 9:23-24 (NIV)*

Put your passion in action by allowing Jesus to live His life in and through you. Give Jesus the reins to your life and let Him have His way in you. Surrender to His Lordship and submit to His prompting. Your passion will be evidenced by your obedience.

March 7
FRIENDS SENT BY GOD

"We sent Timothy, who is our brother and God's fellow worker in spreading the gospel of Christ, to strengthen and encourage you in your faith, so that no one would be unsettled by these trials. You know quite well that we were destined for them." 1 Thess 3:2-3 (NIV)

Paul had a deep abiding love for the church at Thessalonica. The new believers were developing in their faith and understanding of God's will. After a season of separation, Paul sent Timothy to reconnect with the congregation in order to strengthen and encourage them in the midst of their trials.

Living out the Christian faith in the sin dominating culture of Thessalonica was not easy. The believers were persecuted for their faith in Jesus. The magnetic pull of their former lifestyle continued to pull at them. The believers were unsettled by the persistence of their trials. Timothy invested time and energy in them to strengthen their faith and to encourage their faithfulness.

God does not intend for you to live the Christian life without His enablement. God has empowered you by the Person of the Holy Spirit living in you. Stand firm in your faith by surrendering to the control of the Holy Spirit. Allow Him to fuel your faith and to ignite your enthusiasm.

You need Christian friends to live the life God has for you in this fallen world. Don't fly solo! Don't try to accomplish God's will without the people God brings into your life to encourage you and to strengthen you. Remember, to have a friend, you need to be a friend. As you serve others, watch how God brings godly friends into your life to encourage you along the way.

Take a moment to list and thank God for the Christian friends He has brought into your life.

March 8
Faith Tested by Temptation

"For this reason, when I could stand it no longer, I sent to find out about your faith. I was afraid that in some way the tempter might have tempted you and our efforts might have been useless." 1 Thess 3:5 (NIV)

Paul cared about the status of the faith of the church of the Thessalonians. He sent Timothy to encourage them in their faith and to measure their progress. Paul knew the power of the evil one to dilute passion and to diffuse spiritual power. The tempter might have tempted them to return to the lifestyle God had delivered them from.

As you walk with the Lord each day, be alert to the strategy of the evil one to distract you from your passion for God's will. The enemy will seek to divert your focus from godliness to worldliness, from selflessness to selfishness, and from eternal things to temporal things. Satan's goal is not to get you to move twenty miles off mission. He just wants you to move an inch today. And then, tomorrow he will seek to get you to move away from God another inch. Before you know it, you will have drifted far from God and lose your passion for the things of God.

- *"But the Lord is faithful, and he will strengthen and protect you from the evil one." 2 Thess 3:3 (NIV)*

Stand firm by anchoring your faith to the rock of God's character. The Lord is faithful. He will not waver in the storms of life. God will not shift in the assault of Satanic attacks on your faith. The Lord will strengthen you in the midst of the battle. He will protect you from the flaming arrows of the evil one. God's grace is more than sufficient for the temptation you encounter and the battles you fight.

March 9
FAITH REVEALED BY TRIALS

"Therefore, brothers, in all our distress and persecution we were encouraged about you because of your faith. For now we really live, since you are standing firm in the Lord." 1 Thess 3:7-8 (NIV)

God allows trials to come into your life to reveal your faith. Whatever is on the inside of you will come out during trials. When trials come, your faith is featured in the display window of life. If doubt, bitterness, and resentment are lingering inside of you, they will seep out during the season of trials. God will purge you of anything that does not bring honor to His Name.

God also uses trials to develop your faith. As you know, God does not waste the trials He allows into your life. God will develop your faith to match the assignment He has for you. The testing of your faith will develop perseverance (James 1:2-3). Spiritual muscles are built through the resistance trials produce. Without pain, there is no growth. God will convert the pain into something beneficial to accomplish His plan.

Paul, Silas, and Timothy were immensely encouraged by the faith of the church of the Thessalonians. Their faith had been revealed through the trials they endured. Living out their Christian faith in a pagan culture was not without resistance. God developed their faith to match the assignment He had for them. Standing firm in the Lord was their faith response to living in an anti-Christian environment.

What do the trials you are facing reveal about your faith? Are you standing firm in the Lord? You have the Holy Spirit living in you making intercession on your behalf. Jesus is at the right hand of our Father interceding for you. No need to retreat. Advance through adversity by standing firm in the Lord.

March 10
REVEALING GOD'S GLORY

"And whatever you do, whether in word or deed, do it all in the name of the Lord Jesus, giving thanks to God the Father through him." Col 3:17 (NIV)

You have the power to conceal or reveal God's glory.

God reveals His glory to you as you worship Him privately and corporately. Whether you encounter God personally through private worship or in a setting with other believers, God reveals His glory. He wants you know His nature and His character. God wants you to come to know Him by experience.

As God reveals Himself to you, your relationship deepens. Your understanding of God's purposes and ways grows as you spend time with Him. What are you going to do with what God reveals to you? Are you going to conceal His glory or reveal His glory?

Authentic worship is a lifestyle. It is not what you come to on Sunday morning or what you go away from on Sunday afternoon. Worship is living a life that honors God as you are doing life in this fallen world. Everything you do should be an act of worship. Even menial tasks can be used to reveal God's glory.

- *"Therefore, I urge you, brothers, in view of God's mercy, to offer your bodies as living sacrifices, holy and pleasing to God--this is your spiritual act of worship." Romans 12:1 (NIV)*

God will orchestrate opportunities today for you to reveal His glory to others. What will others come to know about God's nature and character through your willingness to reveal His glory?

March 11
SHINING HIS LIGHT

"You are the light of the world. A city on a hill cannot be hidden. Neither do people light a lamp and put it under a bowl. Instead they put it on its stand, and it gives light to everyone in the house. In the same way, let your light shine before men, that they may see your good deeds and praise your Father in heaven." Matt 5:14-16 (NIV)

Uncover your candle.

Jesus has transformed your life so that you will become an agent of transformation in the world. Jesus has illuminated your life so that you will reflect His light and extend His love to a lost and dying world. As a child of God, you are the light of the world. God has strategically placed you in a dark culture in order to shine His light in you and through you. You are alive right now on purpose. You live, work, study, and play right where God has placed you to know Jesus and to make Him known.

Is your light shining? Is your candle burning brightly for the Lord? God has created people who need the light you have. God has brought them into your life and placed them in your sphere of influence so that you can let your light shine before them.

Don't fear the open doors God places before you. Don't divert from the path God has placed you on. Don't neglect crossing the bridges God has built for you.

You will come into contact with people today who need the light God has placed within you. Will you uncover the candle? Will you allow the light of Jesus to shine through you in order to reveal His love to others?

March 12
MOUNTAINTOP EXPERIENCES

"After six days Jesus took with him Peter, James and John the brother of James, and led them up a high mountain by themselves. There he was transfigured before them. His face shone like the sun, and his clothes became as white as the light." Matt 17:1-2 (NIV)

If only life was a perpetual mountaintop experience. Wouldn't it be wonderful to be on a constant spiritual high and never come down? Peter, James, and John had a once in a lifetime experience with Jesus on the top of a mountain. Jesus was transfigured before them. Peter wanted to build three shelters in order to stay on the mountaintop and live in the radiance of Jesus' glory.

Jesus used the experience to teach Peter, James, and John the necessity to come down the mountain to meet the needs of people in the valley. In other words, God surprises us with mountaintop experiences to reveal His glory so that we can go into the world to reveal God's glory to others.

Consider the terrain of your spiritual journey. Can you recall the mountaintop experiences you have had with God? Did God reveal His glory to you in those moments so that you would stay in the moment? No! God gave you those special glimpses into His nature and character so that you could go into the valley of life to connect with people in desperate need of God's salvation.

God moments can be difficult to transfer to others. Often, the God moments are for you to be encouraged and strengthened personally. The experience should motivate you to go into the world to declare the message of reconciliation to a world alienated from God.

March 13
DEFINING YOUR GOAL

"So we make it our goal to please him, whether we are at home in the body or away from it." 2 Cor 5:9 (NIV)

We tend to live our lives trying to please others. Just about the time we feel as though we have reached the pinnacle of pleasing others, they change their mind. Trying to please others will be an endless pursuit.

After hosting Dr. Robert Smith of Beeson Divinity School for a few days, he shared with me an amazing concept. He said, "Don't fall in love with the Body (Body of Christ); fall in love with the Head. The Body is fickle. They will be singing 'Hosanna' on Monday and then 'crucify' on Thursday. The Father is faithful."

Does anything else matter more than living to please God? Is there any other pursuit that supersedes that of pleasing God? What are you currently giving your life to?

What does a life that pleases God look like? It includes living worthy of the Lord, bearing fruit in every good work, growing in the knowledge of God, speaking as one approved by God and entrusted with the gospel, and believing that God exists and rewards you as you earnestly seek Him (Col. 1:10, 1 Thes. 2:4, Heb. 11:6).

Make God's smile the goal of your life today. You may want to place a smiley face sticker on your dashboard near the speedometer in your vehicle to serve as a daily reminder of why you exist. You are alive to make God smile. Keep looking up to God and focus your energy on bringing pleasure to Him.

March 14
Reflecting God's Heart

"My brothers, as believers in our glorious Lord Jesus Christ, don't show favoritism." James 2:1 (NIV)

James gives perspective to the believers who have been dispersed by the persecution in Jerusalem. He is writing to the Jews of the Diaspora. They are living outside of their homeland. They are being exposed to different cultures and to different philosophies for living. James reminds them that they are believers in our glorious Lord Jesus Christ. Their position in Christ is to inform their behavior toward others.

We have been transformed by God's grace and adopted into His forever family. Our identity is that of being believers in our glorious Lord Jesus Christ. Our lives take on new meaning as we embrace the way of Jesus. His life and His mission become our reality. Jesus wants to transform the culture through us. Thus, we are not to show favoritism. We are not to value one person over another. We are not to favor one people group over another people group.

- *"'Do not pervert justice; do not show partiality to the poor or favoritism to the great, but judge your neighbor fairly.'" Lev 19:15 (NIV)*
- *"I charge you, in the sight of God and Christ Jesus and the elect angels, to keep these instructions without partiality, and to do nothing out of favoritism." 1 Tim 5:21 (NIV)*

The spirit of favoritism does not reflect the heart of God. As His children, we are not to show favoritism. God has called us to extend His love to every people group on earth. That means to impartially radiate His love and compassion to every person regardless of their skin color or social status. A great start would be for you to begin praying for people who are not like you.

March 15
SEEING OTHERS THROUGH THE CROSS

"Suppose a man comes into your meeting wearing a gold ring and fine clothes, and a poor man in shabby clothes also comes in. If you show special attention to the man wearing fine clothes and say, 'Here's a good seat for you,' but say to the poor man, 'You stand there' or 'Sit on the floor by my feet,' have you not discriminated among yourselves and become judges with evil thoughts?"
James 2:2-4 (NIV)

The corporate worship setting is sacred. When we gather with fellow believers to express our love to God in corporate worship, we are obeying God and demonstrating a reverence for His glory. The worship environment is conducive to encouraging each other and edifying the body of Christ. However, the corporate setting for worship can also be an environment where discrimination seeps in.

Making a judgment about one's appearance based on their attire is condescending to the very one Christ died for. For us to give preferential treatment to those endowed with financial prowess would be tragic in the eyes of God. For us to consider withholding our love, affirmation, acceptance, and inclusion of those less fortunate would break the heart of God. We become the judges when we start ranking human beings and attaching varying levels of worth based on externals.

Preferential treatment misrepresents the character of God. We need to embrace God's perspective on those He created and sent His Son to die for. God took the initiative to establish our value through the atoning work of Jesus on the cross. Every person matters to God. As followers of Jesus Christ, we are to place the same value on others that God does. We are to see others through the saving work of Jesus on the cross.

Is there anyone you are currently looking down on? Have you minimized the value God places on others? Let's be reminded of where we were when God found us in our sin.

March 16
REDEFINING WEALTH

"Listen, my dear brothers: Has not God chosen those who are poor in the eyes of the world to be rich in faith and to inherit the kingdom he promised those who love him? But you have insulted the poor. Is it not the rich who are exploiting you? Are they not the ones who are dragging you into court? Are they not the ones who are slandering the noble name of him to whom you belong?"
James 2:5-7 (NIV)

What is your definition of rich? As you view those in your circles, whom would you identify as rich? In our materialistic culture, we tend to rank wealth based on the acquisition of possessions or the accumulation of exorbitant funds. If only we could operate from God's perspective.

God defines rich based on faith and not funds. In God's economy, the poor in the eyes of the world are made rich in faith and inherit the eternal riches of God's treasure by faith in Jesus. God is the equalizer. God elevates the poor. God can also easily dissipate the rich in the eyes of the world.

Maybe we just need to reflect on life from God's perspective. Maybe we need to contemplate what true wealth is. You can be rich as far as the world's standards are concerned and yet be destitute in God's economy. Forsaking God's offer of eternal life would keep a person in total desperation regardless of his or her earthly assets.

Calculate the value you currently place on others. Do you allow their social status to dictate how you treat them? Do you allow their appearance to formulate your view of them? What if you began to view others from God's perspective?

March 17
LOVING YOUR NEIGHBOR

"If you really keep the royal law found in Scripture, 'Love your neighbor as yourself,' you are doing right." James 2:8 (NIV)

We are by nature self-absorbed, self-centered, and self-focused. When anything happens around us our first question is: How will this affect me? In many ways, we act as though the earth really does rotate around us. The reality of our fallen nature pops up from time to time like a ground hog trying to catch a glimpse of daylight.

Jesus acknowledges the presence of our self-love. We truly love ourselves. As one of my colleagues would often say, "Sometimes you just have to be good to yourself!" We have no problem being good to ourselves do we? We value comfort. We value pleasure. We value looking good and feeling good and sleeping good.

As we begin viewing others from God's perspective, we will begin to value others the way God values them. The resulting choice will be to love others as we love ourselves. In other words, we will begin to treat others the way we want to be treated. We will love others with the same kind of love that we desire to receive.

James identifies that we are doing right when we love others as we love ourselves. Longing to do right is not enough. Putting our faith in action by loving others brings honor to God.

Do you love others as much as you love yourself? Ouch! That's a painful question.

March 18
FAVORITISM AND SIN

"But if you show favoritism, you sin and are convicted by the law as lawbreakers. For whoever keeps the whole law and yet stumbles at just one point is guilty of breaking all of it. For he who said, 'Do not commit adultery,' also said, 'Do not murder.' If you do not commit adultery but do commit murder, you have become a lawbreaker." James 2:9-11 (NIV)

Have you ever heard of the domino effect? If you accidentally tip one domino, it triggers an effect that ultimately impacts every other domino. Tip toeing through life in a fallen world is very similar to the domino effect. It doesn't take much to sin. One impure thought is sin. Failing to do what God wants you do is sin. Doing what God does not want you to do is sin.

- *"For all have sinned and fall short of the glory of God." Romans 3:23 (NIV)*
- *"If we claim to be without sin, we deceive ourselves and the truth is not in us." 1 John 1:8 (NIV)*

Our sin nature causes a chain reaction. The more we sin the more our sin nature craves sin. Whatever you feed grows and whatever you starve dies. Crucify the flesh! Make no provision for sin!

Favoritism is a sin that we can succumb to subtly. It can sneak up on us. We can drift from having God's perspective and then fail to see others through His eyes.

Let's commit to stay sensitive to the presence of sin. Sometimes favoritism is not as tangible in our own lives. We may not even realize that we are showing favoritism. Let's ask God to help us detect even a fraction of favoritism resident in our lives.

March 19
BEING MERCIFUL TO OTHERS

"Speak and act as those who are going to be judged by the law that gives freedom, because judgment without mercy will be shown to anyone who has not been merciful. Mercy triumphs over judgment!" James 2:12-13 (NIV)

Imagine being transferred instantly before the throne of God. You are standing before God right now and you fall on your face before God and He asks you to give an account for your treatment of others. Where would that place you in the area of God's approval and affirmation? How would you measure up to God's standard of perfection?

God is a God of justice. And yes, God is a God of mercy. Without God's justice, mercy would not exist. Without God's mercy, justice would not exist. God declared His justice on your sin when Jesus took upon Himself God's wrath for your sin on the cross. God demonstrated His mercy by providing for the forgiveness of your sin. How will you treat others in light of what God has done for you?

- *"'Blessed are the merciful, for they will be shown mercy.'" Matt 5:7 (NIV)*
- *"'Do not judge, or you too will be judged. For in the same way you judge others, you will be judged, and with the measure you use, it will be measured to you.'" Matt 7:1-2 (NIV)*

Our tendency is to use binoculars when judging our lives and using a microscope when judging the lives of others. Thank God for His mercy. God wants our conversation and our conduct to reflect the mercy we have received from Him. God is not asking us to do anything in our relationship with others that He has not already done for us.

March 20
THE FRAGRANCE OF MERCY

"Speak and act as those who are going to be judged by the law that gives freedom, because judgment without mercy will be shown to anyone who has not been merciful. Mercy triumphs over judgment!" James 2:12-13 (NIV)

Grace is getting what we do not deserve. We do not deserve God's love. We do not deserve God's gift of eternal life. We do not deserve our new identity in Christ. We do not deserve having our names written in the Lamb's Book of Life. Yet, God graced us with these and many other spiritual realities.

Mercy is not getting what we deserve. Because of our sin, we deserve separation, punishment, and alienation. Because of our sin, we deserve eternal damnation. Because of our sin, we deserve total isolation from God's abiding Presence. Yet, God extends His mercy to us and did not give us what we deserved. Instead, God has blessed us, redeemed us, included us, sealed us, and lavished us with His love.

Because of God's mercy, we have a song to sing and a message to declare. As recipients of God's mercy, we have been given a clean canvas upon which we join God in His redemptive activity.

May God's merciful treatment of us radically transform our conversation and our conduct! May our words and our walk exhibit mercy to others as God has exhibited to us!

- *"May the words of my mouth and the meditation of my heart be pleasing in your sight, O LORD, my Rock and my Redeemer." Psalm 19:14 (NIV)*

Viewing others from God's perspective will produce the fragrance of mercy in our lives. May that aroma bring others closer to the love of God that we have found in Christ!

March 21
PUTTING FEET TO YOUR FAITH

"What good is it, my brothers, if a man claims to have faith but has no deeds? Can such faith save him?" James 2:14 (NIV)

What does it take for a person to be saved? Is it possible to have saving faith without deeds? Will my faith be demonstrated by my deeds? So many have embraced an "easy believism" theology that can produce a false sense of security. You can spend your entire life on the earth thinking that you are saved and in reality, be lost. You can profess Christ and not possess Christ.

- *"'Not everyone who says to me, "Lord, Lord," will enter the kingdom of heaven, but only he who does the will of my Father who is in heaven.'" Matt 7:21 (NIV)*
- *"Therefore, my brothers, be all the more eager to make your calling and election sure. For if you do these things, you will never fall, and you will receive a rich welcome into the eternal kingdom of our Lord and Savior Jesus Christ." 2 Peter 1:10-11 (NIV)*

Your eternal destiny is determined by how you respond to God's offer of salvation found in Christ alone. Knowing about Christ is not sufficient for salvation. You must know Christ personally through faith in the completed work of Jesus on the cross.

Take inventory of your spiritual condition. Don't rely on feelings. Trace your steps and identify the moment you had a life-changing experience. Clarify your conversion experience. When did you come to realize your sin and your need for God's forgiveness? When did you acknowledge that Jesus is God's Son and the only way to heaven? When did you receive God's gift of eternal life?

March 22
DEMONSTRATING GENUINE FAITH

"Suppose a brother or sister is without clothes and daily food. If one of you says to him, 'Go, I wish you well; keep warm and well fed,' but does nothing about his physical needs, what good is it? In the same way, faith by itself, if it is not accompanied by action, is dead." James 2:15-17 (NIV)

Your actions speak so loudly I can't hear what you're saying.

If you have been born from above, adopted into God's family, and filled with the Holy Spirit, shouldn't the reality of your salvation be evidenced? If you have experienced transformation on the inside, shouldn't that show up on the outside? Faith void of action is dead. Your faith is to be demonstrated by action.

- *"In the same way, let your light shine before men, that they may see your good deeds and praise your Father in heaven." Matt 5:16 (NIV)*
- *"The Lord's message rang out from you not only in Macedonia and Achaia--your faith in God has become known everywhere. Therefore we do not need to say anything about it, for they themselves report what kind of reception you gave us. They tell how you turned to God from idols to serve the living and true God, and to wait for his Son from heaven, whom he raised from the dead--Jesus, who rescues us from the coming wrath." 1 Thess 1:8-10 (NIV)*

God has put you in the display window of life to demonstrate your faith in practical ways. Find a need and meet it. Shine the light of Jesus and share the love of Jesus.

Pray continually, give sacrificially, and worship passionately. May those who know you but don't know Jesus, come to know Jesus because they know you. May your faith be that convincing! May your faith be activated and demonstrated to a watching world!

March 23
RECAPTURING GOD'S PERSPECTIVE

"Do not be anxious about anything, but in everything, by prayer and petition, with thanksgiving, present your requests to God." Phil 4:6 (NIV)

Anxiety is the great distraction. All of your emotional energy is diverted to fuel the vast demands anxiety produces. Incessant worry evaporates the tranquil waters of peace and contentment. Instead of living to benefit and bless others, you marshal strength to combat the gravitational pull of self-absorption. During these seasons, the small things of life that would usually not phase you appear as giants. Anxiety has a way of distorting your perspective.

What is the antidote to anxiety? How do you recapture God's perspective on your circumstances? The first step is to replace your anxious thoughts with intentional prayer. You have the precious gift of unhindered and uninterrupted access to your Heavenly Father through the avenue of prayer. The more specific you are in your prayer life, the more dynamic your experience of God's peace will be. Be prayerful. Be specific. Be thankful in the midst of your circumstances as you cast your cares upon the Lord.

Consider writing or typing the items in your life right now that are generating anxious thoughts and feelings. Cry out to God in prayer over each item and express your desperation for God's perspective and God's provision. God wants you to seek Him and to long for Him. Your abiding relationship with Him is the most important relationship. Draw near to God.

Begin to anticipate God's response as you specifically present your requests to God in prayer. Watch to see how God brings clarity to your confusion. Take note of the renewed strength God provides to help you navigate the troubled waters. God may eliminate the obstacles or empower you to overcome the obstacles. Either way, you will come to know God by experience!

March 24
THE PROMISE OF PEACE

"And the peace of God, which transcends all understanding, will guard your hearts and your minds in Christ Jesus." Phil 4:7 (NIV)

Choose to replace your anxious thoughts with intentional prayer. Your focus will shift from the gravity of your circumstances to the enormity of God's power. You will gain God's perspective on the obstacles you face and you will be fortified by God's peace.

The peace of God is not the absence of adversity, but the presence of Divinity. God's peace transcends understanding in that it is difficult to fathom. How can a believer have such peace in the midst of a raging storm? The peace of God is not subdued by the intensity of your circumstances. God dispenses His peace in proportion to your need. The stronger the waves of resistance you encounter, the greater the allotment of God's peace you experience.

God's peace will guard your heart. The enemy knows that if he can rob you of your passion for God in the midst of your adversity, he will have stolen a piece of your heart. The peace of God will guard your heart from the toxic assaults unleashed by the enemy. You have given your heart to Christ and His peace will reign in you.

During seasons of adversity, the enemy seeks to pollute your mind with thoughts of fear, timidity, and doubt. God's peace will guard your mind. As you replace your thoughts with intentional prayer, the peace of God will shield your mind. Fear will be replaced by faith, timidity will be replaced with courage, and doubt will be replaced with assurance.

How's your heart? How's your mind? Are you experiencing the peace that transcends all understanding? Let the peace of God provide relief to your soul.

March 25
LEARNING CONTENTMENT

"I know what it is to be in need, and I know what it is to have plenty. I have learned the secret of being content in any and every situation, whether well fed or hungry, whether living in plenty or in want." Phil 4:12 (NIV)

The landscape of living in a fallen world is littered with inconsistencies, fluctuation, and instability. Selfishness and sin permeate our planet. People let us down. Deception, injustice, and greed fuel the choices made throughout the earth on a daily basis. Sound hopeless? Don't lose heart.

Paul understood the cultural current of living on a broken planet. He experienced the extremes of life including being a persecutor of the church and then becoming a preacher of the gospel. Paul knew adversity on a first name basis. Read 2 Corinthians 11:23-28 for a snapshot of his resume of rejection, ridicule, and rigorous suffering. While incarcerated by the Roman government, Paul writes this personal love letter to the church at Philippi to remind them of his love for them and to encourage them in their faith.

You may not be able to control your circumstances, but with Christ's help, you can control how you respond to your circumstances. You may not be able to control how people treat you, but you can control how you respond to their treatment. Contentment is learned in the laboratory of life. God works through the daily grind in your life to form you and to fashion you. Don't miss what God is seeking to do in your life in the midst of your adversity.

Are you learning the secret of being content in any and every situation? What's the secret? "I can do everything through him who gives me strength" (Phil 4:13 NIV). Christ Jesus is the curator of contentment!

March 26
Claiming God's Promise

"'For I know the plans I have for you,' declares the LORD, 'plans to prosper you and not to harm you, plans to give you hope and a future.'" Jer 29:11 (NIV)

God has plans for your life. Where are you currently in relation to God's plans? Have you had some bumps along the way? Have you experienced any delays or detours? God factored in your response to His plans before you were ever born. God knew how you would navigate the path He has for you. Remember, nothing catches God by surprise. God sees the totality of your life from beginning to end. He knew when you would be born and where you would live and even the personality you would express. God's plans always prevail.

- *"But the plans of the LORD stand firm forever, the purposes of his heart through all generations." Psalm 33:11 (NIV)*
- *"Many are the plans in a man's heart, but it is the LORD's purpose that prevails." Prov 19:21 (NIV)*

You can anchor your life in God's plans. His plans are to prosper you, to give you hope and a future. Your future goes beyond this present life. Your future includes eternity. God's plans stand firm forever. Where Satan puts a period, God puts a comma. God's purpose prevails.

You may not know what tomorrow holds, but you know who holds tomorrow! Turn this verse into a prayer. "Lord, I know that You know the plans you have for me. Your plans are to prosper me and not to harm me. Thank You precious Lord that Your plans are to give me hope and a future. I entrust my present and my future to Your care. In Jesus' name, Amen."

March 27
Trusting God's Plan

"One day Jesus said to his disciples, 'Let's go over to the other side of the lake.' So they got into a boat and set out." Luke 8:22 (NIV)

God will get you to the other side. His plan for you is personal. God designed you with His purpose in mind. You are not an accident. Before you were born, God knew you (Jer. 1:5). You are here at this very moment because God ordained your existence. God has a special plan for your life that includes your past, present, and future.

God's plan factors in your choices. You are not an impersonal robotic creature. You are a personal relational being with the purpose of God in your heart. God knows you by name and even the hairs upon your head are numbered (Luke 12:7).

God's plan for you is eternal. There's more in store than what you see in the here and now. God has placed eternity in your heart to position you for eternal life (Eccl. 3:11). Your life goes beyond the grave. God's plan for you extends beyond the immediate and includes eternal life. As you receive the gift of eternal life by faith, your forever is changed. Heaven becomes the place where you will live with God forever.

The disciples responded to Jesus by getting into a boat and setting out. Jesus said, "Let's go over to the other side." Jesus did not say, "Let's see if we can make it to the other side." When Jesus is in your boat, there's nothing to fear. Jesus will get you to the destination safely and right on time. Enjoy the journey! Trust God's plan!

March 28
PROGRESSIVE REVELATION

"In the past God spoke to our forefathers through the prophets at many times and in various ways, but in these last days he has spoken to us by his Son, whom he appointed heir of all things, and through whom he made the universe." Heb 1:1-2 (NIV)

God is a God of revelation. He unveils that which was once hidden. God passionately reveals His truth so that we can know Him and serve Him and fulfill His plan. His revelation is progressive in that God chose to reveal His general revelation through nature (Rom 1:20) and His special revelation by Jesus (John 1:14). God became like us so that we can become like Him.

Our God is a God who speaks. He desires to communicate His love to His creation. Henry Blackaby, in his study, Experiencing God, taught us that God speaks by the Holy Spirit through the Bible, prayer, circumstances, and the church to reveal Himself, His purposes, and His ways. The Holy Spirit enables the believer to understand and apply God's Word.

- *"But the Counselor, the Holy Spirit, whom the Father will send in my name, will teach you all things and will remind you of everything I have said to you." John 14:26 (NIV)*

Notice how the Holy Spirit is identified as a Teacher and a Reminder. God, through the Holy Spirit gives us wisdom to appropriate His Word in our daily living. The Holy Spirit teaches us God's Word and reminds us of what God has spoken.

As you read God's Word, ask God to give you the Spirit of wisdom so that you may know Him better. Are you growing in your knowing? Have you placed your faith in the completed work of Jesus on the cross?

March 29
ENTERING OUR BOX

"The Word became flesh and made his dwelling among us. We have seen his glory, the glory of the One and Only, who came from the Father, full of grace and truth." John 1:14 (NIV)

Why did Jesus leave the glory of heaven to come to earth? What motivated Him to leave an environment of pure and persistent worship to dwell among sinful and rebellious humanity? God chose to become like us. God robed Himself in flesh.

Religion is man's attempt to break out the box of the natural and to seek to enter the realm of the supernatural. Man's attempt is futile at best. Knowing that we could not enter the realm of the supernatural, God chose to enter our natural realm. God entered our box in the Person of Jesus.

Jesus lived a sinless life and died a sacrificial death to atone for our sins. Jesus did for us that which we could not do for ourselves. Our righteousness does not measure up to the standard of God's holiness. Even on our best day, we completely miss the mark of God's perfection. The Good News is that the Word became flesh and made His dwelling among us. Jesus identified with us so that we could identify with Him.

Jesus came from the Father full of grace. His grace provides us with the gift of eternal life that we could never earn, nor deserve. His grace enables us to accept His acceptance of us.

Jesus also came from the Father full of truth. The truth of our condition without Christ is that of utter hopelessness. We stand bankrupt before our Holy God. Jesus demonstrated the truth of forgiveness, righteousness, and restoration. The truth is that our sin debt has been paid in full.

March 30
CULTIVATING INTIMACY WITH THE LORD

"My sheep listen to my voice; I know them, and they follow me." John 10:27 (NIV)

You can live your life at a distance relationally and experience the absence of meaningful relationships with others. The relational deficit will soon erode your joy and remove your smile. God made us for relationships.

The shepherd and sheep relationship is very prominent in the Bible. Dependent on the shepherd's care, the sheep learns to respond to the shepherd's voice. There is a connection that develops through the consistent exposure to the voice of compassion and concern.

- *"We all, like sheep, have gone astray, each of us has turned to his own way; and the LORD has laid on him the iniquity of us all." Isaiah 53:6 (NIV)*
- *"For you were like sheep going astray, but now you have returned to the Shepherd and Overseer of your souls." 1 Peter 2:25 (NIV)*

Jesus is the Shepherd of our souls. He took on the full wrath of God for our sin. Jesus invites us into an intimate love relationship that is personal and eternal. We participate in the cultivation of that relationship once we turn from our sin and turn to Christ alone for salvation. Each day as we spend time in prayer and Bible reading, the love relationship deepens and our faith increases.

Learn to recognize the voice of Truth. God speaks to us in alignment with His Word and His will. You will hear the still small voice of the Lord speaking to you as you practice His Presence throughout each day. Be sensitive to the prompting of the Holy Spirit living in you. Tune out the noise of worry and worldliness and tune in to the voice of the One who sought you and bought you with His own blood.

March 31
EMBRACING MORAL PURITY

"For God did not call us to be impure, but to live a holy life." 1 Thess 4:7 (NIV)

Is it possible to stay clean while living in a dirty world? Every possibility for contaminating our lives is available to us. Sin is rampant. We face trials from without and temptation from within. The cultural current is moving in the opposite direction of the Christ honoring flow. We must make a conscious and continuous decision to walk in purity.

- *"Since we have these promises, dear friends, let us purify ourselves from everything that contaminates body and spirit, perfecting holiness out of reverence for God." 2 Cor 7:1 (NIV)*
- *"Don't let anyone look down on you because you are young, but set an example for the believers in speech, in life, in love, in faith and in purity." 1 Tim 4:12 (NIV)*

Purify yourself and perfect holiness. Purify your heart and set an example for the believers in purity. In Christ, you are positionally pure. In Christ, you are a new creation. Live out practically what you are presently and positionally in Christ. The only way to reign in this life is to allow Christ to reign in your life.

Staying clean while living in a dirty world is only possible in the strength Christ provides. Jesus has already set the example. Jesus has demonstrated the life of purity in a sin-polluted culture. Jesus lived a sinless life and died a sacrificial death so that you can walk in victory.

Embrace moral purity by yielding to the Lordship of Christ. Make Jesus the Lord of your life. God called you to live a holy life. Now give Jesus His rightful place in your life and allow Him to live His life through you.

April 1
Measuring Your Value

"I am the good shepherd. The good shepherd lays down his life for the sheep."
John 10:11 (NIV)

Because He is the Good Shepherd, you are valued.

Your value is not determined by your portfolio. Your value is not determined by your performance. Your value is not determined by your personality. Your value is determined by what God has done on your behalf. Before you could do anything with God or for God, in His mercy and grace, God decided what to do with you and for you.

Your value was established before you were born. God knew you before He formed you in your mother's womb (Jer. 1:5). God chose to provide a tangible demonstration and validation of your value by becoming man (John 1:1,14).

Is the Lord your Shepherd (Ps. 23)? Have you allowed Him to be the Shepherd and Overseer of your soul? Now think about your value in God's economy. You are the apple of God's eye. You are His treasure. Look around! Do you see other people in your weekly routine? Guess what? God values them, too.

Communicate God's love to others. Show them how much the Good Shepherd loves them by emulating His personal touch. Slow down and show how much you care about others. Let them see the Shepherd's heart inside of you. God values those you interact with each day.

April 2
RESTORING RUPTURED RELATIONSHIPS

"All kinds of animals, birds, reptiles and creatures of the sea are being tamed and have been tamed by man, but no man can tame the tongue. It is a restless evil, full of deadly poison." James 3:7-8 (NIV)

Doing life requires restraint. There are countless temptations used of Satan to entice us to compromise our Christianity. His goal is to get us to drift from our devotion to God. One of Satan's favorite tools is an unbridled tongue. He knows that our words can do more damage than our actions alone.

Have you ever said something you deeply regretted? Have you had one of those moments when you spoke before you had time to really think through and process what you were going to say? Ouch! It is impossible to retrieve words once spoken. If only we could snatch them out of the air before they made contact with the tympanic membrane of someone's ear. If you have ever allowed words to slip and wound someone, then embrace this great word from God on how to respond.

- *"If you have been trapped by what you said, ensnared by the words of your mouth, then do this, my son, to free yourself, since you have fallen into your neighbor's hands: Go and humble yourself; press your plea with your neighbor!" Prov 6:2-3 (NIV)*

Has God placed someone on your heart that you have wounded with your words? Are you willing to go to them in humility in order to apologize and ask for their forgiveness? God will honor your obedience to His word. God will make a way for you to experience restoration. Restoration is God's specialty! Don't delay. Make things right!

April 3
RELYING UPON GOD

"Some trust in chariots and some in horses, but we trust in the name of the LORD our God." Psalm 20:7 (NIV)

This verse became dear to my heart when I was pastoring my seminary church in 1992. My wife, Tonya, and I went through the Experiencing God study along with our deacons and their wives. My journey of faith has been enhanced by the concept of trusting in the name of the Lord our God.

Trust is a fragile item in the life of a believer. Trust is like the petal of a rose. Trust can beautify a difficult path and create an aroma pleasing to Christ. Trust can also wilt when betrayed. Like a gem in the hand of a jeweler, trust in God can lead to an irresistible life in which God's glory radiates.

What do you trust in? In our society draped with affluence, it is so easy to trust in materialism. If we can only acquire one more object of our affection or jump into one more activity that produces an adrenaline rush, then we will be fulfilled...so we think. The things of this world just don't deliver what they promise. The chariots of our culture and the horses of our entertainment are not trustworthy.

Only God can deliver on the magnitude of His promises. God always lives up to the level of His nature and character of perfection. There is no lack! There is no discrepancy! God is all sufficient and more than enough! Fully rely upon God.

April 4
Perpetual Obedience

"Commit your way to the LORD; trust in him and he will do this: He will make your righteousness shine like the dawn, the justice of your cause like the noonday sun." Psalm 37:5-6 (NIV)

A few months after I surrendered to preach at age sixteen, God placed a true man of God in my life. His name was J.D. Scott. He had been preaching for over 55 years and was serving as an interim pastor. Pastor J.D. invited me to ride with him to his church and allowed me to preach in his pulpit. It was only my third time to ever preach. A few days later, I received a personal thank you letter in the mail from Pastor J.D. and next to his signature he wrote, "Psalm 37:5-6." As you can imagine, I immediately opened my bible to read those verses to see what God wanted to say to me.

Your responsibility is to commit your way to the Lord and trust Him to do what He said He will do. God will take the imputed righteousness of Christ within your life and make it shine so that others may be drawn to Christ in you. Surrender your ambition, your desires, and your dreams to God and trust Him to shine His penetrating light through you to touch the nations.

God will make the justice of your cause like the noonday sun. As you put feet to the purposes of God in your life, God will produce the momentum and establish the magnitude of your impact for His glory. Trust in God. Remember that God can do more through your life fully surrendered to His Lordship in a matter of minutes than you can do on your own. Let God have full reign in your life.

Will others see Jesus in you today? Will others be drawn to the Savior of the world because of your perpetual obedience and surrender to Him? You can trust Jesus with your life!

April 5
HAVING A SONG TO SING

"He put a new song in my mouth, a hymn of praise to our God. Many will see and fear and put their trust in the LORD." Psalm 40:3 (NIV)

What is your life song? Has God put a new song in your mouth? As children of God, we have the life transforming message of Jesus. If you have been redeemed by the blood of Jesus, then you have a song to sing. It does not matter how musically inclined you are. What matters is that you have a song to sing! Your life in Christ is a song that others will observe.

Will others see Christ in your life song? Will they see and revere Jesus because of your life song? Will others place their trust in Jesus as a result of the song that your life sings? God has given us the wonderful and awesome privilege to be the tangible portrait of His grace on this planet. The conversations and interactions that you engage in on a daily basis are chords that vibrate the rhythm of God's love.

When you study the life of Jesus you will notice that Jesus maximized the opportunities presented to Him each day. Jesus lived a life that radiated the love of God. People were drawn to Jesus because His life song declared the magnitude of God's abundant grace and mercy.

Maybe you are in a season currently that has inhibited the song in your mouth. Maybe you have not had a song to sing due to hurt, anger, or disappointment. Ask God to renew your mind and to renew your strength. Ask God to put a new song in your mouth to help you persevere and experience a breakthrough. God knows right where you are and exactly what you need. Trust God!

April 6
LIVING IN VICTORY

"I do not trust in my bow, my sword does not bring me victory; but you give us victory over our enemies, you put our adversaries to shame." Psalm 44:6-7 (NIV)

When you identify an area that you are gifted in or an activity that comes naturally to you, it is easy to place your confidence in that area or activity. Sometimes our competence becomes our confidence. We begin to trust the gifts and abilities that God has given us to the neglect of relying upon His strength. Sometimes we may even forget how we have become victorious. What do you trust in? Who are you relying upon to live the victorious Christian life?

- *"'But blessed is the man who trusts in the LORD, whose confidence is in him. He will be like a tree planted by the water that sends out its roots by the stream. It does not fear when heat comes; its leaves are always green. It has no worries in a year of drought and never fails to bear fruit.'" Jer 17:7-8 (NIV)*
- *"No, in all these things we are more than conquerors through him who loved us." Romans 8:37 (NIV)*

God gives us the victory. The credit does not belong to us for weathering the storms of life. God gives us the grace we need to both live and die. God provides us with His ample supply of manna and quail. God multiplies the loaves and fish to nourish us.

Spend a few moments thanking God for coming to your rescue. Be mindful of how needy you are and how generous God is. Weigh the privilege of trusting God and using the gifts and abilities He has given in order to live for His glory. Don't miscalculate the value God places on your life and on your obedience.

April 7
THE BATTLE IS THE LORD'S

"Those who trust in the LORD are like Mount Zion, which cannot be shaken but endures forever." Psalm 125:1 (NIV)

Can God use a shepherd boy to slay a giant? We all face giants in this life. Sometimes the giants are related to health, sometimes related to family or friends, and sometimes related to finances. The giants before us are not obstacles to overcome but rather opportunities for our trust in the Lord to be developed and displayed. God gets the glory when the victory is won. When David faced his giant, Goliath, God received the glory.

- *"David said to the Philistine, 'You come against me with sword and spear and javelin, but I come against you in the name of the LORD Almighty, the God of the armies of Israel, whom you have defied. This day the LORD will hand you over to me, and I'll strike you down and cut off your head. Today I will give the carcasses of the Philistine army to the birds of the air and the beasts of the earth, and the whole world will know that there is a God in Israel. All those gathered here will know that it is not by sword or spear that the LORD saves; for the battle is the LORD's, and he will give all of you into our hands." 1 Sam 17:45-47 (NIV)*

Repeat this phrase aloud, "The battle is the Lord's." Just speaking forth that phrase reminds us that the battle is not about us, but about God and what He wants to accomplish in us and through us. The opposition you face in this life provides you with multiple opportunities to trust in God and demonstrate His ability to enable you to endure difficult circumstances. As long as you anchor your trust in God, you will not be shaken. The evidence of stability will be realized as you place your trust in God.

Now consider your giants. Is there anything you are facing that God cannot handle? Remember, the battle is the Lord's.

April 8
FORGIVING OTHERS

"Be kind and compassionate to one another, forgiving each other, just as in Christ God forgave you." Eph 4:32 (NIV)

Extending forgiveness is intentional and perpetual. The words "just as" are powerful. In our key verse above, they mean to imitate and to emulate God's forgiveness. We are to forgive each other just as in Christ God forgave us. Let's consider going on a personal journey together in order to extend forgiveness to those who have wounded us.

Ask God to bring to your mind someone you need to forgive. This may induce feelings of hurt, betrayal, or neglect. Now that you have someone in mind, take that person with you to the cross in prayer. In fact, you may even need to take them by the hand as you kneel with them at the foot of the cross. Remember that Jesus knows him or her better than you do. Jesus loves him or her more than you do. Also, Jesus paid the full price for his or her complete forgiveness.

In prayer, say to the Lord, "Jesus, as You have graciously forgiven me, I now choose to forgive (insert his or her name)." Release that person from the prison of your unforgiveness. Genuinely extend forgiveness as in Christ God forgave you. Now entrust that person and your future to God. "'And when you stand praying, if you hold anything against anyone, forgive him, so that your Father in heaven may forgive you your sins'" (Mark 11:25 NIV). Forgiveness is always the best decision.

April 9
DYING TO LIVE

"He himself bore our sins in his body on the tree, so that we might die to sins and live for righteousness; by his wounds you have been healed." 1 Peter 2:24 (NIV)

Jesus died so we could live. Our destiny was destruction. Our identity was diluted by sin. Our iniquity was placed upon Jesus (Is. 53:6). Jesus became sin for us so that we could be recipients of His righteousness (2 Cor. 5:21). Jesus bore our sins on the cross. The penalty for our sin was atoned for. Jesus paid our sin debt in full. It is finished (Jn. 19:30).

- *"He is the atoning sacrifice for our sins, and not only for ours but also for the sins of the whole world." 1 John 2:2 (NIV)*
- *"This is love: not that we loved God, but that he loved us and sent his Son as an atoning sacrifice for our sins." 1 John 4:10 (NIV)*

God took the initiative to communicate His unconditional love (Rom. 5:8). The cross is a visible and tangible demonstration of God's redeeming love. Jesus died as the sinless atoning sacrifice for you. You can now die to sin and live for righteousness. His physical wounds spiritually heal you.

When God sees you, He views you through the shed blood of Jesus. Your life is now hidden with Christ (Col. 3:3). God's love is made complete in you. What if you started living in light of that reality? In Christ, you are a new creation (2 Cor. 5:17).

April 10
REMOVAL OF SIN

"Just as man is destined to die once, and after that to face judgment, so Christ was sacrificed once to take away the sins of many people; and he will appear a second time, not to bear sin, but to bring salvation to those who are waiting for him." Heb 9:27-28 (NIV)

In the Old Testament sacrificial system, the high priest would enter the holy of holies once a year on the Day of Atonement to offer sacrifices for the sins of his family and for all the people. One goat would be chosen to be sacrificed for the Lord and one goat would become the scapegoat (Lev. 16:10). The blood from the goat sacrificed as a sin offering would be sprinkled throughout the altar, sanctuary, and tent of meeting to remove defilements of the past year. The high priest would then place his hands on the head of the scapegoat and symbolically transfer the sins of the people to it. The scapegoat, also known as the goat of removal, would be led away from the people into the desert to picture the removal of sins.

Jesus bore our sins on the cross to pay the penalty for our sin. Jesus took our punishment for sin to satisfy God's justice. In His mercy, Christ was sacrificed to remove our sins. Our sin debt has been paid in full and our salvation purchased through the atoning work of Jesus on the cross. Jesus became our scapegoat to take away our sins.

Have you confessed your sins? Have your received God's provision for the forgiveness of your sins? Spend some time thanking Jesus for the removal of your sins.

April 11
THE MIRACLE OF RECONCILIATION

"But now he has reconciled you by Christ's physical body through death to present you holy in his sight, without blemish and free from accusation." Col 1:22 (NIV)

Does life make sense to you? Are you clear about why you exist and why God has placed you right where you are? Do you understand where you fit in God's story?

It all begins with God and His invitation for you to be reconciled to Him. Discipleship is both initial and perpetual. You make an initial commitment to Christ by confessing your sin and receiving God's provision for the forgiveness of your sin. You are reconciled to God and your old life of sin is exchanged for the new life Christ provides. Your commitment to Christ is perpetual in that following Christ is an ongoing moment-by-moment conscious decision to continue following Christ.

God's redemptive story includes you. If you choose to become a follower of Jesus Christ, you come into alignment with God's purpose and plan. Life will never make sense until you come to the place of turning your life completely over to Jesus. Allow Him to be the Lord of your life. Bring Jesus to the center of your destiny and your daily decisions.

In Christ, you are reconciled to God and considered holy in His sight. You are now without blemish and free from accusation through the death of Christ. His sacrifice brought forth your new identity in Christ.

April 12
HE HAS RISEN

"He is not here; he has risen! Remember how he told you, while he was still with you in Galilee: 'The Son of Man must be delivered into the hands of sinful men, be crucified and on the third day be raised again.'" Luke 24:6-7 (NIV)

In a world saturated with the confetti of bad news, as followers of Jesus Christ, we have the privilege of operating on the basis of the good news of the resurrection. Jesus has risen! He is alive! The tomb is empty!

Our message to the world is a message of hope. Our message to the world is a message filled with resurrection power and a demonstration of God's unconditional love. Just as we have experienced the reality of the resurrected Christ, we can share that wonderful news with a world living in darkness and doubt.

For the believer, everyday is Easter. We operate our lives in light of the reality of the resurrection of Jesus from the dead. The grave couldn't hold Him and death couldn't defeat Him. Jesus conquered sin, the grave, and death. Jesus brought forth life eternal to those who believe in Him.

Are you living in light of the resurrection? Is your life a perpetual demonstration of resurrection power? Share the good news of the resurrection. Live each moment in the resurrection power God provides. The same power that raised Jesus from the dead is available to you. You cannot live the Christian life in your own power. Righteous living requires resurrection power.

April 13
RESURRECTION REALITY

"Jesus said to her, 'I am the resurrection and the life. He who believes in me will live, even though he dies; and whoever lives and believes in me will never die. Do you believe this?'" John 11:25-26 (NIV)

Belief brings ultimate relief. Believing in Jesus brings the ultimate relief of knowing that you will never die. In Christ, you will never experience the sting of death (1 Cor. 15:55-57). Those who choose to live and believe in Jesus will never die. For the Child of God, death is not a wall to climb, but rather an open door to enter. Jesus has built the bridge to transfer a believer from life on earth to life in heaven.

Martha was troubled by the death of her brother, Lazarus. She did not understand why Jesus delayed in coming to the rescue. Jesus comforted Martha and affirmed that He was the resurrection and the life. Martha placed her faith in Jesus (John 11:27). Jesus called Lazarus forth from the grave and he came out wrapped in grave clothes. Jesus commanded that his grave clothes be removed. Lazarus experienced Jesus as the resurrection and the life. Martha witnessed the miracle of resurrection.

As a child of God, you are armed with the powerful message of eternal hope and security. You can personally deliver the good news that whoever confesses Christ will never die. You can participate with God in His redemptive activity by sharing the saving news of Jesus with the lost. Heaven and eternal life are fixtures in the life of every believer.

April 14
RESURRECTION POWER

"With great power the apostles continued to testify to the resurrection of the Lord Jesus, and much grace was upon them all." Acts 4:33 (NIV)

How is resurrection power evidenced in your life? The apostles demonstrated resurrection power as they testified of the bodily resurrection of the Lord. They combated immense opposition to share the gospel. They were willing to risk everything for the sake of witnessing to the reality of the resurrected Lord. As they gave witness of the Lord's resurrection, the grace of God was upon them.

Could it be that God reserves His resurrection power for the most important task? Is it possible that God unleashes His resurrection power when you join Him in His redemptive activity? When you testify of His redeeming love, God releases His power in you to accomplish His task of spreading the fragrance of Christ. When you enter the spiritual battlefield for the souls of men, women, boys, and girls, God empowers you for the mission.

Are you attempting anything that requires resurrection power? Are you living on mission with God to the extent that you are desperate for His divine enabling? God has given you everything you need for life and godliness (2 Peter 1:3). As you share the gospel, remember that it is the power of God for the salvation of everyone who believes (Rom. 1:16).

There's no need to be ashamed. Operate in the resurrection power God provides. Allow God to take you places you have never been in your love relationship with Him. Trust God to give you the boldness and the courage to confront the culture and to present the wonderful saving news of Jesus.

April 15
REIGNING IN LIFE

"And if the Spirit of him who raised Jesus from the dead is living in you, he who raised Christ from the dead will also give life to your mortal bodies through his Spirit, who lives in you." Romans 8:11 (NIV)

Is He in you? Is the Holy Spirit living in you? If you are a child of God, then you are the walking tabernacle of the presence of Almighty God. Your body is the temple of the Holy Spirit (1 Cor. 6:19-20). The Holy Spirit is your Counselor, the Spirit of truth, who lives with you and in you forever (John 14:16-17). At the moment of your conversion, you received the Holy Spirit as a deposit guaranteeing what is to come (2 Cor. 5:5). You were saved the moment you confessed Jesus as Lord and believed in your heart that God raised Him from the dead (Rm. 10:9-10). The Holy Spirit is the deposit guaranteeing your eternal inheritance (Eph. 1:14).

This same Spirit, the Holy Spirit, who raised Jesus from the dead, gives life to your mortal body. Your body is in a constant motion of decay. Your mortal body is not made to last forever. One day, you will receive a glorified body. Until then, you are to allow the Holy Spirit to live in you and through you to accomplish God's mission on earth.

You cannot reign in this life unless you allow the Holy Spirit to reign in your life. Surrender to His control. Be filled with the Holy Spirit by yielding to His leadership in your life (Eph. 5:18). Live by the Spirit (Gal. 5:16). Allow the Holy Spirit to bear His fruit (Gal. 5:22-23). Stay connected to the Vine and bear much fruit for the glory of God (John 15:5).

April 16
ROLLING THE STONE AWAY

"When the Sabbath was over, Mary Magdalene, Mary the mother of James, and Salome bought spices so that they might go to anoint Jesus' body. Very early on the first day of the week, just after sunrise, they were on their way to the tomb and they asked each other, 'Who will roll the stone away from the entrance of the tomb?'" Mark 16:1-3 (NIV)

What's on your mind this morning? Is there anything that has been troubling you and draining your emotional energy? On their way to the tomb, Mary Magdalene, Mary the mother of James, and Salome were troubled by the challenge of removing the massive stone covering the entrance to the tomb. They were perplexed by the apparent dilemma. The question lingered in their minds, "Who will roll the stone away?"

Perhaps you are facing a challenge that defies your ability to bring about resolution. Maybe there is an obstacle keeping you from living the victorious Christian life God offers. Who will roll the stone away for you? Your stone may be financial, relational, or vocational. Your stone may be medical, emotional, or familial. Whatever your stone represents, God has the power to roll your stone away.

When the women arrived at the tomb, they saw that the stone had been rolled away (Mark 16:4). The very thing that had worried them most was alleviated first. God had rolled the stone away, not to let Jesus out, but to let the women in. God had already provided for their victory. God did for the women that which they could not do for themselves.

Have you given your stone to the Lord? In prayer, spend some time releasing your stone of adversity, your stone of worry, or your stone of uncertainty. Receive the comfort God provides. Embrace the resolution God prompts. Trust God's timing to accomplish His will His way. God knows the obstacles in your path. God sees the terrain of your pain. Place your confidence in the One who created you for His glory.

April 17
Resurrection Faith

"Who is he that condemns? Christ Jesus, who died--more than that, who was raised to life--is at the right hand of God and is also interceding for us." Romans 8:34 (NIV)

What did Jesus do? He lived a sinless life, He died a sacrificial death, and He rose bodily from the dead. After His resurrection, Jesus appeared to over five hundred eyewitnesses (1 Cor. 15:6). Then, Jesus ascended back to His Father in heaven (Lk. 24:51).

Now what? What does Jesus do? Jesus intercedes for us. He is at the right hand of God praying for us. Jesus always lives to intercede for us (Heb. 7:25). Not only do we enjoy the fruit of His death, resurrection, and ascension, but we also continue to benefit from Jesus' ministry of intercessory prayer. Jesus is alive and actively fulfilling God's agenda.

You can receive God's offer of salvation by grace through faith (Eph. 2:8-9). You can be adopted into God's family (Eph. 1:5). Your name can be written in the Lamb's book of life (Rev. 21:27). Your sins can be forgiven (1 Jn. 1:9). You have access to everything you need for life and godliness (2 Pt. 1:3).

As you abide in Christ and grow in your love relationship with Him, you have the permanent indwelling of the Holy Spirit within you. In Christ, your salvation is secure and Jesus makes intercession for you. Not a moment goes by in which Jesus is not praying for you. Your name, your life, your circumstances, and your future continually go before our Heavenly Father through the compassionate lips of Jesus. Jesus died for you and Jesus lives to intercede for you.

April 18
LIVING IN THE POWER

"He is not here; he has risen, just as he said. Come and see the place where he lay." Mt. 28:6 (NIV)

Are you living in the power of the resurrection? Jesus is alive! The redemptive act of God has ushered forth new life and a new beginning. God is who He says He is and does what He says He will do. The resurrection of Jesus from the dead changes everything. The darkness has turned to light. Sin and death no longer have mastery over us. Both have been defeated.

Have you allowed the empty tomb to become a reality in your daily living? Are you walking in perpetual consciousness of God's redemptive activity? There's more to Easter than just dressing up and going to church. The fact that Jesus rose from the dead establishes our eternal destiny and enables us to proclaim His redemption story throughout the earth.

Praise the Living God today! He rules and He reigns! Allow Jesus to have full access to your hurts, your habits, and your hang ups. Allow Him to bring His resurrection power to every area of your life so that you can live in fullness everyday. The same power that raised Jesus from the dead is available to you. Live in His resurrection power.

April 19
SERVING IN RESURRECTION POWER

"And I tell you that you are Peter, and on this rock I will build my church, and the gates of Hades will not overcome it." Matt 16:18 (NIV)

God ordained marriage and God ordained the church. We are married to Christ and our union is expressed through His Body, the church. Peter confessed that Jesus was the Christ, the Son of the living God. Jesus affirmed that He would build His church on that reality.

In order to become a follower of Jesus Christ and become a member of His Body, the church, a person must confess Jesus as the Christ, the Son of the living God. This profession of our faith is essential to salvation (Rom. 10:9-10). Jesus builds His church by adopting us into His family (Eph. 1:5). Only those who are born again enter into His Kingdom (John 3:3).

Jesus builds His church. Our job is to be the church. Jesus saves people from their sin. Our job is to share the Good News of Jesus so that others can know Jesus personally and eternally. Jesus saves us, not sit, but to serve. Our role in the Body of Christ, the church, is to empty hell and to populate heaven.

How many people will be in heaven because of you?

April 20
SPIRITUAL BLESSINGS IN CHRIST

"Paul, an apostle of Christ Jesus by the will of God, to the saints in Ephesus, the faithful in Christ Jesus:" Eph 1:1 (NIV)

In her book, *Breaking Free*, Beth Moore reminds us of our position in Christ in the following affirmations:

God is who He says He is.

God can do what He says He can do.

I am who God says I am.

I can do all things through Christ.

God's Word is alive and active in me.

Seek to memorize these five statements and speak them aloud each morning to start your day off in the right frame of mind. It will affect your outlook and attitude in a life-giving way. Focus with me on the third affirmation: I am who God says I am. Repeat that phrase to yourself and allow it to sink in. Let's notice the connection of this truth with the spiritual blessings we have in Christ.

If you are in Christ, then God says that you are a saint. A saint is one who has been set apart by God. Your faith in the atoning work of Christ on the cross transfers your identity to that of a saint. It does not mean that you are perfect and immune to the presence of sin. It means that God positions you as a saint. God did for you that which you could not do for yourself. You have a new standing before God and with God. If you are in Christ, then you are a new creation (2 Cor. 5:17). God made Jesus to become sin so that you could become the righteousness of God in Christ (2 Cor. 5:21).

April 21
BLESSED TO BE A BLESSING

"Praise be to the God and Father of our Lord Jesus Christ, who has blessed us in the heavenly realms with every spiritual blessing in Christ." Eph 1:3 (NIV)

You are God's treasure. Can you imagine the Creator of the universe being the reason for your existence? You are not an accident. God purposed for you to be born. You were planned by God. Another reality of being in Christ is that you are blessed. If you are in Christ, then you can say, "I am blessed." Go ahead and say it aloud!

God has blessed you in the heavenly realms with every spiritual blessing in Christ. God's resources are unlimited. He never runs out! He never runs dry! His shelves are never empty! Our God of abundance has blessed you with every spiritual blessing in Christ.

When someone asks you today, "How are you doing?"...don't say, "Oh, I'm doing alright." Instead, say with conviction and confidence and assurance, "I am blessed!" Doesn't that make you want to shout? Don't ever forget who you are in Christ. You are a child of the King! You are blessed and highly favored by the Lord. Walk in the new identity you have in Christ.

You are blessed to be a blessing to others. Regardless of your circumstances, your identity in Christ is safe and secure. Your identity is fashioned by God. You are blessed by God to be a blessing for God.

April 22
CHOSEN BY GOD

"For he chose us in him before the creation of the world to be holy and blameless in his sight." Eph 1:4 (NIV)

Have you ever wondered what makes people do good things? Why would someone choose the way of truth? Why would someone set their heart on God's laws? Perhaps a person's behavior is related to his or her position in Christ. In Christ, you are a saint, you are blessed, and you are chosen.

Did you choose God or did God choose you? You were chosen by God long before you were even born. The song says, "While He (Jesus) was on the cross, I was on His mind." Even before Jesus came to earth to live a sinless life, die a substitutionary death, and defeat sin and death, you were chosen by God. Before God splattered the stars in the universe, you were chosen. Before God spoke light into existence, you were chosen. Before God separated the day from the night, you were chosen.

- *"You did not choose me, but I chose you and appointed you to go and bear fruit--fruit that will last. Then the Father will give you whatever you ask in my name." John 15:16 (NIV)*
- *"But we ought always to thank God for you, brothers loved by the Lord, because from the beginning God chose you to be saved through the sanctifying work of the Spirit and through belief in the truth." 2 Thess 2:13 (NIV)*

Why were you chosen? You were chosen by God to bear fruit that will last. You were chosen by God to be saved. Can you pull that off by yourself? No! Does God expect you to pull that off by yourself? No! Jesus came so that you could live the life of choseness.

April 23
Adopted into God's Family

"For he chose us in him before the creation of the world to be holy and blameless in his sight. In love he predestined us to be adopted as his sons through Jesus Christ, in accordance with his pleasure and will--to the praise of his glorious grace, which he has freely given us in the One he loves." Eph 1:4-6 (NIV)

If you are in Christ, then you have been adopted into God's family. God gave the right for you to become a child of God. In love, God predestined you to be adopted as His child in Jesus Christ. "Yet to all who received him, to those who believed in his name, he gave the right to become children of God" (John 1:12 NIV).

God's grace is the gateway to your adoption into His family (Eph. 2:8-9). Your adoption is formalized at conversion. God takes the initiative to draw you by convicting you of sin and convincing you of His righteousness. God gives you the freedom to choose Him or refuse Him. His salvation is available to all but only effective for those who place their trust in the completed work of Jesus on the cross.

Adoption is not an option. Adoption is the spiritual blessing for those who are in Christ. Spend some time thanking God for His willingness to adopt you into His family. God selected you. You are God's choice. In spite of your sin, in spite of your inadequacies, and in spite of your inconsistencies, God chose to adopt you into His family.

Be sensitive to opportunities this week to express your adoption. God has made this eternal adoption transaction available to all. Will you be available to be used by God to share His offer of salvation to those who are disconnected from Christ?

April 24
ACCEPTING HIS ACCEPTANCE

"...to the praise of his glorious grace, which he has freely given us in the One he loves." Eph 1:6 (NIV)

How do you respond to rejection? Do you allow the rejection to inject you with insecurity or do you challenge the rejection? Rejection is painful. We long for acceptance. The wonderful news is that in Christ, you are accepted. God has accepted you on the basis of His redeeming love for you. Remember, in Christ, you are a saint, you are blessed, you are chosen, you are adopted, and you are accepted.

Have you accepted God's acceptance of you? He took the initiative to demonstrate His acceptance of you by freely giving you His grace in Jesus. Do you measure up to His standard of righteousness? No! However, God declared you righteous when you accepted the atoning work of Jesus on the cross.

When rejection surfaces, combat the lies with the truth of God's acceptance of you. Your peace in this life will be proportionate to your acceptance of God's acceptance of you. Your acceptance of God's acceptance of you will give you lasting peace and eternal security. Some people may reject you. At times, people may misunderstand you. However, you can respond to rejection by living in light of your acceptance of God's acceptance of you. "But God demonstrates his own love for us in this: While we were still sinners, Christ died for us" (Romans 5:8 NIV).

Your acceptance has permanence! Choose to accept God's acceptance of you.

April 25
REDEEMED BY THE BLOOD

"In him we have redemption through his blood, the forgiveness of sins, in accordance with the riches of God's grace that he lavished on us with all wisdom and understanding." Eph 1:7-8 (NIV)

Our position of being "in Christ" unlocks the treasure chest of His resources. It is imperative that you make certain that you are in Christ. Your union with Jesus will release the spiritual blessings He has for you. In Christ, you are a saint, you are chosen, you are adopted, you are accepted, and you are redeemed.

Redemption in the language of the New Testament carries the idea of purchasing or redeeming a slave in order to set him free. Jesus purchased you with His blood in order to set you free. He ransomed you through His death.

Do you realize how valuable you are in God's sight? Do you understand that Jesus paid your sin debt in full? You have been redeemed!

I am reminded of the song, "He paid a debt He did not owe. I owed a debt I could not pay. I needed someone to wash my sins away." Thank God for His redeeming love! Rejoice in your new identity that Christ purchased!

April 26
FORGIVENESS FOREVER

"For he has rescued us from the dominion of darkness and brought us into the kingdom of the Son he loves, in whom we have redemption, the forgiveness of sins." Col 1:13-14 (NIV)

If you are in Christ, then you are forgiven. Because of Christ's atonement, you have been declared righteous. Your sins have been forgiven.

- "In him we have redemption through his blood, the forgiveness of sins, in accordance with the riches of God's grace that he lavished on us with all wisdom and understanding." Eph 1:7-8 (NIV)
- "In fact, the law requires that nearly everything be cleansed with blood, and without the shedding of blood there is no forgiveness." Heb 9:22 (NIV)

Jesus shed His blood to pay the debt of your sin in full. Have you received God's forgiveness? Confess your sins and God will forgive you of your sins (1 Jn 1:9). Jesus atoned for your sin by dying on the cross as the perfect and sinless sacrifice. His payment for your sin was sufficient to provide for your cleansing. Now walk in the reality of being in Christ. You are forgiven.

You have a right standing before God because of your faith in the atoning work of Christ on the cross. You are forgiven because He was forsaken. Jesus bore the penalty for your sin. Jesus provided for the forgiveness of your sins. Heaven and eternal life define your future because of what Jesus did on your behalf. You are forgiven. Your sins have been removed as far as the east is from the west (Ps. 103:12).

April 27
SAFE AND SEALED

"Now it is God who makes both us and you stand firm in Christ. He anointed us, set his seal of ownership on us, and put his Spirit in our hearts as a deposit, guaranteeing what is to come." 2 Cor 1:21-22 (NIV)

Perhaps you have heard the expression, "Life has no guarantees!" Well, that's just not true. In Christ, you have a guarantee that no one can disrupt. God guarantees your safe and secure eternal destiny. How does God indicate the security of our future? "Now it is God who has made us for this very purpose and has given us the Spirit as a deposit, guaranteeing what is to come" (2 Cor 5:5 NIV).

God gives His Holy Spirit to us at conversion. The moment we confess Jesus as Lord and embrace the reality that God raised Jesus from the dead; we are saved and filled with His Holy Spirit. The Holy Spirit indwells us permanently. The Holy Spirit does not move in and then move out. His indwelling Presence becomes our guarantee.

You are made fit by God for the Holy Spirit's habitation. At the moment of your conversion, the Holy Spirit comes to live inside of you. You become the walking Tabernacle of His Presence. The Holy Spirit guarantees what is to come. Your eternal security is enveloped by the indwelling Presence of the Holy Spirit.

Have you received God's deposit? Read Ephesians 1:13-14 and reflect on the spiritual blessing God has bestowed upon you. You are safe and sealed for eternity.

April 28
UNVEILING THE MYSTERY

"And he made known to us the mystery of his will according to his good pleasure, which he purposed in Christ, to be put into effect when the times will have reached their fulfillment--to bring all things in heaven and on earth together under one head, even Christ." Eph 1:9-10 (NIV)

The mystery Paul is speaking of is not mysterious. He is speaking about something once hidden now made known. God is a God of revelation. As Henry Blackaby says, "God reveals Himself, His purposes, and His ways." God wants you to know His will. God invites you into a relationship through which you come to learn how to walk with Him.

Have you noticed the activity of God in your life? There's no mystery here! God is at work! It brings God pleasure to reveal His will to you. God is moved by the relational interaction between Himself and the one He pursues. You are that one! God pursues you with His everlasting love in order to bring you into harmony with His purpose and plans. You are treasured by God.

Spend some time tracing the activity of God in your life. You may want to write down some spiritual markers in your life that help you identify God's activity in and through your circumstances. Be sure to include spiritual markers such as salvation and baptism. Think about seasons of uncertainty that you navigated with God. Slow down and feel the love God has shown you. Be reminded of the faithfulness of God to reveal Himself to you in the midst of adversity. God has never left you and He will never forsake you.

April 29
UNDERSTANDING GOD'S WILL

"Get wisdom, get understanding; do not forget my words or swerve from them."
Prov 4:5 (NIV)

We know more than we obey. Wisdom is to know and comprehend. Understanding is to apply what we know and comprehend. Application of God's Word indicates fullness in Christ.

Just as a treadmill will not benefit your health unless you get on it and use it, God's Word will not bring understanding until you apply it. Application leads to clarification, maturation, and transformation. Wisdom and understanding become evidenced through application. Put God's Word and God's wisdom into practice.

Where do you start? You start by reading God's Word. Next, you meditate on God's Word. Then, you apply God's Word. Instead of leaning on your own understanding, trust in the Lord and acknowledge His ways (Prv. 3:5-6). Instead of swerving from God's Word, get His wisdom and His understanding (Prv. 4:5). Instead of coasting through life, diligently get understanding (Prv. 4:7).

Obey what you know! Apply what God has spoken into your life with understanding! Walk in the light God gives you! The adventure continues as you walk with God and entrust your life to His care. God has special plans for you that will bring you into a closer relationship with Him. You will need God's wisdom and understanding to participate with Him in His agenda.

April 30
God's Orchestration

"In him we were also chosen, having been predestined according to the plan of him who works out everything in conformity with the purpose of his will, in order that we, who were the first to hope in Christ, might be for the praise of his glory." Eph 1:11-12 (NIV)

Has your life ever become complicated and messy? Have you traveled down a road you never thought you would navigate? Living in a fallen world tends to cause us to experience unexpected turns in life. Sometimes we make poor choices and sometimes the decisions of others negatively affect us. It could be that a relationship has diverted into unhealthy patterns or personal behaviors have drifted away from God's best.

The good news is that God is sovereign. He rules and He reigns. He always has the final say in any and every situation. Even when you make a disastrous move, God can orchestrate your path for your good and His glory. Notice how our Bible verse says that God works out everything in conformity with the purpose of His will. He is God! There is nothing that is impossible with Him. He can handle your situation. He can handle your relationships.

God orchestrates everything we encounter to bring about His will. Right now your current challenge may seem like an uphill climb dragging two dead elephants. God can take any difficult situation and orchestrate the details to conform to His plan.

Are you willing to surrender your hurts, your frustrations, your disappointments, and your fears to God? Release them and entrust them to God's sovereign care. He is the master conductor in the orchestra called life.

May 1
ENTRUSTED WITH GOD'S TREASURE

"On the contrary, we speak as men approved by God to be entrusted with the gospel. We are not trying to please men but God, who tests our hearts." 1 Thess 2:4 (NIV)

God has called us to speak on His behalf. When others hear from us, they need to hear from God. God has saved us, is sanctifying us, and will be glorifying us. We speak as those who have been approved by God.

God has entrusted us with the precious treasure of the gospel. The Good News that brings forth eternal life and the forgiveness of sins has been entrusted to us by God and for God. Our assignment is to share God's plan of salvation with the lost. Every person on the planet is lost without Christ. Our mandate from God is to shine His light and to share His love with all people groups.

What is our motivation? Is it to please men? Is it to receive the applause of men? No, we spread the fragrance of Christ to bring pleasure to God. We are ambassadors for Christ because God is making His appeal through us (2 Cor. 5:20). We live to please God. Our Heavenly Father has given us eternal life through His Son, Jesus.

Are you convinced that lost people go to hell? Does your life give evidence to the reality of heaven and hell? You have been approved by God and entrusted with the Good News of Jesus Christ. Make it your ambition to please God. Express your appreciation to God by sharing His message of reconciliation with those disconnected from Christ. Make the smile of God the goal of your life.

May 2
SHARING YOUR SALVATION STORY

"Many of the Samaritans from that town believed in him because of the woman's testimony, 'He told me everything I ever did.' So when the Samaritans came to him, they urged him to stay with them, and he stayed two days. And because of his words many more became believers." John 4:39-41 (NIV)

God uses human instrumentality in the redemptive process. There is nothing like the power of a changed life. When someone turns from sin and to Jesus for salvation, that transformed life touches other people. The Samaritans knew the shadowy past of the woman at the well. They were familiar with her lifestyle and most impacted by her transformation.

The woman at the well was willing to go back into her city to share her salvation story. She was willing to go back to her fellow Samaritans to share her testimony. The Lord Jesus had transformed her life and she was compelled to let her new life in Christ be an instrument to bring others to salvation. "They said to the woman, 'We no longer believe just because of what you said; now we have heard for ourselves, and we know that this man really is the Savior of the world'" (John 4:42 NIV).

Are you helping people come to know Christ? Are you sharing your personal testimony? Do your family members know your salvation story? Look for opportunities this week to share your testimony and watch how God uses your life to draw others to Christ.

May 3
ACTIVELY SHARING YOUR FAITH

"I pray that you may be active in sharing your faith, so that you will have a full understanding of every good thing we have in Christ." Philem 1:6 (NIV)

Our participation in God's redemptive activity includes actively sharing our faith. We are commissioned by God and for God to share His redemptive love to all 12,500 people groups on this planet. God has saved us and set us free so that we can shine His light and share His love with every individual. God wants us to share our faith with those He brings into our path. God also wants us to build bridges to people we have never met in order to share our faith with them.

Are you willing to seize the opportunities that God gives you? Are you willing to go on a short term mission trip in order to share your faith in other cultures? Your home is your mission field. Your neighborhood is your mission field. Your school is your mission field. Your work place is your mission field. Everywhere you go is terrain that God wants you to claim for His glory.

How many people will be in heaven because of you? Will your life impact the population of hell? Will your testimony impact the population of heaven?

God has given you the gift of eternal life so that you can personally share that gift with others. Don't mute your testimony. Don't conceal your testimony. Instead, reveal to others what God has done in your life to bring you to the point of salvation and abundant life.

May 4
Message Worth Sharing

"So do not be ashamed to testify about our Lord, or ashamed of me his prisoner. But join with me in suffering for the gospel, by the power of God, who has saved us and called us to a holy life--not because of anything we have done but because of his own purpose and grace. This grace was given us in Christ Jesus before the beginning of time, but it has now been revealed through the appearing of our Savior, Christ Jesus, who has destroyed death and has brought life and immortality to light through the gospel." 2 Tim 1:8-10 (NIV)

Paul modeled his testimony before his son in the ministry, Timothy. Paul was consumed by the gospel. The Good News of Jesus Christ had radically transformed Paul's life and he unashamedly bore witness to the saving grace of Jesus to a lost and dying world.

- *"I am not ashamed of the gospel, because it is the power of God for the salvation of everyone who believes: first for the Jew, then for the Gentile." Romans 1:16 (NIV)*
- *"And even if our gospel is veiled, it is veiled to those who are perishing." 2 Cor 4:3 (NIV)*

What's there to be ashamed about? Jesus has saved you and called you to a holy life by His own purpose and grace. Jesus has destroyed death and has brought forth life through His gospel. You are armed with the most powerful message on planet earth. The gospel impacts life in the now and the hereafter.

God has given you an eternal message empowered by His eternal Spirit that brings forth eternal life to everyone who believes. You have been given the keys to unlock hell and open heaven for every person who turns from their sin and to Jesus alone for salvation. Hallelujah! Praise the Lamb of God!

May 5
READINESS

"Therefore, prepare your minds for action; be self-controlled; set your hope fully on the grace to be given you when Jesus Christ is revealed." 1 Peter 1:13 (NIV)

We are at war. As followers of Jesus Christ, we have to confront the reality of spiritual warfare. The kingdom of light and the kingdom of darkness are in opposition. As children of the light, we must combat the forces of evil. God's agenda is our agenda. God's mission is our mission. Loyalty to Christ will produce opposition from Satan and his demonic forces.

Be proactive by preparing your mind for action. Fill your mind with the Word of God and choose to claim God's promises. God has revealed His plan and provided His spiritual armor for the spiritual battle. Prepare your mind for the warfare of combating temptation, sin, and compromise.

Be self-controlled. This is no time for apathy or lethargy. Don't drift into complacency. Submit to the control of the Holy Spirit and allow Him to bear the fruit of self-control in you. Yield to the Spirit's prompting for perpetual victory over sin and Satan.

Where have you anchored your hope? Your life in Christ is established on the basis of God's grace. The grace that saved you is the grace that keeps you secure in the midst of opposition. God's grace will sustain you whether you are in the valley of intense spiritual warfare or on the mountain of heavenly bliss.

May 6
Entrusting Your Life

"When they hurled their insults at him, he did not retaliate; when he suffered, he made no threats. Instead, he entrusted himself to him who judges justly." 1 Peter 2:23 (NIV)

Hurting people hurt people. Those who have been wounded often wound others. There's something about our fallen nature that seeks revenge. When someone has inflicted pain onto us, we want them to experience the same measure of pain in return. Retribution saturates the landscape of our lives.

Jesus ushered in a new way of living. Jesus demonstrated the proper response to unfair treatment and to adverse circumstances. If there were ever a person who did not deserve one fraction of mistreatment, it would be Jesus. His life was filled with compassion for others, generosity in action, and integrity both in private and in public. Jesus received unjust treatment. He was ridiculed and falsely accused, yet He did not retaliate. As He suffered, He made not threats. Jesus could have called down a legion of angels to eliminate His offenders.

Instead of reacting to His assailants, Jesus responded by entrusting Himself to God. Jesus chose to entrust His life and His circumstances to the Creator of the universe. Jesus affirmed that God is the righteous and just judge. God sees the inequities of life. Sin will be judged. Penalties will be ascribed.

Have you been treated unfairly? Did you choose to react or respond? Entrust your life to God. God created you for His glory. You are God's workmanship (Eph. 2:10). You have a purpose to fulfill and a light to shine in this dark world. Fallen people will continue to act like fallen people until they come into a saving relationship with Jesus. Even after conversion, a person who becomes a follower of Christ can drift into some of the old fleshly patterns that wound and inflict pain. Don't retaliate. Respond by entrusting your life to God.

May 7
Prepared to Share

"But in your hearts set apart Christ as Lord. Always be prepared to give an answer to everyone who asks you to give the reason for the hope that you have. But do this with gentleness and respect, keeping a clear conscience, so that those who speak maliciously against your good behavior in Christ may be ashamed of their slander." 1 Peter 3:15-16 (NIV)

Readiness to share your salvation story is proportionate to Lordship. Your submission to the Lordship of Christ determines your level of readiness to give an answer for the reason of the hope you have. When you make Jesus the Lord of your life, your passion becomes pleasing Him. Your ambition in life is to do what Jesus did. Submitted to the Lordship of Christ, your life becomes oriented to the redemptive activity of God.

What is the reason for the hope you have? What was your life like before Christ became your Savior and Lord? How did you come to know Christ personally? What is different about your life now that you have an abiding love relationship with Him? Be prepared to give an answer. Be prepared to engage others in spiritual conversation. Unveil to others what Christ means to you and what He can do for them.

Sadly, conversation can dilute into being superficial and temporal. What if you began to operate your life in light of eternity? What if your conversation became centered around the reality of God's redeeming love? Give evidence to the Lordship of Christ in your life. With gentleness and respect, declare the hope you have in Christ. Speak of the mercy and grace of God you have been freely given. Allow the light of God's love to radiate from your life and your lips. In Christ, you have the most powerful message on the planet. Are you ready to give an answer?

May 8
WHEN YOU SPEAK

"If anyone speaks, he should do it as one speaking the very words of God. If anyone serves, he should do it with the strength God provides, so that in all things God may be praised through Jesus Christ. To him be the glory and the power for ever and ever. Amen." 1 Peter 4:11 (NIV)

Words have the power to build up or tear down. Words can inspire or discourage creativity. As a follower of Jesus Christ, your calling is to continue the ministry of Jesus on this earth. You are an ambassador for Christ (2 Cor. 5:20). Your conduct and your communication will indicate the health of your love relationship with Christ. When you speak, you have the opportunity to be an irresistible influence for Christ. Your speech has the potential to impart life to a person who has been searching for meaning and purpose in life. The way you interact with others can bring them into a living connection with Jesus.

Under the inspiration of the Holy Spirit, Peter exhorts us to remember that when we speak, we are speaking the very words of God. Consider the weight of your words. The manner in which you converse with others is of vital importance. Your speech gives clear evidence of that which is in your heart (Luke 6:45). If your speech becomes toxic and demeaning, then your heart has become hard and indifferent. If your speech is gentle, considerate, and life giving, then your heart is tender and teachable.

Does your daily conversation bring praise to God? As God listens to the words that come from your lips, does He smile? Let's be conscientious about the words we speak. Our words have immense power. Maybe that's why James says we ought to be quick to listen and slow to speak (James 1:19). When we do speak, let's be cognizant of the privilege of speaking the very words of God. Being God's voice in a noisy world is an awesome responsibility to behold.

May 9
SUFFERING AS A CHRISTIAN

"However, if you suffer as a Christian, do not be ashamed, but praise God that you bear that name." 1 Peter 4:16 (NIV)

When you received the gift of eternal life, you were saved by the grace of God. Your name was written in the Lamb's book of life and your eternal security was sealed by the Holy Spirit. Your position in Christ is that of having a right relationship with God and a right relationship with others. The sacrificial death of Christ upon the cross provided you with a new identity, in Christ, as a child of God.

Receiving the benefits of salvation is a joy. However, what you may not have realized is that being a follower of Jesus Christ includes suffering. You cannot be on mission with God and give your life to fulfilling the Great Commission and live out the Great Commandment without an element of suffering. Going against the current of culture will produce a level of suffering. Combating the satanic opposition from the kingdom of darkness will generate a level of suffering. Denying yourself and crucifying the flesh in order to walk in the Spirit will spawn an encounter with suffering.

Do not be ashamed if you suffer as a Christian. Maybe you work in a difficult environment where Christianity is not well received. Maybe your home is not conducive to the reality of your Christianity. Perhaps being a Christian on your campus, at work, or in your home places you in the minority. Do not be ashamed. Give praise to God that you have high honor and privilege of bearing that name. You are Christ on your campus. You are Christ at your work. You are Christ in your home. Everywhere you go, you are representing Jesus! You are continuing the ministry of Jesus on the earth by doing what He did. You wear His name and you bear His identity. Remember, you may be the only Jesus others see!

May 10
MOTHER'S DAY

"Charm is deceptive, and beauty is fleeting; but a woman who fears the LORD is to be praised." Prov 31:30 (NIV)

Our culture places immeasurable value on beauty. Teenage girls and women combat incalculable pressure to compete with the enhanced images of celebrities frequenting magazine covers. The pressure escalates as trends vacillate from month to month. What is considered a beautiful trait now may not measure up next month. Swirling in plurality, our culture redefines beauty as often as the shifting of sand upon the seashores.

The Bible defines beauty in relationship to how one reveres God. From God's perspective, beauty is an internal reality instead of an external commodity. Your authentic walk with God determines your level of beauty. External beauty is fleeting. From the moment we are born, our physical body begins to deteriorate. This shell that we live in continues to age. How we respond to God determines our inner beauty.

Fearing God is the key to beauty. Fearing God means to revere Him, to adore Him, and to esteem Him. To fear God is to value what He values, to love what He loves, and to hate what He hates. Fearing God involves being perpetually aware of His holiness and purity.

If your mother is still living, have you praised her for fearing the Lord? If your mother has already gone to heaven, spend some time in prayer thanking God for blessing you with a mother who feared the Lord. You are blessed to have such a rich heritage. I am so grateful to God for blessing me with a mother who fears the Lord. Her life has been a continual source of inspiration. My brother and I arise and call her blessed (Prv. 31:28).

May 11
The God of All Comfort

"Praise be to the God and Father of our Lord Jesus Christ, the Father of compassion and the God of all comfort, who comforts us in all our troubles, so that we can comfort those in any trouble with the comfort we ourselves have received from God." 2 Cor 1:3-4 (NIV)

God redeems pain.

When you look into the rear view mirror of your life, you can probably recall painful experiences that you have had in your past. Some of those experiences may be the direct result of poor choices that you made and some of those experiences may be related to poor choices that someone else made. You may look back and recognize painful experiences that were not attached to poor choices at all. It may be that you simply encountered pain as a result of living in a fallen world.

Grief is an ongoing pain that resides within us as we try to navigate a path without someone who has meant so much to us. Grief can be encountered as a result of job loss, a shift in our personal health status, or a shattered dream. Are you currently experiencing any level of grief in your life? Can you identify the source of your grief?

God is the Father of compassion. He is the God of all comfort. God comforts us so that we can comfort others. God blesses us with experiences that elevate our need for Him. We come to realize our dependency upon God and how desperate we really are for God

God does not bring comfort into our lives so that we can become comfortable. God brings comfort into our lives during seasons of pain and difficulty so that we can comfort others who go through trying circumstances. We come to know God by personal experience. We become better equipped to bring comfort to others. Who are you building a bridge of comfort to? Who has God brought into your path lately who simply needs to know God's comfort through you?

May 12
READY FOR BATTLE

"Be self-controlled and alert. Your enemy the devil prowls around like a roaring lion looking for someone to devour. Resist him, standing firm in the faith, because you know that your brothers throughout the world are undergoing the same kind of sufferings." 1 Peter 5:8-9 (NIV)

The enemy is persistent in his pursuit of your loyalty. The devil is on a mission to neutralize your faith and to tranquillize your passion for God. Prowling around like a roaring lion, the devil seeks to distort your vision of God. If the enemy can rob you of your passion and your vision, then he has accomplished his mission. The devil cannot attack God, so he chooses to attack God's family. As a child of God, you are on Satan's radar.

Persist to resist. You do not have to succumb to the attacks of the devil. You do not have to yield to his temptation to doubt God's Word. You do not have to surrender to the enemy's agenda to thwart God's will. Remember, you are a child of the King! Jesus purchased you with His own blood. You have received the imputed righteousness of Christ. The Holy Spirit lives in you and there is no vacancy for the devil. The enemy is not welcome in your mind. The devil has no place in the landscape of your life devoted to the Lord.

Stand firm in the faith. Remember the confidence you placed in the completed work of Jesus on the cross. Stand firm in the reality of your new identity in Christ. Allow the fruit of the Spirit, self-control, to be released in your life. Starve the flesh and feed the Spirit. Guard your heart. Put on the full armor of God. Be alert! Don't drift into apathy. Don't coast into complacency. Stand firm in the faith God has given you.

May 13
EVERYTHING YOU NEED

"His divine power has given us everything we need for life and godliness through our knowledge of him who called us by his own glory and goodness." 2 Peter 1:3 (NIV)

God does not expect you to live the Christian life outside of His enablement. In fact, it is impossible to be a fully devoted follower of Christ without God's provision. You need God's fuel to accomplish God's will for your life. God's mission demands supernatural power that you don't have outside of His resources. To operate in God's economy requires God's energy.

God's divine power has given you everything you need for life! Your union with Christ connects you to the supernatural power needed for living out your faith. Being salt and light on this broken planet will require that you to stay in a vibrant, healthy, and growing relationship with Christ. As you come to know the Lord intimately, your progressive relationship will unlock God's power in your life.

God's divine power has given you everything you need for godliness! To be godly is to be like God. His heart becomes evident in your heart. His love becomes evident in the way you love others. His compassion becomes apparent as you extend His compassion to those in need. In Christ, you become the conduit through which God displays His power and His grace. Everything you need for godliness is made available to you through your abiding relationship with Christ.

Stay connected! Keep your love relationship tender, open, and progressive. Confess known sin. Receive God's forgiveness. Feed on God's Word daily and practice His presence throughout the day. Be conscious of God's activity in you, through you, and around you. God is working His power in you so that He can display His power through you.

May 14
PARTICIPATING IN THE DIVINE NATURE

"Through these he has given us his very great and precious promises, so that through them you may participate in the divine nature and escape the corruption in the world caused by evil desires." 2 Peter 1:4 (NIV)

We are blessed to have the promises of God at our fingertips. The Bible we treasure is the instrument through which God communicates His Word to us. We are so blessed to have access to the very Word of God. Each promise in God's Word gives us traction for participation in His divine nature. As we read, study, meditate on, memorize, and apply God's Word, we unleash His power and realize His nature.

God is holy. God is immutable. God is omnipotent, omniscient, and omnipresent. God is eternal. He was never born and He will never die. God is love. God is mercy, grace, and peace. God is infinite; we are finite. God is flawless; we are flawed.

How do you escape the corruption in the world? Escaping corruption is made possible as you claim God's promises and participate in God's divine nature. God the Father, God the Son, and God the Holy Spirit make up the Trinity. You declare the fullness of God as you apply God's Word. You participate in the divine nature as you seek to fulfill the Great Commission and live out the Great Commandment. Loving God and loving others requires employing the promises of God. Participating in God's divine nature takes place when you walk in the Spirit and choose to deny the cravings of the sinful nature.

Proximity to God's promises matters. Begin to recite the promises of God that you have memorized over the years. Open your Bible and search for specific promises related to your current situation. Let God speak and choose to participate with God in His divine nature.

May 15
Don't Bypass Jerusalem

"The following night the Lord stood near Paul and said, 'Take courage! As you have testified about me in Jerusalem, so you must also testify in Rome.'" Acts 23:11 (NIV)

Paul experienced intense opposition as he shared the gospel in Jerusalem. He caused turbulence in the Temple among the crowd and chaos as he faced the court, the Sanhedrin. His body was almost torn into pieces by the mob and almost flogged by the military. Paul's encounters in Jerusalem produced the fruit of failure from the worldly perspective. However, God was at work in the midst of severe adversity.

Don't bypass Jerusalem; God will use it to get you to Rome. Our natural proclivity is to take the path of least resistance. We dodge the potholes of life and seek the terrain of minimal pain. Yet, God often allows us to go through adversity to get us where He wants us. God will use the hammer of adversity and the chisel of suffering to conform us into the image of Christ and to prepare us for our next assignment.

Moses had to leave the luxury of the palace to go to the desert. There are some things God wanted to teach Moses in the desert that he could not learn in the palace. By the way, the bush wasn't burning in the palace. God used the desert to train Moses in shepherding to equip him to lead the children of Israel out of Egyptian bondage. Moses had to go through his personal Jerusalem, the desert, to get to his Rome.

If God allows adversity in your life, He will use it for your good and for His glory. Jesus comforted Paul with the assurance of testifying in Rome. Paul had a longing to go to Rome to preach the gospel. God was giving Paul the desires of his heart. Just when Paul thought that Jerusalem was the end of the road, God built a bridge through adversity to Rome.

May 16
Asking the Right Question

"Consider it pure joy, my brothers, whenever you face trials of many kinds, because you know that the testing of your faith develops perseverance. Perseverance must finish its work so that you may be mature and complete, not lacking anything." James 1:2-4 (NIV)

Have you ever been perplexed by a season of adversity? You look for answers. You search for the source of your adversity and then you try to figure out why this is happening to you. Your mind is flooded with questions.

Adversity can immobilize your faith or activate your faith depending on the questions you ask. Instead of asking why, ask what! Humble yourself before the Lord and ask Him what He wants to do through your season of adversity. If God permits adversity to come your way, He will use it to build you into the man or woman of God He desires you to be.

Spiritual maturity is not instant. Spiritual maturity is developed slowly through the process of walking with God in the midst of the diverse terrain of life. God will utilize the hammer of adversity and the chisel of suffering to perfect the character of Christ in you. If God allows adversity to come into your life, He will use it to conform you into the image of Christ (Romans 8:28-29) and to develop your spiritual maturity.

Consider the adverse circumstances you are currently facing. Is it more beneficial for you to know why you are experiencing this season of adversity or to know what God is up to? God knows where you are. God knows how you feel. He knows your fears, your frustrations, and your anxious thoughts. God knows where you will be on the other side of this adversity. Draw near to God (James 4:8) and allow Him to accomplish His work in you. You are God's workmanship (Eph. 2:10). Perseverance is being developed through the testing of your faith. Will you be mature and complete?

May 17
THE OBJECT OF YOUR AFFECTION

"And God said, 'I will be with you. And this will be the sign to you that it is I who have sent you: When you have brought the people out of Egypt, you will worship God on this mountain.'" Exodus 3:12 (NIV)

How's your worship? Is God the object of your affection and the recipient of your relentless pursuit? God wants you to worship Him and no other. God wants you to display your love and affection for Him both in private worship and in public worship.

Moses encountered God at the burning bush. This divine appointment was a life-changing experience for Moses. God provided Moses with the blessing of an Egyptian upbringing and now God is teaching Moses some things in the desert that he couldn't learn in the palace. God reveals Himself to Moses. Moses comes to know God in His holiness and righteousness. God instructs Moses to deliver the children of Israel out of Egyptian bondage and to bring them to the mountain to worship God corporately.

God demands our worship. God deserves our worship. Spend some time in private worshiping God for who He is. Express your love to God by praising Him. Make a commitment to take your private worship to church. Join other believers in public worship. Seek to express your love to God with fellow believers in worship just like you do in your private worship. God alone is worthy of your worship and your praise!

Assess your worship. Is your private worship consistent and persistent? Do you draw near to God? How's your public worship? Are you joining other believers in a weekly celebration of God's Presence? Do you give God your best in your expression of worship?

May 18
TRUST GOD'S TIMING

"In all my prayers for all of you, I always pray with joy because of your partnership in the gospel from the first day until now, being confident of this, that he who began a good work in you will carry it on to completion until the day of Christ Jesus." Phil 1:4-6 (NIV)

God is working. His purpose and plan will be accomplished. Satan cannot thwart God's will. Even when you experience doubts, delays, and distractions, God is still fulfilling His agenda. God is sovereign. He rules and He reigns. God factors in our sin. God factors in the reality of demonic opposition. God is not surprised by our surprises.

God's master plan includes you. It is God's will for you to be saved, to grow spiritually, and to join Him in His redemptive activity. Jesus took on the full wrath of God for your sin so that you could be set free to have a vibrant love relationship with God in Christ. You were filled with the Holy Spirit at the moment of your conversion so that you could continue the ministry of Jesus on this broken planet.

God will complete the good work He began in you. What God starts, He always finishes! God is not through with you. You are still in the process of becoming who God has made you to be. God is molding you and shaping you into the man or woman of God He created you to be.

Will you allow God to continue His work in you so that He can accomplish His work through you? Are you willing to trust God's timing? God knows where He wants you. God knows what the finished product of His character development in you looks like. God's timing is perfect. Entrust your life to His care.

May 19
EMBRACING WHOLESOME THINKING

"Dear friends, this is now my second letter to you. I have written both of them as reminders to stimulate you to wholesome thinking. I want you to recall the words spoken in the past by the holy prophets and the command given by our Lord and Savior through your apostles." 2 Peter 3:1-2 (NIV)

The Bible was written over a period of 1,400 years by forty human authors under the inspiration of the Holy Spirit. The Old Testament is made up of thirty-nine books and the New Testament is made up of twenty-seven books. The sixty-six books are God's revelation to us. God has revealed Himself to us through His Word so that we can know His plan and experience His love. The common thread throughout the Bible is God's redemptive love. God pursues us with His everlasting love. In Christ, we are reconciled to God.

In his second letter, Peter writes to remind his readers of the revelation they have received from God through the holy prophets and through the apostles. The message of Christ has been conveyed. Peter reminds them in order to produce unmixed and uncontaminated thinking. In Christ, right thinking produces right behavior.

Wholesome thinking involves knowing God's will and obeying God's will. To be unmixed in your thinking is to operate your life in alignment with God's purpose and plan. God reveals His truth so that you can live out His truth. God reveals His agenda so that you can fulfill His agenda. Recall what you have learned. Recite the Bible verses you have memorized. Apply God's truth in your daily decisions. Prepare for the future by obeying God's Word today.

Are you obeying what God has already revealed to you? Are you walking in the light God has provided? Is your thinking pure, unmixed, and uncontaminated? Where there is purity there is clarity.

May 20
BEING RIGHT WITH GOD

"First of all, you must understand that in the last days scoffers will come, scoffing and following their own evil desires." 2 Peter 3:3 (NIV)

We are living in the last days. Don't be surprised by the turbulence of the times. Those who laugh at the things of God and dismiss the activity of God will continue to increase in number. Scoffers will litter the landscape of this life as we get closer to the coming of Christ. Wickedness will increase and love will deteriorate (Matt. 24:12). The fleshly desires of the unsaved will be fertilized and fed.

Understand your current reality. Where do you fit in the flow of end time events? Are you on the winning team? Have you received God's offer of salvation in Jesus and turned your life over to Him? If you are in Christ, you are secure for eternity. However, you must be cognizant of the features of the end times. Sin will parade the property on this fallen planet. The scoffers will obey the cravings of their sin nature. Their behavior will reflect their disregard for the plan of God.

Be alert to the presence of sin. Be mindful of the pervasiveness of sinful conduct. Satan realizes that his time is short, so he will spare no time to unleash his assault. As the deceiver, the enemy specializes in convincing scoffers to unleash their personal rebellion against God and God's family. If there were ever a time to get right with God, the time is now!

Crucify your flesh and seek to please God with your life and your lips. Make sure that the tongue in your mouth lines up with the tongue in your shoe. Live with integrity as you surrender to the full control of the Holy Spirit in your life. Confess sin. Live above reproach. Stay close and clean.

May 21
LEADING OTHERS TO THE ARK

"By these waters also the world of that time was deluged and destroyed. By the same word the present heavens and earth are reserved for fire, being kept for the day of judgment and destruction of ungodly men." 2 Peter 3:6-7 (NIV)

Sin infected the earth God created. In Noah's day, man's wickedness had become great (Gen. 6:5). In His holiness and righteousness, God judged sin by destroying life on earth.

- *"I am going to bring floodwaters on the earth to destroy all life under the heavens, every creature that has the breath of life in it. Everything on earth will perish. But I will establish my covenant with you, and you will enter the ark--you and your sons and your wife and your sons' wives with you. You are to bring into the ark two of all living creatures, male and female, to keep them alive with you." Gen 6:17-19 (NIV)*

God will not tolerate sin. Rebellion against God will not go unnoticed. God is omniscient, which means that He is all knowing. Nothing escapes the scope of God's view. God judges sin. Just as God's wrath was unleashed in Noah's day with water, God's wrath will be released to destroy the heavens and earth by fire. This day of judgment will bring about the destruction of ungodly men.

God demonstrated His mercy and grace in Noah's day by providing the ark of safety for Noah and his family. Noah was righteous in God's eyes and he was rewarded for his obedience. In the same way, God wants us to live a life of instant obedience. God has lavished us with His love and provided for our salvation. The ark of safety became our reality through the death, burial, resurrection, and ascension of Christ.

Knowing of the future destruction by fire, are you motivated to share God's rescue plan with those who are disconnected from Christ?

May 22
God's Perspective

"But do not forget this one thing, dear friends: With the Lord a day is like a thousand years, and a thousand years are like a day." 2 Peter 3:8 (NIV)

Perspective is everything. When you view life from your own perspective, the view can be incomplete. In our humanity, we may only view ten yards at a time on the football field. God sees the entire field of our lives. God is not limited by time or space.

God is eternal. God was never born and God will never die. God is not decaying nor growing old. God is immutable in that He is the same yesterday, today, and forever (Heb. 13:8). In other words, God is.

God is omnipresent. There is nowhere God is not. God is omniscient. There is nothing God does not know. Nothing ever occurs to God. Nothing catches God by surprise. Nothing happens without God's permission. God is sovereign. He rules and He reigns.

From our human perspective, a thousands years is a long time. For us, it is more than twelve times our life expectancy. God views a thousand years like a day. From God's perspective, a day is like a thousand years. God does not operate in the confines of our human perspective. God is not limited by our finite comprehension of His eternal nature.

Choose to live your life in light of eternity. Realize that there is more to this life than what you see. There is life beyond the grave. Every moment counts. Therefore, make every moment of your life count.

May 23
God's Patience

"The Lord is not slow in keeping his promise, as some understand slowness. He is patient with you, not wanting anyone to perish, but everyone to come to repentance." 2 Peter 3:9 (NIV)

Have you ever lost your patience? Waiting in a fast food line for an extended period of time has a way of testing your capacity to embrace patience. In our instant gratification saturated society, we just don't wait well. Our lifestyles have been conditioned through advancing technology to expect everything to come to fruition in a matter of seconds.

Aren't you thankful that God is patient with us? God has graciously given us time to respond to His salvation love gift. God has been patient with us in the process of our spiritual development. In the midst of our sins of omission and sins of commission, God patiently conforms us into the image of Christ. God forgives us of our sins and cleanses us of our unrighteousness (1 John 1:9). God's patience means salvation!

The heart of God is for everyone to come into a vibrant love relationship with Him through Christ. God does not want anyone to spend eternity in hell. God wants everyone to come to repentance. Yet, God has given us the freedom to choose Him or to reject Him. God did not create us to be robotic, but rather to be relational.

Will some perish and experience eternal separation from God? Yes! Those who fail to confess Jesus as Lord and believe in their heart that God raised Jesus from the dead will spend eternity in hell (Rom. 10:9-10). God has provided the way for those who believe in Jesus to not perish (John 3:16). Everlasting life has been made available by God's grace alone through faith in Christ alone.

Have you come to repentance? Will you invest the rest of your life helping others come into a growing relationship with Jesus? Remember to be patient with others just as God has been patient with you.

May 24
EXHIBIT THE MIRACLE

"Therefore, if anyone is in Christ, he is a new creation; the old has gone, the new has come!" 2 Cor 5:17 (NIV)

Exhibit the miracle; you are a new creation.

In Christ, you are a new creation. The light of God's love has illuminated your life and transformed your forever. You are no longer bound by the past. You are no longer a prisoner of sin. You have been purchased with the shed blood of Jesus.

God has placed you in the display window of life to present to others the grace He has lavished on you. You are a living exhibit of the grace of God. You were shown mercy in order that Christ Jesus might display His unlimited patience in you as an example to others (1 Tim. 1:15-16). Portray the grace you have received. Encourage others in their journey by displaying the new creation God has redeemed you to be.

The new has come. In Christ, you have been re-created to bear His image and to bring forth His message of salvation. God has chosen you to exhibit the miracle you are in Christ. Don't hide the grace God has extended you. Don't conceal the mercy you have received. Continue to grow in your love relationship with Christ and choose to glow in this dark world. Allow the light of God's love to radiate through the brokenness in your life. Portray the love of God by treating others the way God has graciously treated you.

You are a living miracle of the gracious work of God. He has pursued you with His unfailing love and rescued you from eternal damnation. God has made you a new creation. Exhibit the miracle you are in Christ.

May 25
Extend the Ministry

"All this is from God, who reconciled us to himself through Christ and gave us the ministry of reconciliation: that God was reconciling the world to himself in Christ, not counting men's sins against them. And he has committed to us the message of reconciliation." 2 Cor 5:18-19 (NIV)

Extend the ministry; you are reconciled to reconcile.

The freedom we enjoy in America comes at a great price. Thousands of men and women have given their lives in service to our country to preserve our freedom. We are blessed to worship God corporately without fear of invasion. Thank God for our fallen warriors and their families.

Christ paid the ultimate sacrifice for our reconciliation. Jesus died to provide for the forgiveness of our sins and to remove the barrier separating us from Holy God. Jesus was obedient to death on the cross to satisfy the righteous requirements of God (Phil. 2:8). As the sinless sacrifice, Jesus provided to us heaven and eternal life.

Now that you have been reconciled to God, extend the ministry of reconciliation to those disconnected from Christ. You are reconciled in order to reconcile. You have been given this life-changing ministry from God. God has empowered you to be a minister of reconciliation.

Build intentional relationships with those who are disconnected from Christ. Join God in reconciling the world to Him. Your reconciliation qualifies you to partner with God in reconciling others through Christ. Extend the ministry as God gives you opportunities this week to bring others into a saving relationship with Jesus.

May 26
EXPRESS THE MESSAGE

"We are therefore Christ's ambassadors, as though God were making his appeal through us. We implore you on Christ's behalf: Be reconciled to God. God made him who had no sin to be sin for us, so that in him we might become the righteousness of God." 2 Cor 5:20-21 (NIV)

Express the message; you became the righteousness of God.

God took the initiative to do for you what you could not do for yourself. God built the bridge you could not build. He established the only way for you to come into a vibrant love relationship with Him. How did God make this eternal relationship possible? God made Jesus to be sin for you so that you could become righteous like Him. At the moment of your salvation, you received the imputed righteousness of Christ. God justified you through your faith in Christ.

As a result of the divine transaction, your identity has shifted from that of a lost person to that of a saved person. You are now in Christ and reconciled to God. In Christ, you have been called and commissioned to share the most important message on the planet. You have been armed with the cure for the cancer of sin. The message of reconciliation that brought you into a growing relationship with Jesus is the same message you are to share with others. You are an ambassador for Christ. God has saved you and filled you with the Holy Spirit to enable you to continue the ministry of Jesus on the earth.

Express the message of reconciliation. Just as you have become the righteousness of God in Christ, you can share the message of reconciliation with others. Will you allow God to use you as an ambassador for Christ? Will you continue the ministry of Jesus on this broken planet full of broken people?

May 27
RAPTURE READY?

"For the Lord himself will come down from heaven, with a loud command, with the voice of the archangel and with the trumpet call of God, and the dead in Christ will rise first. After that, we who are still alive and are left will be caught up together with them in the clouds to meet the Lord in the air. And so we will be with the Lord forever." 1 Thess 4:16-17 (NIV)

If you are a child of God, then there is no need to fear death. You will either experience the Rapture or the resurrection. If you are still alive when Jesus comes for His Bride, you will be raptured. You will be snatched up from your earthly existence. However, if you die before the Rapture occurs, you will not experience the sting of death (I Cor. 15:55). To be absent from the body is to be present with the Lord (2 Cor. 5:6-8). The moment you take your last breath on earth, you are ushered instantaneously into the Presence of the Lord.

Are you Rapture ready? Have you solidified your spiritual status? Do you have the assurance of salvation? The Bible is clear that you can know that you have eternal life.

- *"And this is the testimony: God has given us eternal life, and this life is in his Son. He who has the Son has life; he who does not have the Son of God does not have life." 1 John 5:11-12 (NIV)*
- *"I write these things to you who believe in the name of the Son of God so that you may know that you have eternal life." 1 John 5:13 (NIV)*

Revisit the day of your salvation. Spend some time tracing the spiritual markers in your life. Thank God for His assurance of your salvation. Now that you are Rapture ready, invest your life in making a Kingdom impact for the glory of God. Make your life count for eternity!

May 28
COMING BACK FOR YOU

"'And if I go and prepare a place for you, I will come back and take you to be with me that you also may be where I am.'" John 14:3 (NIV)

God has so much more in store for you than what you have currently in view. There's so much more on the other shore. God is growing you and grooming you in this life in preparation for the life to come. God's nature is that of integrity. God keeps His word. He is the real Promise Keeper.

As a follower of Christ, you will go to heaven either through the doorway of death or the reality of the Rapture. You will either go to Jesus upon your death or Jesus will come to you via the Rapture of the church. If you live, Christ lives with you. If you die, you live with Christ. As a believer, it is a win-win!

You will experience the ultimate reunion with Christ and your believing loved ones who have gone before you. The ultimate trade-in will occur as you trade-in your current body for the glorified body that God has for you. There will be no more cancer, no more arthritis, no more heart disease, no more diabetes, no more multiple sclerosis, no more Alzheimer's, no more macular degeneration, no more mosquitoes, and no more humidity.

Jesus has prepared a place for you. There isn't a place on earth to compare to the glorious mansion Jesus has built for you in Heaven. Jesus has also provided the way for you to get to Heaven. Jesus is the way, the truth, and the life (John 14:6).

Are you ready for Jesus to come back?

May 29
SOVEREIGNTY OF GOD

"You intended to harm me, but God intended it for good to accomplish what is now being done, the saving of many lives." Gen 50:20 (NIV)

The sixty-six books of the Bible provide us with a string of pearls demonstrating God's redemptive activity. Long before we were born, God took the initiative to rescue us from our fallen condition. God factors in our poor choices and even the decisions others make that affect our lives. How refreshing to know that God has the final say. Your past, present, and future circumstances will never circumvent the mighty acts of God.

Joseph had a life changing experience through the gateway of betrayal. Joseph's brothers sold him into slavery and tried to cover up their sin through deception. God elevated Joseph to Potipher's house where he was later falsely accused by Potipher's wife. Joseph went from the pit to the palace and then to prison. His life's circumstances appeared to be most unfortunate. Yet, God knew right where Joseph was and what Joseph needed most.

God was with Joseph and delivered him from prison and promoted him to second in command over Egypt in preparation for the upcoming famine. When Joseph's path intersected that of his brothers, he demonstrated the life giving grace of God. Instead of having his brothers pay for their sin, Joseph forgave them and acknowledged God's sovereignty.

Have you had the ultimate life changing experience by placing your faith in the completed work of Jesus on the cross? Are you living out the reality of God's transforming power? Have you experienced God's forgiveness at the level of being able to forgive others in the same measure?

May 30
PREPARATION FOR YOUR NEXT ASSIGNMENT

"But Moses said to God, 'Who am I, that I should go to Pharaoh and bring the Israelites out of Egypt?'" Ex 3:11 (NIV)

Who am I? Why am I here? These two basic questions are innate in every human being. We long to know who we are and we strive to discover why we are placed on the earth. Our security is proportionate to our understanding of our identity.

God allowed Moses to experience forty years in the palace and then forty years in the desert. God wanted Moses to learn some things about his personal identity through a desert experience that he could not learn in the palace. God was preparing Moses to deliver the children of Israel from Egyptian bondage. The burning bush encounter was a life changing experience for Moses. The encounter enabled Moses to come to know God in a personal way. God revealed His holiness to Moses and then unveiled His plan for Moses to embrace.

As you can imagine, Moses could not visualize himself as the deliverer of the children of Israel. They had been slaves for over 400 years. Moses began making excuses and tried to deny his usefulness to God. Moses began to focus on what he lacked and missed the reality of God's ability to do the extraordinary through ordinary people.

Have you ever doubted your usefulness to God? Have you ever tried to convince God that you are not fit for His plan? God is not impressed with our abilities or our inabilities. God is not limited by our limitations. Are you willing to yield to God's control and allow Him to have His way in your life? God is willing to take you through a desert experience to prepare you for His assignment.

May 31
Available for God's Use

"Then I heard the voice of the Lord saying, 'Whom shall I send? And who will go for us?' And I said, 'Here am I. Send me!'" Isaiah 6:8 (NIV)

Isaiah had a life changing experience. He looked up and saw the Lord in all of His holiness. Isaiah looked inward and recognized his own sinfulness in light of God's holiness. Isaiah then looked outward and detected the sinful condition of others. In this life changing experience, Isaiah heard God's call and responded with instant obedience. Isaiah said, "Here am I. Send me!"

Will you make an impact upon every generation? Are you willing to allow God to call you to a new level of living? God's grace always matches His assignment for your life. Where God guides He always provides. There is never a better moment than now to obey God instantly and make yourself totally available for His use. God can do more in you and through you in the next six months than all the previous years of your life combined.

God values the work He does in you more than the work He does through you. Before God used Isaiah to make an eternal impact, God had to do an internal work in Isaiah's life. The internal work always impacts the external and the eternal work.

Don't bypass what God wants to do in you. Isaiah came face to face with the holiness of God in worship. Isaiah's worship led to a personal assessment of his own morality and then the morality of those around him. After God did this great work in Isaiah, He invited Isaiah to join His world redemptive activity.

You have a chance to make an eternal impact. Are you available? Look upward! Look inward! Look outward!

June 1
FAITH IN THE FIRE

"Shadrach, Meshach and Abednego replied to the king, 'O Nebuchadnezzar, we do not need to defend ourselves before you in this matter. If we are thrown into the blazing furnace, the God we serve is able to save us from it, and he will rescue us from your hand, O king. But even if he does not, we want you to know, O king, that we will not serve your gods or worship the image of gold you have set up.'"
Dan 3:16-18 (NIV)

Has your faith ever been tested? Have you ever been in an environment that provided you with an opportunity to make a bold stand for the Lord? Maybe your home is a place where your faith is put to the test. Maybe your work environment has been a difficult place for you to express your faith. Swimming upstream is always a challenge. Whenever you decide to go in the opposite direction of the cultural current, you will face resistance and opposition.

In the midst of impending death if they chose not to abide by the king's command, Shadrach, Meshach, and Abednego where willing to obey God at all costs. Instead of bowing to the golden image erected by king Nebuchadnezzar, they chose to honor God even if it meant death. They demonstrated their belief in God's ability to save them from the blazing furnace. They went a step further by declaring that even if God did not deliver them that they would not worship the image of gold.

Do you have that kind of "but even if God does not" faith? Are you willing to obey God in the face of opposition and in the face of being misunderstood by your family or peers? Even if God does not deliver you from your difficult circumstances, are you willing to obey Him and honor Him?

The good news is that God delivered Shadrach, Meshach, and Abednego. They did not bow, they did not bend, they did not budge, and they did not burn! God brought them through the blazing furnace.

June 2
DISPLAYING GOD'S SPLENDOR

"Then will all your people be righteous and they will possess the land forever. They are the shoot I have planted, the work of my hands, for the display of my splendor." Isaiah 60:21 (NIV)

Salvation is a gift, not a reward. You cannot perform enough good works to earn salvation. You receive the gift of eternal life by the grace of God through faith in the completed work of Jesus on the cross. If salvation is a gift, how do good works add value?

He graciously gave His best, Jesus, to pay the sin debt you owed. It is a gift. If you try to pay for the gift one has given, then you cheapen the gift. What can you add to the finished work of Jesus on the cross? His atoning work is complete.

You were uniquely designed by God and for God. You are His masterpiece, His treasure, and the apple of His eye. You are His workmanship. He formed you and fashioned you for His glory. You are not an accident! You are here on purpose!

- *"For we are God's workmanship, created in Christ Jesus to do good works, which God prepared in advance for us to do." Eph 2:10 (NIV)*

You cannot add to the salvation that God provided to you by His grace alone through faith alone. However, as His workmanship, you are created to do good works. You don't work for salvation; you work as a result of the salvation gift you have received. Good works are a result of a grateful heart. Gratitude for what God has initiated and what our faith has activated results in good works.

Are you willing to display God's splendor today? You are His workmanship created in Christ Jesus to do good works! Who will benefit from your life today?

June 3
TRAINING YOURSELF TO BE GODLY

"Have nothing to do with godless myths and old wives' tales; rather, train yourself to be godly. For physical training is of some value, but godliness has value for all things, holding promise for both the present life and the life to come."
1 Tim 4:7-8 (NIV)

Godliness involves a lifestyle oriented around living to please God. The believer's life is marked by godliness when the constant pursuit is that of maintaining a vital relationship with God through Christ. Becoming godly includes a disciplined life centered on fulfilling God's agenda and practicing God's presence. Training yourself to be godly requires an awareness of the claims of Christ on your life. You do not drift into godliness. Godliness is the byproduct of the intentional daily surrender to the Lordship of Christ.

- *"But godliness with contentment is great gain."* 1 Tim 6:6 (NIV)
- *"But you, man of God, flee from all this, and pursue righteousness, godliness, faith, love, endurance and gentleness."* 1 Tim 6:11 (NIV)

What are you pursuing? You will become what you are becoming right now. Take care of your body, the temple of the Holy Spirit (1 Cor. 6:19-20). Don't neglect your health. Eat properly, exercise consistently, and rest completely. Physical training is of some value. However, choose to nurture your inner life. Nourish your soul through a vibrant, healthy, and growing relationship with Christ. Maintain a living connection to Christ and allow Him to live His life through you (Gal. 2:20).

Godliness impacts eternity. Your life in Christ continues beyond the grave. You will trade-in your physical body for the glorified body God has for you. Your love relationship with Jesus continues for eternity. Pursue godliness by loving what God loves, hating what God hates, and valuing what God values.

June 4
LOVING GOD'S WAY

"If anyone says, 'I love God,' yet hates his brother, he is a liar. For anyone who does not love his brother, whom he has seen, cannot love God, whom he has not seen." 1 John 4:20 (NIV)

Is it possible to love God and hate your brother? Can you have the love of God residing in you and at the same time have hatred toward others festering in your spirit? The duplicity seems to be incongruent to the life of love that God calls us to and that Jesus exemplified on the earth.

Turn inward for a moment and examine your own current reality. Is there anyone you are fertilizing hatred toward? Do you have someone in your life to whom your love has been extinguished and your hatred has been ignited? Doing life in a fallen world is inundated with landmines of hatred. You will not lack opportunities to be wounded by hurtful words and by harmful people. People will let you down.

You cannot love God and hate others at the same time without your relationship with God being affected. God's love in you demands expression. When you choose to hate the people God created and the people Jesus died for, you restrict God's love within you. God wants you to hate what He hates and love what He loves. God passionately hates sin, but passionately loves the sinner.

Who is your brother? Who is your sister? How would God define your level of love? You will notice daily tests that reveal the authenticity of your love for others. Do you love God? Do you love others?

Loving God and loving people is the entirety of the Bible for present day expression.

June 5
RICH IN GOOD DEEDS

"Command them to do good, to be rich in good deeds, and to be generous and willing to share." 1 Tim 6:18 (NIV)

Jesus is our model to follow. Teaching, preaching, casting out demons, praying, and extending personal touch ministry marked Jesus' life on earth. He was never in a hurry and never late. Jesus maintained a balanced life centered on doing God's will. Loving God and loving others was the central focus of His life.

Jesus came to our planet to reconcile us to God. He willingly gave His life as the sinless sacrifice for our redemption (Col. 1:20). Jesus lived, died, was buried, rose on the third day, and forty days later ascended to heaven. Sitting at the right hand of the Father, Jesus intercedes on our behalf (Romans 8:34).

Your purpose in this life is to continue the ministry of Jesus. You have been saved by grace alone through faith alone to join God in His redemptive activity. God has entrusted every moment of your day to you for careful stewardship. What are you doing with the time God gives you? How are you responding to the opportunities God places before you to continue the ministry of Jesus?

Be rich in good deeds. Invest your life by adding value to others. Serve others from a heart of purity seasoned by daily intimacy with Christ. If you are going to continue the ministry of Jesus, then you must operate in His power. Adding value to others will require spiritual nourishment and spiritual energy.

Maintain a living connection with Christ through feeding on God's Word and seeking His face daily. To do what Jesus did mandates that you nurture your love relationship with God. The outflow of your living connection with Christ will be doing good, being generous, and willing to share.

June 6
RESURRECTION AND LIFE

"Jesus said to her, 'I am the resurrection and the life. He who believes in me will live, even though he dies; and whoever lives and believes in me will never die. Do you believe this?'" John 11:25-26 (NIV)

You are born, you live, you die, and then you go to heaven or hell. There's more to this life than the here and now. There's more to this life than what is visible. In light of eternity, life on planet earth is brief. Yet, there is life on the other side of the grave.

Everyone will face God and acknowledge that Jesus is Lord. Those who make that confession before death will go to heaven. Those who fail to make that declaration before death will face God, confess that Jesus is Lord, and then spend eternity separated from God in the literal place called hell.

There's hope! Because Jesus is the resurrection and the life, you are invited to spend eternity in heaven. You are invited to respond to God's offer of salvation by placing your faith in the redemptive act of Jesus dying on the cross to pay the penalty for your sin. You are invited to receive the gift of eternal life.

- *"For it is by grace you have been saved, through faith--and this not from yourselves, it is the gift of God--not by works, so that no one can boast." Eph 2:8-9 (NIV)*

Receive the gift of eternal life and then spend your remaining days upon the earth inviting others to receive the gift of eternal life before it is too late. How many people will be in heaven because of you?

June 7
STAYING CONNECTED

"'I am the vine; you are the branches. If a man remains in me and I in him, he will bear much fruit; apart from me you can do nothing.'" John 15:5 (NIV)

God will never ask you to do anything without equipping you to do it. God has an assignment for you to complete during your time on this blue and green planet called earth. God's assignment requires His empowerment. You cannot fulfill God's agenda without God's provision. God's assignment for your life flows out of your abiding relationship with Christ. God's command is not for you to bear fruit, but rather to focus your energy on abiding in Christ.

Your fruitfulness will be proportionate to your level of intimacy with Christ. Don't bypass your love relationship with Christ in order to seek to bear fruit. Your passion is not to be channeled in the area of bearing fruit. As you stay connected to Christ and allow His energy, His strength, and His life to flow through you, you will bear much fruit

Because He is the vine, you are fruitful. Jesus is the source! Stay connected to Him. Guard your love relationship with Him. Protect your daily walk with Christ. Don't allow anything or anyone to rob your relationship with Him. Ensure that your abiding relationship with Christ gets your best and not your leftovers. Don't give Jesus your crumbs. He deserves your passionate pursuit.

Are you connected? Are you abiding? You are the branch. Remain in Him and He will bear His fruit through you. Focus on abiding!

June 8
Soul Nourishment

"Then Jesus declared, 'I am the bread of life. He who comes to me will never go hungry, and he who believes in me will never be thirsty.'" John 6:35 (NIV)

Jesus had fed the multitudes with a boy's lunch consisting of two small fish and fives loaves of bread. As S.M. Lockridge used to say, "God is the only One who can multiply two times five and get five-thousand." The people were fixated on the miracle of multiplication and bypassed the miracle worker, Jesus. Instead of believing in the One who provided the bread, they were content to have their appetites fulfilled with earthly bread.

- *"Jesus said to them, 'I tell you the truth, it is not Moses who has given you the bread from heaven, but it is my Father who gives you the true bread from heaven. For the bread of God is he who comes down from heaven and gives life to the world.'"* John 6:32-33 (NIV)

Jesus is the true bread from heaven. He has come to give life to the world. Jesus is the bread of life. Because He is the bread of life, I am nourished. My soul is satisfied. The hole in my heart has been filled. My life is now complete. My life now makes sense. As John Piper says, "God is most glorified when we are most satisfied in Him." Have you come to that place of recognizing Jesus as the bread of life? Has Jesus become your Source for life? Are you most satisfied in Him?

Because Jesus is the bread of life, you are nourished. By placing your faith in the atoning work of Christ on the cross, you become a child of God. Your new identity includes that of Jesus becoming the bread of your life. Jesus is now your nourishment. He is now your reason for living. Jesus is your Source!

Are you daily nurturing the life of Christ in you? Close your eyes and spend some unhurried time alone with God in prayer. Thank Him for being your provider, your peace, and your protector. Allow Jesus to nourish your soul.

June 9
ILLUMINATING YOUR WORLD

"When Jesus spoke again to the people, he said, 'I am the light of the world. Whoever follows me will never walk in darkness, but will have the light of life.'"
John 8:12 (NIV)

Everything changed on March 28, 1979, when I received God's gift of eternal life. Jesus, the light of the world, took up residence in my heart and has illuminated my life both inwardly and outwardly. My ambitions, my desires, and my outlook took on a new perspective. The character of Christ has been daily formed in me. Throughout the years, His light has informed me of areas that need to be brought under His Lordship.

- *"For you were once darkness, but now you are light in the Lord. Live as children of light."* Eph 5:8 (NIV)
- *"For he has rescued us from the dominion of darkness and brought us into the kingdom of the Son he loves, in whom we have redemption, the forgiveness of sins."* Col 1:13-14 (NIV)

Jesus wants to not only shine in you but also to shine through you. His light through your life alters the world around you. Every interaction becomes intentional. Each conversation becomes an opportunity to allow Jesus to shine His light through you. Just as light influences darkness, Jesus has saved you and set you apart to influence others. Because He is the light of the world, you are illuminated. Now, illuminate the environments that God places you in. Allow the light of Jesus to shine brightly through your life today. Eternity is at stake!

June 10
ETERNAL SECURITY

"Therefore Jesus said again, 'I tell you the truth, I am the gate for the sheep.'"
John 10:7 (NIV)

My security in Christ is not based on my feelings. There are days when my emotional security may be threatened. There are days when I just don't feel safe and secure. Fortunately, my security is not anchored to my feelings. My eternal security is found in Jesus completely.

- *"'I am the gate; whoever enters through me will be saved. He will come in and go out, and find pasture. The thief comes only to steal and kill and destroy; I have come that they may have life, and have it to the full.'" John 10:9-10 (NIV)*

Because He is the gate, you are secure. After placing your trust in the completed work of Jesus on the cross, you are completely saved. Your eternal security is not based on your daily performance, but on the finished work of Jesus on the cross. You didn't earn salvation and you cannot lose your salvation. The same One who saved you is the One who keeps you.

As a believer, if you choose to sin, you will face consequences. You don't lose your salvation, but your fellowship with Jesus will be strained and your ability to bear the fruit of the Spirit will be inhibited. Confess your sin now. Specifically agree with God concerning your sin. Remember what you were saved from!

Now walk with Jesus and He will help you find pasture. Jesus will help you develop authentic relationships with other believers and He will help you develop spiritual disciplines to nurture His life in you. Jesus will help you build intentional relationships with unsaved people so that you can shine His light and share His love with them.

June 11
VALUED BY THE SHEPHERD

"'I am the good shepherd. The good shepherd lays down his life for the sheep.'"
John 10:11 (NIV)

Your value is not determined by your portfolio. Your value is not determined by your performance. Your value is not determined by your personality. Your value is determined by what God has done on your behalf. Before you could do anything with God or for God, in His mercy and grace, God decided what to do with you and for you.

Your value was established before you were born. Then, God provided a tangible demonstration and validation of your value when He became man.

- *"The Word became flesh and made his dwelling among us. We have seen his glory, the glory of the One and Only, who came from the Father, full of grace and truth."* John 1:14 (NIV)
- *"God made him who had no sin to be sin for us, so that in him we might become the righteousness of God."* 2 Cor 5:21 (NIV)

Is the Lord your Shepherd? Have you allowed Him to be the Shepherd and Overseer of your soul? Now think about your value in God's economy. You are the apple of God's eye. You are His treasure. Look around! Do you see other people in your weekly routine? Guess what? God values them, too.

June 12
THE ONLY WAY

"Jesus answered, 'I am the way and the truth and the life. No one comes to the Father except through me.'" John 14:6 (NIV)

Often I have heard people insert their belief that "we are all trying to get to the same place, just taking different paths to get there." Scripture does not affirm that belief. In fact, there is only one way to get to heaven. Jesus is the only way! Now that is both exclusive and inclusive. Those who reject Jesus as the only way don't receive the benefit of eternal life in heaven. They are excluded from heaven for failing to accept Jesus as their personal Lord and Savior.

Be informed, since Jesus is the only way to heaven, you can know for certain that you have the gift of eternal life. Everyone who trusts in Jesus alone for salvation is included in the eternal benefits of that decision.

- *"For God so loved the world that he gave his one and only Son, that whoever believes in him shall not perish but have eternal life." John 3:16 (NIV)*
- *"That if you confess with your mouth, 'Jesus is Lord,' and believe in your heart that God raised him from the dead, you will be saved." Romans 10:9 (NIV)*
- *"Salvation is found in no one else, for there is no other name under heaven given to men by which we must be saved." Acts 4:12 (NIV)*

Have you met the Way? Have you embraced the Truth? Have you experienced the Life? Be informed and be transformed by the only One who can make an eternal difference in your life, Jesus.

June 13
ABIDING IN GRACE

"Although I am less than the least of all God's people, this grace was given me: to preach to the Gentiles the unsearchable riches of Christ, and to make plain to everyone the administration of this mystery, which for ages past was kept hidden in God, who created all things." Eph 3:8-9 (NIV)

Have you ever met someone who was great and they didn't know it? In other words, they were simply being who God made them to be and didn't build a tower of recognition for themselves.

Paul was great and didn't know it. He understood that his usability was proportionate to God's dispensing of immeasurable grace. His validation came through recognition of his desperation for God's mercy and grace. Paul was only great because of the greatness of God's grace.

Only through Paul's humility and dependency upon God was he enabled to hyper-focus on the mission of bringing clarity to the mystery of the gospel for the people in need of salvation. Abiding in God's grace was vital to Paul's effectiveness in ministry. Paul recognized God's grace at work through his life (Gal. 2:20).

Does your behavior bring clarity to the gospel for those watching your life? Are you drawing people to Christ or repelling them from Christ? May the fog lift and the gospel clearly go forth through opportunities God gives you this week to make Jesus known. Is there any greater vision to give your life to than that of bringing the gospel to the nations beginning right where you are?

The grace you have received is the grace needed to bring salvation to those disconnected from Christ. As you abide in God's grace, allow God to use you in the redemptive process. Put God's grace on display.

June 14
BEING A TRUE WORSHIPER

"'Yet a time is coming and has now come when the true worshipers will worship the Father in spirit and truth, for they are the kind of worshipers the Father seeks. God is spirit, and his worshipers must worship in spirit and in truth.'"
John 4:23-24 (NIV)

In His interaction with the woman at the well, Jesus confronted the reality of her relational choices. She shifted the focus of their conversation from her personal life to the subject of religion. She expressed her views on worship. Her theology of worship centered on the place of worship rather than the purpose of worship.

Jesus defined true worshipers as those who worship the Father in spirit and truth. Religion is not sufficient to develop a person into a true worshiper. In fact, just as a flu shot will give you just enough of the flu to keep you from getting the real thing, religion can inoculate you from developing a vibrant love relationship with God. Religion, ritual, and routine are not adequate. Without a personal relationship with Jesus Christ, a person cannot become a true worshiper of the living God.

Once you become a follower of Christ, you are to become the kind of worshiper the Father seeks. Express your love to God through personal and corporate worship. Ascribe worth to God by making Him your top priority and embracing Him as the object of your affection.

Are you the kind of worshiper the Father seeks? Do you worship in spirit and in truth? Do you go to church to worship or do you go to church worshiping?

June 15
SALVATION WORKS

"You foolish man, do you want evidence that faith without deeds is useless ? Was not our ancestor Abraham considered righteous for what he did when he offered his son Isaac on the altar? You see that his faith and his actions were working together, and his faith was made complete by what he did." James 2:20-22 (NIV)

Your good works will not produce salvation.

If only you could work your way to heaven! Then the challenge would be knowing how much work would be required by God for you to deserve entrance into heaven. How would you know if you have done enough to get there? What if you almost made it, but fell short by one good deed? Fortunately, God does not base your salvation on your works.

The Bible does not present a works salvation, but a salvation that works. You cannot work for your salvation, but your salvation will be evidenced by good works. In response to God's gracious gift of salvation, you will want to express your appreciation to God through deeds of righteousness. Your deeds will not produce righteousness, but your righteousness in Christ will produce righteous deeds. Your "want to" changes as a result of your salvation.

- *"God made him who had no sin to be sin for us, so that in him we might become the righteousness of God."* 2 Cor 5:21 (NIV)
- *"Those who obey his commands live in him, and he in them. And this is how we know that he lives in us: We know it by the Spirit he gave us."* 1 John 3:24 (NIV)

Your salvation is a gift from God and is marked by a life of obedience.

June 16
Appearing Before the Judgment Seat

"For we must all appear before the judgment seat of Christ, that each one may receive what is due him for the things done while in the body, whether good or bad." 2 Cor 5:10 (NIV)

Everyone will live forever somewhere.

What you do with Christ during your brief stay on planet earth will determine whether you spend eternity in heaven or hell. Your response to God's offer of salvation is the deciding factor to your eternal destination. As Bruce Wilkinson says, "Your belief determines where you will spend eternity; your behavior determines how you will spend eternity."

- *"You, then, why do you judge your brother? Or why do you look down on your brother? For we will all stand before God's judgment seat." Romans 14:10 (NIV)*
- *"Therefore God exalted him to the highest place and gave him the name that is above every name, that at the name of Jesus every knee should bow, in heaven and on earth and under the earth, and every tongue confess that Jesus Christ is Lord, to the glory of God the Father." Phil 2:9-11 (NIV)*

Every human being will stand before God to give an account for his or her life. Every person will bow and confess that Jesus Christ is Lord! Those who reject God's offer of salvation while living on earth will still bow and confess that Jesus Christ is Lord, but it will be eternally too late. Believers will go to the Judgment Seat of Christ to receive reward and heaven while unbelievers will go to the White Throne Judgment (Rev. 20:11-15) to receive punishment and hell.

Live circumspectly! Live in full awareness of God's holiness, purity, and justice! Take as many people with you to heaven as you possibly can in full surrender to the Spirit's control. Make the most of every opportunity!

June 17
GIVING AN ACCOUNT

"So then, each of us will give an account of himself to God." Romans 14:12 (NIV)

God sees every moment of your life. God will hear every word you speak today. Each act of kindness will not go unnoticed. Your thoughts, your motives, and your attitude will not escape His attention. God is all knowing and all seeing. Has it ever occurred to you that nothing ever occurs to God? Nothing catches God by surprise.

One day you will stand before God to give an account for your life. As a follower of Christ, your sins have been forgiven. The penalty for your sin debt has been paid in full. Jesus took your sin upon Himself and received the full wrath of God for your sin. As a believer, you will not stand before God to determine your eternal destiny. Where you spend eternity is solidified by your belief in the atoning work of Christ on the cross. Salvation is not in question.

When you stand before God, you will give an account for how you invested the life God has given you. You are a steward of the blessings and opportunities God gives you. What have you done with all that God has entrusted to your care? Have you been faithful to join God in His redemptive activity? Have you employed your spiritual gifts in service to God through His local church?

Every moment matters to God; so make every moment count. Don't squander your life. Live in light of standing before God one day to give an account. Make decisions based on what God has said in His Word and what God will say when you stand before Him.

June 18
A Night of Wrestling

"So Jacob was left alone, and a man wrestled with him till daybreak. When the man saw that he could not overpower him, he touched the socket of Jacob's hip so that his hip was wrenched as he wrestled with the man." Gen 32:24-25 (NIV)

Have you ever wrestled with God? Who won? Wrestling is part of being God's workmanship. Jacob, as God's workmanship, came to know God in a new way after a night of wrestling. Just like in weight training, without resistance there is no growth.

God allows us to go through seasons of uncertainty. God allows us to experience seasons of silence and yes, even seasons of suffering. We wrestle with God in those seasons. Our faith is challenged and often our prayer life is stretched. We come to know God by experience. Sometimes that experience involves pain.

As God's workmanship, Jacob came away from the night of wrestling with a limp and a new name. You don't come into close proximity with the living God and leave the same. God gave Jacob the name Israel, which means God prevails. Jacob was known as a deceiver, but God gave him a new name to live up to. Jacob would become the patriarch of the twelve tribes of Israel.

God is for you. He is willingly to go to any length to bring you into a vibrant, intimate, and growing relationship that is eternal. God will pursue you and groom you so that you will be conformed into the image of Christ. Your life matters to God.

June 19
RECEIVING GRACE

"A father to the fatherless, a defender of widows, is God in his holy dwelling." Psalm 68:5 (NIV)

"But he gives us more grace. That is why Scripture says: 'God opposes the proud but gives grace to the humble.'" James 4:6 (NIV)

Grace is getting what we do not deserve. We do not deserve God's forgiveness, salvation, reconciliation, favor, blessing, and heaven. But God demonstrates His love by gracing us with that which we do not deserve. God stands in opposition to the proud but responds with grace to the humble. So what does humility look like? As we examine the life of Jesus, we see humility defined. Jesus willingly put others before Himself. Jesus lived selflessly and died sacrificially. Jesus came to this earth to serve and to save. How will you respond?

- *"Humble yourselves before the Lord, and he will lift you up."* James 4:10 (NIV)
- *"Humble yourselves, therefore, under God's mighty hand, that he may lift you up in due time."* 1 Peter 5:6 (NIV)

We are to humble ourselves. As an act of the will, we are to choose to humble ourselves. God can navigate circumstances to bring humility into our lives to remind us of our dependency upon Him. Yet, God wants us to choose the way of humility without the influence of outward circumstances. Based on our love relationship with God, we are to respond to His grace by exemplifying a life of humility.

Is there an element of pride in your life? Have you exhibited the sin of pride through your conversation or your conduct? Trying to do life your way instead of God's way is an expression of pride. Embrace the way of humility, which places God's agenda above your own agenda. Anticipate God's grace to flow like a river!

June 20
TAKE PRIDE FOR A RIDE

"Blessed are the poor in spirit, for theirs is the kingdom of heaven." Matt 5:3 (NIV)

Delays, detours, and distractions are common in this life. Sin, sickness, and sorrow permeate the landscape of our humanity. Is it possible to find happiness while living in a fallen world? The keys to happiness are found in the Beatitudes. Jesus is the greatest preacher who ever lived and preached the greatest sermon ever preached.

The happiness Jesus speaks of in the Beatitudes is not based on circumstances or external conditions. Happy, blissful, and blessed are those who recognize their spiritual bankruptcy before a holy God. Pride has no part in Christ's kingdom. The door into His kingdom is low, and no one who stands tall in pride will ever go through it.

The world emphasizes self-reliance, self-confidence, and self-expression. Jesus went into the display window of life and changed all the price tags. Jesus countered what the world values and ushered in the kingdom values that bring honor to God.

- *"The LORD detests all the proud of heart. Be sure of this: They will not go unpunished."* Prov 16:5 (NIV)
- *"Pride goes before destruction, a haughty spirit before a fall."* Prov 16:18 (NIV)

Take pride for a ride. Instead of an ego trip, we need to go on an integrity trip. Get honest about your destitution and your spiritual poverty before God. Identify and eliminate any fraction of pride in your life. Embrace the way of humility and recognize your dependency upon God and His abundant grace.

Uncover the poison of pride. You will never reach your full redemptive potential while fertilizing pride in your life. Pride has no place in the Christian life fully yielded to the Lordship of Christ.

June 21
THE HAVEN OF HUMILITY

"Blessed are the poor in spirit, for theirs is the kingdom of heaven.'" Matt 5:3 (NIV)

The highway of happiness is paved with humility. Happiness and humility go together. Jesus modeled a life of humility by submitting to the Father's agenda and by living to benefit others. In humility, Jesus sacrificed His life on the cross to provide for the forgiveness of our sins and to reconcile us back to God.

What is meant by poor in spirit? It means a complete absence of pride, a complete absence of self-assurance and self-reliance. It means a consciousness that we are nothing in the presence of God. To be poor in spirit is the tremendous awareness of our utter nothingness as we come face to face with God.

Discover the haven of humility. Admit that you don't have it all together. Admit that you haven't arrived. Recognize that you haven't learned all that God wants you to learn and you haven't completed everything God wants you to do. Make an accurate assessment of yourself before a holy God in light of His holiness.

- *"Do not think of yourself more highly than you ought, but rather think of yourself with sober judgment, in accordance with the measure of faith God has given you." Romans 12:3 (NIV)*
- *"Therefore, as God's chosen people, holy and dearly loved, clothe yourselves with compassion, kindness, humility, gentleness and patience." Col 3:12 (NIV)*

Give up your kingdom so you can inherit God's kingdom! Clothe yourself with humility. Being poor in spirit is a mark of spiritual maturity as you acknowledge your utter dependency upon God and His grace to help you live as a citizen of His kingdom. You cannot live the life God has for you without His supernatural enablement. His power comes to you through the doorway of humility.

June 22
WORTHY OF TRUST

"Some trust in chariots and some in horses, but we trust in the name of the LORD our God." Psalm 20:7 (NIV)

This verse became dear to my heart when I was pastoring my seminary church in 1992. My wife, Tonya, and I went through the Experiencing God study along with our deacons and their wives. My journey of faith has been enhanced by the concept of trusting in the name of the Lord our God.

Trust is a fragile item in the life of a believer. Trust is like the petal of a rose. Trust can beautify a difficult path and create an aroma pleasing to Christ. Trust can also wilt when betrayed. Like a gem in the hand of a jeweler, trust in God can lead to an irresistible life in which God's glory radiates.

What do you trust in? In our society draped with affluence, it is so easy to trust in materialism. If we can only acquire one more object of our affection or jump into one more activity that produces an adrenaline rush, then we will be fulfilled...so we think. The things of this world just don't deliver what they promise.

The chariots of our culture and the horses of our entertainment are not trustworthy. Only God can deliver on the magnitude of His promises. God always lives up to the level of His nature and character of perfection. There is no lack! There is no discrepancy! God is all sufficient and more than enough!

Trust God with your life. He knows your fears and your future. His timing is perfect.

June 23
THE RHYTHM OF GOD'S LOVE

"He put a new song in my mouth, a hymn of praise to our God. Many will see and fear and put their trust in the LORD." Psalm 40:3 (NIV)

What is your life song? Has God put a new song in your mouth? As children of God, we have the life transforming message of Jesus. If the blood of Jesus has redeemed you, then you have a song to sing. It does not matter how musically inclined you are. What matters is that you have a song to sing! Your life in Christ is a song that others will observe.

Will others see and revere Jesus because of your life song? Will others place their trust in Jesus as a result of the song that your life sings? God has given us the wonderful and awesome privilege to be the tangible portrait of His grace on this planet. The conversations and interactions that you engage in on a daily basis are chords that vibrate the rhythm of God's love.

When you study the life of Jesus you will notice that Jesus maximized the opportunities presented to Him each day. Jesus lived a life that radiated the love of God. People were drawn to Jesus because His life song declared the magnitude of God's abundant grace and mercy.

Maybe you are in a season currently that has inhibited the song in your mouth. Maybe you have not had a song to sing due to hurt, anger, or disappointment. Ask God to renew your mind and to renew your strength. Ask God to put a new song in your mouth to help you persevere and experience a breakthrough. God knows right where you are and exactly what you need.

June 24
PLACING VALUE ON PARTICIPATION

"He went to Nazareth, where he had been brought up, and on the Sabbath day he went into the synagogue, as was his custom. And he stood up to read." Luke 4:16 (NIV)

You make room for what you value. When you value participating in the ministry of your local church, you will make room in your life for that ministry. If you value short-term mission trips, then you will make room in your annual calendar of events to go on a short-term mission trip. Whatever you value will receive your time, energy, and attention. Whatever you value will be a guarded priority in your life.

Jesus valued the weekly worship experience in the synagogue on the Sabbath (Saturday). The synagogue had been a consistent part of His life for thirty years at this particular point. After His baptism and 40 days of temptation in the desert, Jesus returned to Galilee and went to His hometown of Nazareth. As was His custom, He went into the synagogue.

Much of Jesus' identity was connected to the synagogue. He had grown up being exposed to the reading of Scripture each Sabbath in the local synagogue. On this day, He stood to read. He participated in the flow of the service and contributed to the experience.

You are the sum total of your habits. In other words, you will become what you habitually invest your life in. You are in the process of becoming who you are in Christ. Value weekly participation in the local church. Value connecting with God in worship with other believers. Value weekly interaction with other believers in a small group Bible study. Make it your custom to grow in your love relationship with Jesus. Your identity is found in Christ.

June 25
CLARIFYING YOUR IDENTITY

"All spoke well of him and were amazed at the gracious words that came from his lips. 'Isn't this Joseph's son?' they asked." Luke 4:22 (NIV)

Jesus shared from Isaiah 61:1-2 in the hearing of those in the synagogue and identified Himself as the fulfillment of that prophecy. The people spoke well of Him. Amazed at Jesus' gracious words, they tried to reconcile His professed identity by asking, "Isn't this Joseph's son?"

The people were confused. Their understanding of the coming Messiah did not position them to anticipate a carpenter's son from Nazareth as the Messiah. The humanity and humility of Jesus did not line up with their view of the Messiah. They were expecting a mighty military leader with position and prominence who would restore Israel.

As followers of Christ, we can identify with His dual identity. Though virgin born, Jesus had an earthly father and a Heavenly Father. We too have an earthly father and our Heavenly Father.

- *"Our fathers disciplined us for a little while as they thought best; but God disciplines us for our good, that we may share in his holiness."* Heb 12:10 (NIV)
- *"How great is the love the Father has lavished on us, that we should be called children of God! And that is what we are! The reason the world does not know us is that it did not know him."* 1 John 3:1 (NIV)

Your identity in Christ is formed and fashioned by your Heavenly Father. God has created you for His glory. You are God's workmanship (Eph. 2:10) and you belong to God (I Pt. 2:9). If you ever forget who you are in Christ, look up! You are a child of the King!

June 26
SHAPED BY HIS HAND

"All the people in the synagogue were furious when they heard this. They got up, drove him out of the town, and took him to the brow of the hill on which the town was built, in order to throw him down the cliff. But he walked right through the crowd and went on his way." Luke 4:28-30 (NIV)

Jesus communicated to His hearers in the synagogue that a prophet is not accepted in his hometown. He was implying that many would miss the fact that He was the Messiah and forfeit the benefits just as many in Israel did not enjoy the benefits of the ministry of Elijah. The people were so furious with Jesus that they tried to throw him down the cliff. Jesus' popularity in His hometown was not very positive!

Your identity is not based on what people say about you. Your identity in Christ is based on what God says about you. You are shaped by God's hand. Your destiny is determined by the loving provision of your Heavenly Father. In the midst of opposition and being misunderstood, you can stand firm in the security of your identity in Christ.

- *"'You did not choose me, but I chose you and appointed you to go and bear fruit--fruit that will last. Then the Father will give you whatever you ask in my name.'" John 15:16 (NIV)*
- *"'If the world hates you, keep in mind that it hated me first.'" John 15:18 (NIV)*

Find a place of solitude and begin to eliminate the voices of falsehood and tune in to the voice of Truth! Speaker and author, Beth Moore, likes to say, "God is who He says He is. God can do what He says He can do. I am who God says I am. I can do all things through Christ. God's Word is alive and active in me. I'm believing God!"

Now listen for God's voice and allow Him to affirm your identity in Christ. Remember who you are in Christ!

June 27
JESUS WAS BAPTIZED

"When all the people were being baptized, Jesus was baptized too." Luke 3:21 (NIV)

Jesus was baptized too? Why was it necessary for Jesus to be baptized? I thought He was sinless. What would Jesus need to repent of? The Bible affirms His sinlessness.

- *"For we do not have a high priest who is unable to sympathize with our weaknesses, but we have one who has been tempted in every way, just as we are--yet was without sin." Heb 4:15 (NIV)*
- *"For you know that it was not with perishable things such as silver or gold that you were redeemed from the empty way of life handed down to you from your forefathers, but with the precious blood of Christ, a lamb without blemish or defect." I Peter 1:18-19 (NIV)*

Jesus did not allow John to baptize Him as an act of repentance. Jesus had no sin to repent of. So why did Jesus participate in this public baptism? Jesus set an example for us to follow. Jesus modeled the value of honoring God. The baptism of Jesus established the clear portrait of turning from sin and turning to Christ alone for salvation.

Just as my wedding ring does not make me married, it lets others know that I am married. So it is with baptism in that baptism does not save you; it lets others know that you have been saved. Your baptism by immersion is a public display of the internal reality of your salvation experience. The reality of your covenant relationship with Christ is demonstrated through your act of obedience in following Jesus in believer's baptism. Your baptism is the public profession of your faith in Jesus.

Have you been baptized, too?

June 28
OBEDIENCE IN BAPTISM

"When all the people were being baptized, Jesus was baptized too. And as he was praying, heaven was opened and the Holy Spirit descended on him in bodily form like a dove. And a voice came from heaven: 'You are my Son, whom I love; with you I am well pleased.'" Luke 3:21-22 (NIV)

Did you notice the activity of the Trinity in this passage? Read it again and see if you can locate God the Father, God the Son, and God the Holy Spirit. The word "Trinity" is not found in the Bible, but the doctrine of the Trinity can be easily located. At Jesus' baptism, we read about the Holy Spirit descending on Jesus like a dove. We read about the voice of God from heaven affirming Jesus at His baptism.

- *"One witness is not enough to convict a man accused of any crime or offense he may have committed. A matter must be established by the testimony of two or three witnesses." Deut 19:15 (NIV)*
- *"Anyone who rejected the law of Moses died without mercy on the testimony of two or three witnesses." Heb 10:28 (NIV)*

The testimony of God and the testimony of the Holy Spirit gave witness to the Lordship of Christ at the inauguration of His public ministry. Jesus was baptized to identify with those He came to seek and to save (Luke 19:10). Jesus brought glory to His Father by His obedience in baptism.

God created you for His glory. Jesus lived a sinless life and died a sacrificial death to provide you with life abundant (John 10:10) and life eternal (1 John 5:11,13). You have been given the Holy Spirit as a deposit. You are saved, sealed, and secure.

June 29
Affirmation In Baptism

"When all the people were being baptized, Jesus was baptized too. And as he was praying, heaven was opened and the Holy Spirit descended on him in bodily form like a dove. And a voice came from heaven: 'You are my Son, whom I love; with you I am well pleased.'" Luke 3:21-22 (NIV)

Jesus was about thirty years old when He began his ministry (Luke 3:23). The inauguration of Jesus' public ministry featured affirmation from His Heavenly Father. God affirmed that Jesus was His Son. It would be similar to an earthly Father saying to his son, "Son, I'm proud of you!"

God provided Jesus with an affirmation of His love. Jesus would draw on the love of His Heavenly Father as He navigated the path of suffering. In the Garden of Gethsemane, Jesus affirmed His love and loyalty to His Heavenly Father by praying, "Not my will, but Your will be done"(Matt. 26:39-44).

Jesus heard the precious words of affirmation, "with you I am well pleased." Jesus brought pleasure to His Heavenly Father through His obedience and willingness to finish His work (Jn. 4:34). God affirmed Jesus with these words at the inauguration of His public ministry.

You are loved by God. In fact, you are the apple of His eye (Ps. 17:8). Walk in the light of God's redemptive work in your life. God came to your rescue so that you could join Him in rescuing others. You are His workmanship (Eph. 2:10). Be affirmed by God!

June 30
I'm Not Ashamed

"If anyone is ashamed of me and my words, the Son of Man will be ashamed of him when he comes in his glory and in the glory of the Father and of the holy angels." Luke 9:26 (NIV)

Believer's baptism by immersion is a public proclamation of your faith in Jesus. Jesus identified with you through baptism so that you could identify with Him through baptism. Your identification with Christ is a bold and courageous act of obedience. If you have not identified with Christ through baptism, what is keeping you from taking that clear step of obedience? What would you be ashamed of? There's nothing to fear!

- *"I am not ashamed of the gospel, because it is the power of God for the salvation of everyone who believes: first for the Jew, then for the Gentile." Romans 1:16 (NIV)*
- *"Do your best to present yourself to God as one approved, a workman who does not need to be ashamed and who correctly handles the word of truth." 2 Tim 2:15 (NIV)*

There's no need to be ashamed. When you identify with Christ through baptism, you demonstrate your faith in the atoning work of Jesus on the cross. In baptism, you testify of His resurrection power that brought you out of darkness into the kingdom of light. You can bear the name of Christ with honor. He has given His all for you so that you can have an abiding love relationship with Him that is personal and eternal.

Don't be ashamed of Christ. If you have not been baptized by immersion since your conversion experience, then make things right with the Lord by obeying His command.

July 1
LOVING OTHERS

"Love is patient, love is kind. It does not envy, it does not boast, it is not proud. It is not rude, it is not self-seeking, it is not easily angered, it keeps no record of wrongs. Love does not delight in evil but rejoices with the truth. It always protects, always trusts, always hopes, always perseveres." 1 Cor 13:4-7 (NIV)

The "Love Chapter" has been read most often in weddings. Marriage is a portrait of love in that one spouse is to seek to meet the needs of the other spouse. Love is putting others first. Love flows from God because God is love (I John 4:8). As the Source of love, God demonstrated His love to us by allowing Christ to die in our place (Rom. 5:8). As you read the Bible, you will see a common thread of God's love in action to restore fallen humanity. Love takes the initiative just as God took the initiative to bring us into a right relationship with Himself.

Have you experienced God's unconditional love personally? God's love for you is not proportionate to your performance or productivity. God's love for you is based on His nature and character. God loves you with a perfect love that humanity cannot match. Allow God's love in you to inspire you to love others unconditionally.

Is there anyone you find difficult to love? Choose to love that person not based on what they can do for you or based on what they have done for you or to you. Choose to love that person based on what God has done for you. Love is a choice. God chose to love you long before you chose to love Him. Now seek to love those Christ died for.

July 2
EXPERIENCING TRUE LIFE

"When he had said this, Jesus called in a loud voice, 'Lazarus, come out!' The dead man came out, his hands and feet wrapped with strips of linen, and a cloth around his face. Jesus said to them, 'Take off the grave clothes and let him go.'" John 11:43-44 (NIV)

Are you living the life God has given?

Jesus left heaven and came to earth to dwell among us and ultimately give His life in death upon the cross so that we could know and experience true life. Jesus has removed the obstacles and provided the only way to salvation. Jesus is the way.

Death could not prevent Jesus from bringing forth life even to Lazarus, who had been dead four days. As the stench of death permeated the graveyard, Jesus called Lazarus by name to come forth from the dead. As Lazarus came out of the tomb, Jesus commanded them to take the graves clothes off and to let him go.

What is keeping you from living the life God has given? What kind of grave clothes have kept you bound? Release those things which prevent you from walking in the fullness of God's provision. Let go of those thoughts and attitudes that inhibit the flow of the Holy Spirit in your life. Jesus has paid full price for your freedom. Jesus has called you forth from the dead.

- *"As for you, you were dead in your transgressions and sins, in which you used to live when you followed the ways of this world and of the ruler of the kingdom of the air, the spirit who is now at work in those who are disobedient."* Eph 2:1-2 (NIV)
- *"So if the Son sets you free, you will be free indeed."* John 8:36 (NIV)

Take the grave clothes off and walk in the grace God provides.

July 3
Displaying His Fruit

"But the fruit of the Spirit is love, joy, peace, patience, kindness, goodness, faithfulness, gentleness and self-control. Against such things there is no law."
Gal 5:22-23 (NIV)

Which fruit is most lacking in your life? If patience is lacking, then God will often allow challenging circumstances to come into your life to develop that particular fruit of the Spirit in you. If there is a deficit of gentleness in your demeanor, then God will often engineer opportunities for that fruit of the Spirit to be expanded in your life.

God values you and the display of the fruit of His Spirit through you. Sometimes God will allow difficult people to come into your life in order to cultivate the fruit of the Spirit most neglected in your life. Learning how to love difficult people is a fertile environment for that particular fruit of the Spirit to be developed. Loving difficult people with the same love that God chooses to love you with does not come naturally. Loving difficult people necessitates a supernatural enabling that only comes through the Spirit filled life.

God will develop the fruit of His Spirit in you and through you as you yield to His control. Your flesh will battle to be placed in the display window of life. Therefore, you must choose to allow the Holy Spirit to take full possession of your life in order for His fruit to be displayed. The fruit of the Spirit is featured best in the midst of the trying circumstances you face and the difficult people you embrace.

Crucify the sinful nature (Gal. 5:24) and keep in step with the Spirit (Gal. 5:25). Allow God to develop the fruit of the Spirit in your life so that others will be drawn to Christ.

July 4
FORGIVENESS AND FREEDOM

"Be kind and compassionate to one another, forgiving each other, just as in Christ God forgave you." Eph 4:32 (NIV)

After speaking to a men's gathering on the subject of father wounds, a man in his mid-thirties came up to me to say that he was going immediately to his dad's house to forgive him. His dad had been pretty tough on him over his lifetime. The son felt that he could never please his dad. It was never enough! His dad always expected more and demanded more and refused to express affirmation. Bitterness had saturated the son's heart and on this day, he was under deep conviction by the Holy Spirit that it was time to forgive his dad.

Forgiveness brings freedom. When you choose to forgive those who have wounded you or neglected you, there is a tremendous release of tension followed by a refreshing wave of satisfaction. Showing kindness and compassion through forgiving others brings honor to God and relief to your soul. Harboring unforgiveness is like trying to push a parked car up a steep hill. Unforgiveness will shackle your capacity to experience love and will imprison your joy.

God is not asking you to do anything He has not already done for you in Christ. God took the initiative to sacrifice His only Son to pay the penalty of your sin. God chose to forgive you in spite of your rebellion, in spite of your past, and in spite of your proclivity to drift into sin.

Forgive others just as God has forgiven you. Dispense to others the mercy and grace you have freely received from God. Jesus bore your sin on the cross so that you could be forgiven and so that you could have the capacity to forgive others.

July 5
PROCLAIM WITHOUT SHAME

"'If anyone is ashamed of me and my words, the Son of Man will be ashamed of him when he comes in his glory and in the glory of the Father and of the holy angels.'" Luke 9:26 (NIV)

Do you conceal your Christianity? Can you be accused of being a closet Christian? Do those in your sphere of influence know that you are a follower of Jesus Christ? There's nothing to be ashamed of. In Christ, you have been adopted into God's family and sealed by the Holy Spirit (Eph. 1:5,13). You have been rescued from darkness and placed in the kingdom of light (Col. 1:5). God has placed you in the display window of life to portray His grace to a dark and decaying world (1 Tim. 1:16).

Embrace the attitude of Paul who affirmed, "I am not ashamed of the gospel, because it is the power of God for the salvation of everyone who believes: first for the Jew, then for the Gentile" (Romans 1:16 NIV). The gospel that brought you hope and eternal life is the same gospel that you represent in this life. Don't be ashamed of the Good News that transformed your life. Don't withhold the cure to the cancer of sin that will set others free just as you have been set free.

Jesus was not ashamed to identify with the lost by becoming flesh (John 1:14). For a person to be ashamed of Christ and His words is to deny the One who gave His all to provide for the forgiveness of sin. There's no room for shame when it comes to identifying with Christ. To align with Christ is an honor to behold.

Go public with your faith. God has given you the message worth sharing and the light worth shining. You have the capacity to influence others toward Christ. How many people will be in heaven because of you?

July 6
Making an Eternal Difference

"When Jesus reached the spot, he looked up and said to him, 'Zacchaeus, come down immediately. I must stay at your house today.' So he came down at once and welcomed him gladly." Luke 19:5-6 (NIV)

You have a choice. You can be a thermostat and set the environment or you can be a thermometer and reflect the environment. Jesus chose to be a thermostat. Jesus leveraged His influence to transform Zacchaeus and his family. Jesus was intentional about bringing life-change to this chief tax collector and his family.

The people criticized Jesus for His actions. We are introduced to this concept of muttering and grumbling in the Old Testament as the children of Israel grumbled against God, Moses, and Aaron (Ex. 16:6-8). Jesus was willing to be misunderstood and criticized in order to bring eternal life to Zacchaeus and his family. Jesus was willing to endure opposition to present this family with the opportunity to be transformed by His love.

Will you influence your environment or be influenced by your environment? Will you become like those around you or will they become like you? It depends upon your decision to be a thermostat or a thermometer. God has placed you here to be salt and light to influence this decaying and dark world with the purity and the light of His love (Matt. 5:13-16). God has planted you right where you are so that you can bloom for His glory and bring others into the kingdom of light.

Are you willing to be criticized for loving the unlovable? Are you willing to be misunderstood for extending grace to the despised and forgotten? You have the gift of eternal life and the power of the Holy Spirit operative within you. Be a thermostat for the glory of God!

July 7
CONTAGIOUS CHRISTIANITY

"Moved by the Spirit, he went into the temple courts. When the parents brought in the child Jesus to do for him what the custom of the Law required, Simeon took him in his arms and praised God, saying: 'Sovereign Lord, as you have promised, you now dismiss your servant in peace. For my eyes have seen your salvation, which you have prepared in the sight of all people, a light for revelation to the Gentiles and for glory to your people Israel.'" Luke 2:27-32 (NIV)

Have you had a personal encounter with Christ that radically transformed your life? Simeon had positioned his life to encounter Christ. Once he encountered the Messiah, Simeon proclaimed that Jesus was a light for revelation to the Gentiles and for glory to His people Israel. This proclamation was made in front of Joseph and Mary who were simply obeying the requirements of the custom of the Law.

Once Jesus comes into your life and transforms you, it is negligent to be silent. You have been rescued from the flames of hell and positioned in Christ for eternity. Proclaim that reality! You were sinking deep in sin, but Christ paid the penalty for your sin and purchased your salvation. Proclaim that reality!

What if you became contagious in your Christianity? What would happen if you seized the next opportunity God gives you to share your salvation story? Share the wonderful life-changing message of Jesus and help populate the Kingdom of Heaven. Souls are worth saving!

One way to get a pulse on someone's spiritual destiny is to simply transition your conversation to life after death. Be willing to ask people where they plan to spend eternity. Ask them to share their spiritual story with you. If they have one, they will be quick to share it with you. If they don't have a spiritual story, then you can help them establish one by sharing with them how they can know Jesus personally.

July 8
Extending and Receiving Forgiveness

"'For if you forgive men when they sin against you, your heavenly Father will also forgive you. But if you do not forgive men their sins, your Father will not forgive your sins.'" Matt 6:14-15 (NIV)

Would it not be hypocritical to receive God's forgiveness personally and then refuse to extend God's forgiveness to others? We do not earn God's forgiveness by forgiving others, but we demonstrate God's forgiveness as we forgive others. We are to forgive others instantly as a result of our being recipients of God's instant forgiveness.

Forgiving those who have hurt you does not validate their behavior, but rather honors God by mirroring His forgiveness towards you. The grace and mercy that God lavishes on you becomes a blessing that flows through you to those who have wounded you. By extending forgiveness, you are allowing the life of Christ to be evident in you and through you.

Forgiveness is immediate; trust takes time. Just because you forgive someone does not mean that it is safe to trust that person. God is not asking you to extend forgiveness and then embrace a posture of vulnerability and susceptibility. You are to walk wisely. It takes time and multiple opportunities for a person to demonstrate trustworthiness. Just as you would not dare cross a bridge that is not deemed trustworthy, you would not trust an individual who has failed to be trustworthy.

Extend forgiveness immediately and then pray for the person you have forgiven. Ask God to transform the one you have forgiven and to help that person become worthy of your trust. It is possible that you may never trust that person again. However, extending forgiveness is not optional in God's economy.

In my daily quiet time, I came across this question by Henry Blackaby that God is using in my life, "Would you want God to forgive you in the same way you are presently forgiving others?"

July 9
SELFLESS INVOLVEMENT

"But a Samaritan, as he traveled, came where the man was; and when he saw him, he took pity on him. He went to him and bandaged his wounds, pouring on oil and wine. Then he put the man on his own donkey, took him to an inn and took care of him. The next day he took out two silver coins and gave them to the innkeeper. 'Look after him,' he said, 'and when I return, I will reimburse you for any extra expense you may have.'" Luke 10:33-35 (NIV)

Has your day ever been interrupted by an unfortunate event? How did you respond? The Good Samaritan responded to the tragedy by getting involved in the resolution. He demonstrated compassion in action by seeking to meet the needs of the one who had been violated and wounded. While others kept their distance and walked on by, the Good Samaritan walked directly to the man in desperate need to extend a helping hand.

Life is full of opportunities to ignore or meet needs. You can easily become apathetic and slip into a numb state of existence whereby the needs of others no longer tug at your heart strings. What if God wants you to get involved? What if God wants to use you to make an eternal difference in the life of someone in need? How will you respond?

- *"When Jesus landed and saw a large crowd, he had compassion on them, because they were like sheep without a shepherd. So he began teaching them many things." Mark 6:34 (NIV)*

Jesus is our model of compassion. Choose to be like Jesus!

July 10
SEIZING OPPORTUNITIES

"I rejoice greatly in the Lord that at last you have renewed your concern for me. Indeed, you have been concerned, but you had no opportunity to show it." Phil 4:10 (NIV)

God chooses to use people to help us. The Christian life is not a solo flight. God saved us to live in union with Christ and in community with other believers. We need each other. We do better together. As a result of being adopted into God's family, we are to communicate and collaborate as fellow followers of Christ. In Christ, we are family!

Paul was imprisoned in Rome when he wrote this personal letter to the church at Philippi. He had a deep abiding love for them and wanted to encourage them in their faith. Paul identified their willingness to put their compassion into action. They sent their gifts to Paul via Epaphroditus (Phil. 4:18). Paul acknowledged their gift as a fragrant offering pleasing to God.

Spend a moment thanking God in prayer for the people He has placed in your life over the years to be a blessing to you. Think about the individuals God used to encourage you on your faith journey. You may even want to write a letter or type an email to someone God has used to elevate your faith. People matter to God and He delights in bringing people into our lives to bring us closer to Christ.

Are you available for God's use? Would you be willing to be used of God to encourage someone today? Would you be willing to be used of God to model Christ before a watching world? Remember that God blesses you so that you can be a blessing to others. Who will benefit from your life today?

July 11
PRAYING EVANGELISTICALLY

"I urge, then, first of all, that requests, prayers, intercession and thanksgiving be made for everyone--for kings and all those in authority, that we may live peaceful and quiet lives in all godliness and holiness. This is good, and pleases God our Savior, who wants all men to be saved and to come to a knowledge of the truth." 1 Tim 2:1-4 (NIV)

Revival is for believers who have become apathetic toward the things of God. Revival is designed by God to restore a believer's passion and hunger for God and His agenda. When revival comes, it produces a byproduct known as a spiritual awakening. While revival is for believers, a spiritual awakening impacts unbelievers and brings them to the place of transformation.

You can pray for a spiritual awakening to occur by praying evangelistically. You will personally be revived as you renew your passion for lost souls. As your soul consciousness is elevated, your awareness of God's presence and your awareness of His redemptive activity will be heightened.

Pray for everyone, including national leaders and those in authority, that they may come to know the Lord personally. The only way for our nation to genuinely change is for the lost to get saved and have a growing relationship with Jesus Christ.

Be sure to pray a prayer of thanksgiving for those who are already following Christ and leading our nation with character and integrity. This pleases God and brings Him glory. God wants everyone to be saved. He has provided the only way for men, women, boys, and girls to be born again. Jesus is the way!

Can you imagine our nation fully yielded to the Lordship of Christ? Can you envision our nation being passionate about pursuing God daily and living for His glory? Join me in praying for that vision to become a reality.

July 12
REFORMATION AND TENACITY

"Josiah removed all the detestable idols from all the territory belonging to the Israelites, and he had all who were present in Israel serve the LORD their God. As long as he lived, they did not fail to follow the LORD, the God of their fathers."
2 Chron 34:33 (NIV)

God used Josiah to bring forth a reformation in Israel. Here are a few of the reformation verbs found in 2 Kings 22-23 and 2 Chronicles 34-35: removed, burned, did away with, took, ground it to powder, scattered, tore, desecrated, pulled down, smashed, cut down, covered, defiled, slaughtered, got rid of, purged, cut to pieces, broke to pieces, tore down, and crushed. Josiah was willing to tenaciously follow God's lead and remove all the detestable idols.

Like his great-grandfather, Hezekiah, Josiah cleansed the nation of idolatry, repaired the temple, restored the worship, and celebrated a great nationwide Passover. Josiah tenaciously renewed the Covenant and reformed the culture.

What is keeping you from reaching your God-given potential? What are you giving your life to? Where does your life give evidence of tenaciously following God's lead?

God placed you right where you are so that you could be an irresistible influence for God's glory. God allowed you to wake up this morning so that you could spread the aroma of Christ through your conversation and your conduct. God did not call you to reflect the environment, but to set the environment. God did not save you so that you would embrace the way of the world. God saved you so that you would tenaciously follow the way of Christ.

July 13
HUNGERING AND THIRSTING

"Blessed are those who hunger and thirst for righteousness, for they will be filled.'" Matt 5:6 (NIV)

You were born with a hole in your heart that only God can fill. Once you respond in faith to the vertical tug of the convicting work of the Holy Spirit, you become a new creation. Your earthly appetites are replaced with the heavenly delight of knowing God personally through His Son, Jesus. Measure the treasure of desiring God, because this Spirit-prompted desire brought you into fellowship with the Creator of the Universe. Your eternal destiny is determined by the reality of this vertical relationship.

Hungering and thirsting for righteousness is a result of an abiding relationship with Jesus that is real, personal, and eternal. You progress from desiring God in salvation to pursuing God in sanctification. You are in the process of becoming who you are in Christ. Your hunger for righteousness will be filled. Your thirst for righteousness will be satisfied. Move into spiritual maturity by feasting on God.

Righteousness is not an optional spiritual supplement but a spiritual necessity. As you hunger and thirst for His righteousness, your decisions will be guided by God's economy. Doing life God's way will become your passionate pursuit. Nothing will appeal to your more than pleasing God and living a life of integrity.

Righteousness is the condition acceptable to God. In salvation, the atoning work of Christ on the cross makes you acceptable to God positionally. Now you are to work out your salvation practically as you live a life of instant obedience. Hungering and thirsting for His righteousness becomes your perpetual preoccupation. Desiring God is to be the focus of your conversation and your conduct as a byproduct of your salvation.

Continue to grow in your passion for God. Align your life with the heartbeat of God by taking paths that bring Him glory.

July 14
SEEKING GOD

"O God, you are my God, earnestly I seek you; my soul thirsts for you, my body longs for you, in a dry and weary land where there is no water." Psalm 63:1 (NIV)

You are as close to God as you choose to be. You determine the level of intimacy with God. Do you earnestly seek Him? Does your soul thirst for Him? Are you longing for Him as though you were in a dry and weary land where there is no water? Calculate the level of your pursuit.

When you wake up each morning, make pursuing God your top priority. Don't allow the demands of your schedule or the deadlines of the day to rob you of the joy of pursuing God through a meaningful daily quiet time. Select a sacred place and carve out some uninterrupted space to commune with the Lord.

Nothing is more important than your unbroken fellowship with God. Nurture the life of Christ in you through a deliberate and persistent pursuit of God's Presence. Commit to start your day with God. Establish a standing appointment with the Creator of the universe each morning.

Pave the way to satisfy the crave for pure spiritual milk by implementing an intentional Bible reading plan. Commit to read through the Bible in one year by reading four chapters each day for the next 365 days. Daily consumption of God's Word will build strong spiritual muscles to help you know God intimately and to live for His glory radically.

Keep your eyes on the prize of growing in your love relationship with the Lord. There's so much more that God wants to reveal to you. God wants to entrust you with His purposes and plan. Emulate the passionate pursuit of God's presence in your life. Remove distractions and return to your first love.

July 15
Pushing Compassion into Action

"'Blessed are the merciful, for they will be shown mercy.'" Matt 5:7 (NIV)

Have you ever been on the receiving end of the hurtful treatment rendered by an unmerciful person? It was not an enjoyable experience was it? Being unmerciful is a direct result of our fallen nature. However, Jesus ushered in a new way to live life on this broken planet.

As you extend mercy to others horizontally, you will receive mercy vertically. The Lord will be merciful to you as you are merciful to others. When you came to trust in Jesus as your personal Savior and Lord, you received salvation as an act of His mercy. Now that you are saved and filled with the Holy Spirit, you are to extend mercy to others.

Being merciful to others is not simply being possessed of pity, but putting compassion into action. It is not enough to see someone in need and to feel sorry for that individual. It is not enough to pity those who are hurting. Push your compassion into action!

Mercy led Joseph to forgive his brothers and to provide them with food. Mercy led Moses to plead with the Lord to remove the leprosy with which his sister Miriam had been punished. Mercy led David to spare the life of King Saul. Mercy led Jesus to endure the agony and shame of the cross.

Push compassion into action by meeting practical needs. Give food to the hungry, comfort the bereaved, love the rejected, and befriend the lonely. Give time, give forgiveness, give money, and give yourself to others. Find a need and meet it!

Ask God to give you eyes to see people in need and to give you a heart to respond to their needs. Begin to look for opportunities to continue the ministry of Jesus by pushing your compassion into action.

July 16
Positional and Practical Purity

"'Blessed are the pure in heart, for they will see God.'" Matt 5:8 (NIV)

God's standard of perfection is Christ. The purity of Christ is the bull's-eye for the believer. To be pure in heart is to be right with God. You cannot have a right relationship with God without having a relationship with others. You cannot have a right relationship with others without having a right relationship with God.

Purity is impossible without the righteousness of Christ being imparted. The impartation and imputation of the righteousness of Christ takes place at the moment of conversion. The righteousness of Christ is deposited to your account. Your new identity in Christ provides you with a righteousness that you could never produce. In Christ, you are positionally pure and fit for heaven.

The Christian life is a journey of working out what God has worked in. As you grow spiritually, you learn how to exhibit practical purity as a result of your positional purity.

- *"In him we have redemption through his blood, the forgiveness of sins, in accordance with the riches of God's grace that he lavished on us with all wisdom and understanding." Eph 1:7-8 (NIV)*
- *"In the same way, count yourselves dead to sin but alive to God in Christ Jesus. Therefore do not let sin reign in your mortal body so that you obey its evil desires." Romans 6:11-12 (NIV)*

The righteousness of Christ is a grace gift from God. God is holy and demands His followers to be holy. Live in light of your position in Christ. Pursue holiness in private and in public. Stay in God's will by staying in God's Word.

July 17
INCREASING LOVE

"May the Lord make your love increase and overflow for each other and for everyone else, just as ours does for you." 1 Thess 3:12 (NIV)

How do you make your love for others grow? You place the same value on others that God does. If we could ever fully embrace God's perspective on people, then our love for others would increase. Our tendency is to judge people based on externals while God evaluates the heart. We tend to overemphasize the outside and underestimate the inside. God has planted unlimited potential in every human being. The key that unlocks potential is an abiding relationship with Jesus Christ.

- *"'I am the vine; you are the branches. If a man remains in me and I in him, he will bear much fruit; apart from me you can do nothing.'" John 15:5 (NIV)*
- *"We ought always to thank God for you, brothers, and rightly so, because your faith is growing more and more, and the love every one of you has for each other is increasing." 2 Thess 1:3 (NIV)*

Increase your love for others by serving them, praying for them, and viewing them from God's perspective. Sometimes our expression of love for others is inhibited by busyness. Often our love for others is stifled by our self-centeredness. It's difficult to increase our love for others when we become consumed with ourselves.

Read through the Gospels and notice how Jesus had a perfect balance of guarding His love relationship with the Father and meeting the needs of people. As your love relationship with your Heavenly Father grows, your love for others will increase in proportion.

July 18
Praying God's Word

"If my people, who are called by my name, will humble themselves and pray and seek my face and turn from their wicked ways, then will I hear from heaven and will forgive their sin and will heal their land." II Chronicles 7:14

God honors those who seek Him. God took the initiative to bring us into a right relationship with Himself. His heart is for you to know Him intimately. God has done everything needed to enable you to have an intimate love relationship with Him. Will you respond to God's invitation?

If you will humble yourself, pray, and seek God's face and turn from the path of evil, God will respond with blessing from heaven. God promises to hear, forgive, and heal. Are you in need of God's heavenly touch? As you seek God, He responds to your pursuit. Your impact for God will never rise above your prayer life.

Can you imagine where you would be had God not pursued you long before you ever thought about Him? Can you visualize where you would be had God not built the ultimate bridge to come to where you were? You are armed with an opportunity to take your relationship with the Creator of the universe to a whole new level. Seize the opportunity by taking God at His Word. Capture the awesome privilege of connecting with Almighty God through prayer.

Spend some time praying for your family, your church family, your community, your state, your nation, and your world. As you pray, be sensitive to the specific individuals God brings to your attention. Begin to intercede for each person. Give careful attention to the person God gives you a burden for. Invest extra time praying for that person and watch to see how God works!

July 19
POINTING CHILDREN TO CHRIST

"And whoever welcomes a little child like this in my name welcomes me. But if anyone causes one of these little ones who believe in me to sin, it would be better for him to have a large millstone hung around his neck and to be drowned in the depths of the sea." Matt 18:5-6 (NIV)

Jesus loves the little children. As you read these powerful words of Christ, you may be offended by the strong language used. Jesus does not water down His conviction about the vitality and vulnerability of children. Jesus confronts us with the reality that the children are our responsibility. If we choose to mislead them, we will suffer the consequences. If we choose to guide them in the way of the Lord, we will be blessed.

The vast majority of those who come to place their faith in Christ alone for salvation do so before the age of twelve. Children exhibit tenderness toward the things of God. They are so open to what God wants to do in their lives and through their lives. Children are like tender clay in the hands of a potter. God has given us the responsibility to help mold them and shape them into fully devoted followers of Christ.

With this awesome privilege comes tremendous responsibility. Jesus wants us to take our responsibility of influencing children toward Him seriously. Think of what is at stake when children are misled. Not only is their immediate future jeopardized, but also their eternal destiny.

I am so grateful for the godly men and women that God placed in my life during my formative years to point me to Jesus. They faithfully modeled the Christ-centered life. Every generation deserves to be led to the foot of the cross and introduced to a saving relationship with Jesus. Are there children in your sphere of influence that will be in heaven because of you?

July 20
SET THE EXAMPLE

"Don't let anyone look down on you because you are young, but set an example for the believers in speech, in life, in love, in faith and in purity." 1 Tim 4:12 (NIV)

After being involved in a life altering jet ski accident and surrendering to preach at age sixteen, I remember officiating one of my first weddings. I was standing near the altar steps just before the wedding rehearsal was to begin when the mother of the bride asks, "Where's the minister?"

When I announced that I was the minister, you should have seen her face fall. She reacted by darting out the words of surprise that, in her estimation, I was just a kid. Those were the "good old days."

Paul's words of encouragement and instruction to his young son in the ministry have been a life-line over the years of my ministry. Every generation has the honor of participation in God's redemptive activity. Regardless of your current life stage, whether you are in the Bridger, Buster, Boomer, or Builder generation, you have the wonderful invitation from God for participation in God's world redemption story.

Don't allow your inadequacies and insufficiencies to barricade you from joining God in His activity. Your usefulness to God is not based on your particular generational identification. Your usefulness to God is based on your identity in Christ and your availability to Christ.

Surrender to the Lordship of Christ and be an example to others in your conversation, your convictions, and your conduct. Every person in every generation will one day stand before God to give an account for the deeds done while in the body. Set a Christ-honoring example for others. Be a model to follow!

July 21
TRUSTING GOD'S SOVEREIGNTY

"You intended to harm me, but God intended it for good to accomplish what is now being done, the saving of many lives." Gen 50:20 (NIV)

The sixty-six books of the Bible provide us with a string of pearls that demonstrates God's redemptive activity. Long before we were born, God took the initiative to rescue us from our fallen condition. God factors in our poor choices and even the decisions others make that affect our lives. How refreshing to know that God has the final say. Your past, present, and future circumstances will never circumvent the mighty acts of God.

Joseph had a life changing experience through the gateway of betrayal. Joseph's brothers sold him into slavery and tried to cover up their sin through deception. God elevated Joseph to Potipher's house where he was later falsely accused by Potipher's wife. Joseph went from the pit to the palace and then to prison. His life's circumstances appeared to be most unfortunate. Yet, God knew right where Joseph was and what Joseph needed most. God was with Joseph and delivered him from prison to second in command over Egypt in preparation for the upcoming famine. When Joseph's path intersected that of his brothers, he demonstrated the life giving grace of God. Instead of having them pay for their sin, Joseph forgave them and acknowledged God's sovereignty.

Have you had the ultimate life changing experience by placing your faith in the completed work of Jesus on the cross? Are you living out the reality of God's transforming power? Have you experienced God's forgiveness at the level of being able to forgive others in the same measure?

July 22
THE DESERT OF PREPARATION

"But Moses said to God, 'Who am I, that I should go to Pharaoh and bring the Israelites out of Egypt?'" Ex 3:11 (NIV)

Who am I? Why am I here? These two basic questions are innate in every human being. We long to know who we are and we strive to discover why we are placed on this planet called earth. Our security is proportionate to our understanding of our identity.

God allowed Moses to experience forty years in the palace and then forty years in the desert. God wanted Moses to learn some things about his personal identity through a desert experience that he could not learn in the palace. God was preparing Moses for the purpose of delivering the children of Israel from Egyptian bondage. The burning bush encounter was a life changing experience for Moses. The encounter enabled Moses to come to know God in a personal way. God revealed His holiness to Moses and then unveiled His plan for Moses to embrace.

As you can imagine, Moses could not visualize himself as the deliverer of the children of Israel. They had been slaves for over 400 years. Moses began making excuses and tried to deny his usefulness to God. Moses began to focus on what he lacked and missed the reality of God's ability to do the extraordinary through ordinary people.

Have you ever doubted your usefulness to God? Have you ever tried to convince God that you are not fit for His plan? God is not impressed with our abilities or our inabilities. God is not limited by our limitations. Are you willing to yield to God's control and allow Him to have His way in your life? God is willing to take you through a desert experience to prepare you for His assignment.

July 23
AVAILABLE FOR GOD'S USE

"Then I heard the voice of the Lord saying, 'Whom shall I send? And who will go for us?' And I said, 'Here am I. Send me!'" Isaiah 6:8 (NIV)

Isaiah had a life changing experience. He looked up and saw the Lord in all of His holiness. Isaiah looked inward and recognized his own sinfulness in light of God's holiness. Isaiah then looked outward and detected the sinful condition of others. In this life changing experience, Isaiah heard God's call and responded with instant obedience. Isaiah said, "Here am I. Send me!"

Will you make an impact upon every generation? Are you willing to allow God to call you to a new level of living? God's grace always matches His assignment for your life. Where God guides He always provides. There is never a better moment than now to obey God instantly and make yourself totally available for His use. God can do more in you and through you in the next six months than all the previous years of your life combined.

God values the work He does in you more than the work He does through you. Before God used Isaiah to make an eternal impact, God had to do an internal work in Isaiah's life. The internal work always impacts the eternal work. Don't bypass what God wants to do in you. Isaiah came face to face with the holiness of God in worship. Isaiah's worship led to a personal assessment of his morality and then the morality of those around him. After God did this great work in Isaiah, He invited Isaiah to join His world redemptive activity.

You have a chance to make an eternal impact for every generation. Are you available? Look upward! Look inward! Look outward!

July 24
GENUINE FAITH

"Shadrach, Meshach and Abednego replied to the king, 'O Nebuchadnezzar, we do not need to defend ourselves before you in this matter. If we are thrown into the blazing furnace, the God we serve is able to save us from it, and he will rescue us from your hand, O king. But even if he does not, we want you to know, O king, that we will not serve your gods or worship the image of gold you have set up.'" Dan 3:16-18 (NIV)

Has your faith ever been tested? Have you ever been in an environment that provided you with an opportunity to make a bold stand for the Lord? Maybe your home is a place where your faith is put to the test. Maybe your work environment has been a difficult place for you to express your faith. Swimming upstream is always a challenge. Whenever you decide to go in the opposite direction of the cultural current, you will face resistance and opposition.

Shadrach, Meshach, and Abednego, in the midst of impending death if they chose not to abide by the king's command, where willing to obey God at all costs. Instead of bowing to the golden image erected by king Nebuchadnezzar, they chose to honor God even if it meant death. They demonstrated their belief in God's ability to save them from the blazing furnace. They went a step further by declaring that even if God did not deliver them that they would not worship the image of gold.

Do you have that kind of "but even if God does not" faith? Are you willing to obey God in the face of opposition and in the face of being misunderstood by your family or peers? Even if God does not deliver you from your difficult circumstances, are you willing to obey Him and honor Him?

The good news is that God did deliver Shadrach, Meshach, and Abednego. They would not bow, they would not bend, they would not budge, and they would not burn! God rescued them through the blazing furnace. God allowed them to go through the fire unharmed. Now that's a life changing experience!

July 25
UNWAVERING FAITH

"So the king gave the order, and they brought Daniel and threw him into the lions' den. The king said to Daniel, 'May your God, whom you serve continually, rescue you!'" Dan 6:16 (NIV)

Daniel had a track record of faithfulness to God. His loyalty to God was unwavering. After the king signed a decree forbidding Daniel to pray to God, Daniel allowed his devotion to God to supersede his devotion to the king. Daniel was not willing to disobey God in order to obey the king. Instead, Daniel honored God at the expense of the king's retribution. Daniel paid a hefty price for his obedience. He was thrown into the lions' den.

- *"Daniel answered, 'O king, live forever! My God sent his angel, and he shut the mouths of the lions. They have not hurt me, because I was found innocent in his sight. Nor have I ever done any wrong before you, O king.'" Dan 6:21-22 (NIV)*

Your devotion and faithfulness to God may not ever lead you to be thrown into a literal lions' den. However, your lions' den may simply be having others misunderstand you or criticize you for your devotion to God. Your family members may not support you in your walk with God. Your co-workers or neighbors may not fully understand your commitment to serving God. Your lions' den may be when your peers fail to comprehend your level of loyalty to God.

Serve continually! Trust God completely! God can shut the mouths of the lions. God can redeem the hurt you endure. Allow God to use you to make an impact for His glory for every generation. Be comforted by the fact that God is all-knowing and nothing escapes His attention. God knows right where you are and He knows exactly what you need to accomplish His plan.

July 26
SHAPED FOR ETERNAL SIGNIFICANCE

"So I went down to the potter's house, and I saw him working at the wheel. But the pot he was shaping from the clay was marred in his hands; so the potter formed it into another pot, shaping it as seemed best to him." Jer 18:3-4 (NIV)

The safest place for you to be is in the center of God's will. The most dangerous place for you to be is in the center of God's will. When you are living in the center of God's will, you experience His provision and protection. However, you are the greatest threat to Satan when you are living in the center of God's will. When you think about it, being on Satan's radar is an indication of being a threat to his kingdom. You cannot walk in the center of God's will unopposed.

One of my Sunday School teachers who flew an A-10 fighter jet in the Air Force used to say, "The closer you get to the enemy, the greater the conflict." Motion causes friction. When you are living to please God, be ready for that spiritual motion to cause friction and spiritual warfare.

Jeremiah, known as the weeping prophet, experienced the painful reality of being on the potter's wheel. God placed Jeremiah on the potter's wheel to demonstrate His loving and corrective touch. God demonstrated the value He places on purity, holiness, and full surrender. God expects that of every generation and every nation.

Don't resist those seasons of being placed on the potter's wheel. Remember that God is the Potter and you are the clay. God tenderly and lovingly molds you and shapes you for His glory. God removes the impediments in your life that restrict His flow through you. Be still! Rest! Give God access to every area of your life. Allow God to shape you for His eternal significance.

July 27
GUARD YOUR HEART

"Above all else, guard your heart, for it is the wellspring of life." Prov 4:23 (NIV)

God loves you and has a plan for your life. Satan hates you and also has a plan for your life. God's plan is for you to stay close and clean. Satan's plan is for you to stay distant and dirty. God saved you and set you apart so that you can walk in His holiness and enjoy His abiding presence. God rescued you from the dominion of darkness and placed you in kingdom of light so that you can continue the ministry of Jesus before you go to heaven. The enemy, Satan, will not cease trying to devour your devotion to God.

Guard your heart! Don't allow Satan, sin, or selfishness to invade your heart. Blockade your heart with the truth of God's Word and fasten the breastplate of righteousness in place. Don't give the devil access to your heart. Post guard! You are to love God with all your heart and to preserve your heart for His rightful place as Lord!

God wants you to have a pure heart and to embody pure motives. Be single-minded and render undivided loyalty to Christ. Allow Jesus to reign in your life. Invite the Holy Spirit to take full possession of your heart. Leave no room for the enemy to confiscate any fraction of real estate within your heart. Post a "no trespassing" sign at the entrance of your heart to alert the enemy that he is not welcome to occupy any portion of your heart.

Your heart is the wellspring of life. In the language of the Old Testament, the heart represents the inner person, the seat of motives and actions. The heart includes the thinking process and the will. You have the capacity to obey God with all of your heart. Guard His treasure, your heart!

July 28
MONITOR YOUR MOUTH

"Put away perversity from your mouth; keep corrupt talk far from your lips."
Prov 4:24 (NIV)

Have you ever said something that you wish you could retrieve? We have all been there. If only we could have thought about what we were going to say before we said it. Let's use the word THINK as an acrostic to give us some insightful questions to ask before we speak.

Is it True? Now that's a great question for us to consider before speaking. What would our world look like if everyone only spoke the truth? Instead of spreading lies and infusing suspicion, everyone would operate based on integrity and truth.

Is it Helpful? Consider your words. Are they beneficial to others? Does your conversation add value to the lives of other people? Let's commit to speak words that bless and build others up.

Is it Inspiring? God has sealed you by the Holy Spirit so that you can be a vessel of honor. Your life is designed by God to inspire others to come to a saving relationship with Jesus Christ and to mature spiritually. Do your words encourage others to reach their full redemptive potential?

Is it Necessary? Sometimes silence is the best option. When we are about to say something that is not necessary, maybe that's a good time to hit the pause button.

Is it Kind? I remember hearing Dr. Jerry Vines, pastor emeritus of First Baptist Church of Jacksonville, Florida, say that "a Christian never has the luxury of being unkind." Before we speak, we might want to ask the question, "Is it kind?" Will our words reflect the heart of Jesus? Will our words demonstrate the value that God places on others?

July 29
ADVISE YOUR EYES

"Let your eyes look straight ahead, fix your gaze directly before you." Prov 4:25 (NIV)

Eyesight is an amazing feature of the human body. God's creation throughout the earth is awesome to behold whether taking in the sight of the blue sky in the day or the star filled sky at night or observing a butterfly dancing from leaf to leaf. From gazing at the flowing wildflowers in the open field to examining the intricacies of a cell under a microscope, eyesight is a gift from God.

There is so much to look at from day to day. To walk in victory, we must be very selective in what we allow to come into our minds through the open window of our eyes. Some things we view bring honor to God while other things bring dishonor. Differentiating between the two is a mark of spiritual maturity and a byproduct of the fruit of the Spirit, self-control. Walking in victory while living in a fallen world mandates that we advise our eyes.

- *"'But I tell you that anyone who looks at a woman lustfully has already committed adultery with her in his heart.'" Matt 5:28 (NIV)*
- *"I made a covenant with my eyes not to look lustfully at a girl." Job 31:1 (NIV)*

Take the initiative to advise your eyes. Tell your eyes where to look. Look straight ahead. Fix your gaze so that you will not be distracted by the lure of lust and the syrup of sin. Train your eyes to bounce off of anything that does not honor God. As Billy Graham has said, "The first look is natural; the second look is sin."

It is wise to advise your eyes by viewing life from God's perspective. Feed on God's Word so that your eyes will be informed and your heart will remain pure.

July 30
Pick Your Path

"Make level paths for your feet and take only ways that are firm. Do not swerve to the right or the left; keep your foot from evil." Prov 4:26-27 (NIV)

Have you ever peaked into the rearview mirror of life and wondered, "Why did I choose that path?" Perhaps you made a decision to go in a certain direction at a critical time in your life that catapulted you onto a path that took you places you really did not want to go. You may be living with regret even now as you revisit your moment of decision that placed you on the unhealthy path.

Your daily decisions determine the direction of your life. If you don't pick your path, a path will pick you. God wants you to walk in wisdom and to exercise spiritual discernment as you seek to operate in His will. Use Spirit infused discretion in your decision making. Ask yourself, "What is the wise thing to do?" Knowing what you know about God and His ways, make level paths for your feet. Allowing the Holy Spirit to take full possession of your life, take only ways that are firm.

God's way is always the best way. God has a path for you to discover and to experience personally. Sometimes the path God has for you includes delays. You may not understand why you are in a season of uncertainty, but you know that God is with you and that He will allow the fog to lift in His perfect timing. While you are waiting for God to show you the next step on this path, obey what you already know. Enjoy His abiding presence. Share His love and shine His light. Bloom for God's glory on the path God has for you. If you are on the wrong path, make a wise decision to move in the new direction God shows you.

July 31
BUILD THE BRIDGE

"Blessed are the peacemakers, for they will be called sons of God." Matt 5:9 (NIV)

While viewing a leadership talk delivered by pastor Andy Stanley, I was captivated by his statement, "In eternity past, God looked upon our sin-saturated planet and asked, 'What can I do to help?'" That concept painted a vivid image in my mind of God being the ultimate bridge builder. God created us and gave us the freedom to choose Him or to reject Him. God saw our sin and our rebellion and chose to build the ultimate bridge paved with His redeeming love. God took the initiative to come to our rescue. The bridge of hope was constructed by the sacrificial death of Jesus. The gulf of our separation has been bridged by the depth of God's love.

In this seventh Beatitude, Jesus esteems the value of our participation in continuing His ministry on the earth through being peacemakers. Peacemaking involves loving people the way Jesus modeled during His earthly ministry. Being a peacemaker means viewing others through the lens of God's redemptive pursuit. When you place the same value on others that Jesus does, you position yourself as a peacemaker. Instead of being indifferent toward others who aren't like you, you will have a deep abiding burden for them to know Jesus personally. Instead of building a wall to distance yourself from those Christ died for, you build a bridge to engage them with the message of salvation.

Let's choose to walk in the blessing of God by becoming bridge builders. Take the initiative to start loving people with the same redeeming love you have experienced from the heart of God. Join me in looking into the eyes of those God brings into our path and being willing to ask, "What can I do to help?"

August 1
MAKE PEACE WITH GOD

"Therefore, since we have been justified through faith, we have peace with God through our Lord Jesus Christ." Romans 5:1 (NIV)

The first crucial step in becoming a peacemaker is to make peace with God. Until you are in a right relationship with God, your horizontal influence for the kingdom of God will not be fruitful. God took the initiative to provide for the salvation of your soul. Your sin debt was paid in full by the atoning work of Jesus on the cross. Jesus took the full wrath of God for your sin. Jesus took your place. As a result of His work of redemption, you are justified through faith. It is "just-if-I'd" never sinned! When God sees you, He sees you through the shed blood of Jesus.

Have you responded to God's redemptive act by placing your faith in Jesus alone for your salvation? That divine transaction changes your forever. Once you have made peace with God, you become a new creation. You are filled with the Holy Spirit and adopted into God's forever family. Your salvation is sealed by the Holy Spirit. Your security is not based on your human effort, but on God's redeeming grace. No one can snatch you out of the Father's hand.

Now that you are in a right relationship with God, walk in the peace God provides. When that peace is threatened through compromise, confess your sin and purge your life of anything that hinders your love relationship with God. Maintain peace with God by living a life of instant obedience. The convicting work of the Holy Spirit will alert you when something enters your life that does not honor God. Confess sin immediately and allow the Holy Spirit to take full possession of your life. Will others see God's peace in your life today?

August 2
HELP OTHERS MAKE PEACE WITH GOD

"All this is from God, who reconciled us to himself through Christ and gave us the ministry of reconciliation: that God was reconciling the world to himself in Christ, not counting men's sins against them. And he has committed to us the message of reconciliation." 2 Cor 5:18-19 (NIV)

Peacemaking involves helping others make peace with God. As a peacemaker, you have the awesome privilege and responsibility of building a bridge to others to help them come into a saving relationship with Jesus. God reconciled you to Himself so that you could join Him in reconciling others to Himself. You have been rescued to rescue others. God has given you ministry of reconciliation. You may think that you are not called into the ministry. However, every believer is called into the ministry of reconciliation. God has built the ultimate love bridge to you so that you can in turn build His love bridge to others.

As a child of God, you not only have a ministry to fulfill but you also have a message to declare. The message of reconciliation is the wonderful news that God is reconciling the world to Himself, in Christ. The atoning work of Jesus on the cross provides for the complete and absolute forgiveness of our sins. In Christ, God does not count our sins against us. We are forgiven! We are free! We have discovered the cure to the cancer of sin. We have the remedy for the plight of sinful man. God has lavished us with His love and armed us with the most powerful life changing message on the planet.

Are you helping others make peace with God? Will the population of heaven increase because of your participation in the ministry and message of reconciliation?

August 3
HEIGHTENED SENSITIVITY

"'Therefore, if you are offering your gift at the altar and there remember that your brother has something against you, leave your gift there in front of the altar. First go and be reconciled to your brother; then come and offer your gift.'"
Matt 5:23-24 (NIV)

In yielded worship before the Lord, your sensitivity to the things of God is heightened. Your awareness of God's holiness and your personal sin becomes elevated when you are consecrated before the Lord in worship. If during the act of offering your gift at the altar of worship God brings to your mind the reality of a strained relationship, leave your gift and diligently go and be reconciled.

God values unity in the body. God expects us to protect the vitality of our relationships with others. You cannot have a right relationship with God, even in worship, if you are not in a right relationship with others. Living in a fallen world perpetuates the litter of strained relationships. Make reconciliation your "first" response to God in worship. You have been reconciled to God through the finished work of Jesus upon the cross so that you can be an intentional reconciler on this broken planet.

Your gift becomes acceptable to God at the level of your relational purity with God and with others. Guard your relationships. Seek immediate reconciliation! Exhibit humility and brokenness! Ask for forgiveness! Extend forgiveness! Do whatever it takes to make things right between you and God. Do whatever it takes to make things right with others.

August 4
SPIRITUAL PASSION

"Never be lacking in zeal, but keep your spiritual fervor, serving the Lord."
Romans 12:11 (NIV)

What are you passionate about? What are you giving your time, energy, and resources to? What gets the best of you? You answer unveils your zeal.

God placed zeal in you. Your passion is an expression of your spiritual DNA. God gives you the ability to be passionate in this life. However, it is possible to misdirect the passion God gives you. Your passion can be diverted to areas that are unhealthy or unfruitful. You can channel your passion to outlets that dishonor God or even to good things that rob God's best for you.

God's Word teaches us to keep our spiritual fervor. Our passion in action should be vertical in nature. We are to be passionate for God. Our zeal for God and His Kingdom should never experience a deficit. As we nurture our passion for God, we are to keep our passion channeled in the paths that God provides.

Are you passionate about the things of God? Does your life give evidence to the passion God desires from you? Take some time to assess your current reality. See if your passion is misdirected. Examine your life to the level of identifying the source of your passion and the expression of your passion in action.

August 5
Shaped by the Potter

"But the pot he was shaping from the clay was marred in his hands..." Jer 18:4 (NIV)

Whenever you purchase an item that has an "as is" tag on it, you accept the fact that it may be flawed. In other words, the item may not be perfect.

The beauty of salvation is that God accepted us "as is" and brought us into a vibrant love relationship with Himself to move us from "as is" to "what could be" in His hands. Yes! We were marred in His hands. But, He lovingly and patiently removes the imperfections of our attitude, behavior, and speech.

Being on the Potter's wheel can be painful at times. As God allows us to go through suffering and sorrow in this life, the areas of our life that do not reflect Christ-likeness will be dealt with. God will grow us through the pain. He will mold us and shape us through adversity.

Bathsheba endured some difficult seasons in her life. She experienced loneliness, grief, delays, disappointment, and shattered dreams. Yet, God redeemed all of those seasons in her life to bring her into a deeper relationship with Himself. She would have never become a Proverbs 31 woman without the adversity that God allowed her to face. She was marred in His hands. As a result of the loving touch of the Potter's hands, she became a masterpiece!

Are you on the Potter's wheel? Be patient. Allow God to mold you. He took you "as is" and He is shaping you for eternal significance.

August 6
MAKE AN ETERNAL DIFFERENCE

"When Jesus reached the spot, he looked up and said to him, 'Zacchaeus, come down immediately. I must stay at your house today.' So he came down at once and welcomed him gladly." Luke 19:5-6 (NIV)

You have a choice. You can be a thermostat and set the environment or you can be a thermometer and reflect the environment. Jesus chose to be a thermostat. Jesus leveraged His influence to transform Zacchaeus and his family. Jesus was intentional about bringing life-change to this chief tax collector and his family.

The people criticized Jesus for His actions. We are introduced to this concept of muttering and grumbling in the Old Testament as the children of Israel grumbled against God, Moses, and Aaron (Ex. 16:6-8). Jesus was willing to be misunderstood and criticized in order to bring eternal life to Zacchaeus and his family. Jesus was willing to endure opposition to present this family with the opportunity to be transformed by His love.

Will you influence your environment or be influenced by your environment? Will you become like those around you or will they become like you? It depends upon your decision to be a thermostat or a thermometer. God has placed you here to be salt and light to influence this decaying and dark world with the purity and the light of His love (Mt. 5:13-16). God has planted you right where you are so that you can bloom for His glory and bring others into the kingdom of light.

Are you willing to be criticized for loving the unlovable? Are you willing to be misunderstood for extending grace to the despised and forgotten? Be a thermostat for the glory of God!

August 7
AMPLIFY THE VOICE OF TRUTH

"When he had finished speaking, he said to Simon, 'Put out into deep water, and let down the nets for a catch.'" Luke 5:4 (NIV)

Jesus had been teaching the crowd from Simon's boat. The water's surface propelled the teachings of Jesus with clarity to the hearers. Simon was in the boat with Jesus and overheard His teachings. The lesson was going to be directed Simon's way. Jesus challenged Simon's faith by asking him to transition the boat to deeper waters. The request escalated as Jesus exhorted Simon to let down the nets for a catch.

What is a carpenter doing telling a fisherman how to fish? Fishermen in that region knew that fishing the shallow waters at night was the protocol for success. Yet, Jesus issues a seemingly impractical call to fish the deeper waters during the daylight. Simon experienced a crisis of belief. He had to wrestle the words of this carpenter up against his own personal experience as a commercial fisherman. Simon knew the waters and the industry. Would he consider obeying the words of Jesus?

Sometimes life doesn't make sense. Sometimes the way of Jesus is counter to the way of logic. Jesus invites us to join Him in the journey of faith. Faith is not a blind leap in the dark. Faith is trusting that Jesus knows what is best for us. We come to the place of experiencing the crisis of believing our own way or the way Jesus illuminates.

Simon was willing to take Jesus at His Word and to trust Him with the results. Simon silenced the voice of doubt and amplified the voice of Truth.

Is there anything agonizing your inner being and causing you to question the best next step? Are you willing to take God at His Word and trust His prompting? God's way will bring you to a crisis of belief that will require faith and action.

August 8
CAPTAIN OF YOUR BOAT

"Simon answered, 'Master, we've worked hard all night and haven't caught anything. But because you say so, I will let down the nets.'" Luke 5:5 (NIV)

Do you remember those words you frequently heard as a child? You may have challenged something your parent said and then they responded emphatically with, "Because I said so!"

Simon had one of those moments in his own boat with Jesus. After a long night of fishing and coming up "empty-netted," Simon and his partners were in the process of completing the task of washing their nets. Jesus borrows Simon and his boat in order to teach the crowd aligning the shore. Jesus then asks Simon to maneuver the boat into the deep waters and to let down his nets for a catch.

Addressing Jesus as Master, Simon recounted his all-night fishing experience and the fact of catching no fish. Then Simon says to Jesus, "But because you say so, I will let down the nets."

Simon demonstrated loyalty to Jesus. By his actions, Simon was in essence saying, "Jesus, I trust you and whatever is mine is yours and whatever you ask of me I will obey." Embracing Jesus as Captain of his boat, Simon exemplified surrender and submission. He was willing to make Jesus the Lord of his boat and his life.

Have you given Jesus dominion over every area of your life? Is Jesus truly Lord in your life? Have you given Him full authority in your private life? Does Jesus have full reign in the public and visible areas of your life? Your loyalty to Christ is proportionate to your willingness to surrender to the Lordship of Christ. Make Jesus the Captain of your boat! Give Him full access and full authority over every environment of your life!

August 9
Enjoy God's Way

"When they had done so, they caught such a large number of fish that their nets began to break. So they signaled their partners in the other boat to come and help them, and they came and filled both boats so full that they began to sink."
Luke 5:6-7 (NIV)

God's way is always best! You will never go wrong obeying God. He knows you and He knows what is best for you. Everything God invites you to do allows you to participate in His Kingdom activity.

Simon and his fishing partners experienced a miraculous catch of fish because Simon was willing to obey Jesus. Blessing follows obedience. Simon responded to Jesus' invitation to let down his nets for a catch in the deeper waters in the daytime. The fishermen normally fished in the shallow waters at night in that region of the Lake of Gennesaret (also known as the Sea of Galilee). However, Simon was willing to fish Jesus' way and reap the tremendous benefits.

Both boats were filled so full that they began to sink. What a picture of the abundance of God's blessings! Doing life God's way is always the right choice. Even when God's directive doesn't add up in your logical thinking, you can count on God's way to be the best option.

Can God speak through a donkey (Num. 22:30), cause an axhead to float (2 Ki. 6:5-6), and provide water from a rock (Num. 20:8)? Yes, God can! Can God handle your situation? Yes, God can!

Will you trust God and submit to His way? Will you seek the Lord (Is. 55:6) and draw near to Him (James 4:8)? Will you trust in the Lord (Prv. 3:5-6)? Now, walk in the light God gives you!

August 10
ENCOUNTERING THE DIVINE

"When Simon Peter saw this, he fell at Jesus' knees and said, 'Go away from me, Lord; I am a sinful man!' For he and all his companions were astonished at the catch of fish they had taken, and so were James and John, the sons of Zebedee, Simon's partners." Luke 5:8-10 (NIV)

What produced such awe in Simon's heart to cause him to respond to Jesus the way he did? Simon recognized that he was in the presence of the Divine. Jesus was more than a carpenter from Nazareth. Jesus was the Master of the wind, the waves, and the fish. Jesus demonstrated His omnipotence.

Simon and his fishing partners were astonished at the catch of fish they had taken. Yet, Simon was gripped more by Jesus than the catch of fish. Simon recognized his own personal sinfulness in light of the holiness of Jesus. We see similar responses from Isaiah and John when they encountered the Lord.

- *"'Woe to me!' I cried. 'I am ruined! For I am a man of unclean lips, and I live among a people of unclean lips, and my eyes have seen the King, the LORD Almighty.'" Isaiah 6:5 (NIV)*
- *"When I saw him, I fell at his feet as though dead. Then he placed his right hand on me and said: 'Do not be afraid. I am the First and the Last. I am the Living One; I was dead, and behold I am alive for ever and ever! And I hold the keys of death and Hades.'" Rev 1:17-18 (NIV)*

Don't lose the awe of serving your Master, Jesus Christ. He is worthy of your wonder and awe. Jesus is holy and deserves reverence and honor. As you engage in activities throughout the day, whether menial or magnificent, remember the awe of serving Jesus!

August 11
FISHING AND FOLLOWING

"Then Jesus said to Simon, 'Don't be afraid; from now on you will catch men.'" Luke 5:10 (NIV)

If you're not fishing, you're not following. Following Christ will result in faithfully and intentionally fishing for souls. When you follow your Rabbi, Jesus, you go where He goes and you do what He does.

Jesus alleviated Simon's fear by clarifying his life-focus. Instead of fishing for fish, Simon was being invited to a life of fishing for souls.

- *"The fruit of the righteous is a tree of life, and he who wins souls is wise."* Prov 11:30 (NIV)
- *"I pray that you may be active in sharing your faith, so that you will have a full understanding of every good thing we have in Christ."* Philem 1:6 (NIV)
- *"Be merciful to those who doubt; snatch others from the fire and save them; to others show mercy, mixed with fear--hating even the clothing stained by corrupted flesh."* Jude 1:22-23 (NIV)

Focus your life on that which is closest to the heart of Jesus. Souls! Focus your life on fishing for souls. Join God in His redemptive activity by bringing others into a saving relationship with Jesus. Share your personal salvation story (I Pt. 3:15-16) and invite others to become followers of Jesus Christ. Focus your life on souls! Eternity is at stake!

August 12
FATIGUE AND REFRESHMENT

"The LORD said to Moses: 'Bring me seventy of Israel's elders who are known to you as leaders and officials among the people. Have them come to the Tent of Meeting, that they may stand there with you. I will come down and speak with you there, and I will take of the Spirit that is on you and put the Spirit on them. They will help you carry the burden of the people so that you will not have to carry it alone.'" Num 11:16-17 (NIV)

When you love and care for people, you will experience fatigue. Life has a way of draining your energy and depleting your emotional reserves. Relationships can be refreshing and wonderful, yet some can be taxing and demanding. You can become weary to the point of total exhaustion.

Moses hit a low point after caring for nearly two million Israelites. The journey of wandering in the wilderness had taken its toll. The Israelites were irritable and ungrateful for all that God had done and wanted to go back to Egypt. Moses felt the weight of their complaints. His emotional reserves were empty.

God responded to the desperation Moses was experiencing by providing some much needed help. Moses could not bear this burden alone. God instructed Moses to bring a select group of Israel's elders to the Tent of Meeting. God put His Spirit on them and empowered them to help Moses carry the burden of the people.

Are you overwhelmed by life? Have you experienced compassion fatigue? Perhaps your load has exceeded your limit and you have no margin in your life. Ask God to bring some godly people into your life to help you carry the load. Ask God to show you what you need to stop doing, what you need to continue doing, and what you need to start doing.

August 13
Finding Balance

"Moses' father-in-law replied, 'What you are doing is not good. You and these people who come to you will only wear yourselves out. The work is too heavy for you; you cannot handle it alone.'" Ex 18:17-18 (NIV)

Our lives are bombarded with information and endless opportunities to expend our energy. Do you have margin in your life? Margin is the space between your load and your limit. God has designed you to handle a certain amount of His work during your brief stay on this planet called earth. God has given you all the time you need to accomplish His plan.

Moses reached a breaking point due to being overextended and overwhelmed. The masses of people each wanted his time, his attention, and his decision making prowess. Though serving as judge over Israel, Moses failed to exercise proper judgment over his own life.

God came to the rescue by bringing Jethro into Moses' life. Jethro lovingly spoke into Moses' life to declare, "What you are doing is not good." Moses couldn't see the unhealthy path that he was on. Jethro saw it clearly and succinctly. Jethro was willing to help Moses' de-clutter his life.

Has your load exceeded your limit? What are you giving your life to that is outside of God's will? Step back and evaluate your current reality. You may want to ask someone you know and love and trust to help you examine your life. Allow that person to give you feedback on what they see going on in your world. Their perspective could help you see what you are not seeing.

God uses other people to help us walk in obedience to His will. Pray and ask God to bring a Jethro into your life.

August 14
VICTORY IN TEMPTATION

"No temptation has seized you except what is common to man. And God is faithful; he will not let you be tempted beyond what you can bear. But when you are tempted, he will also provide a way out so that you can stand up under it."
1 Cor 10:13 (NIV)

Temptation is an opportunity to honor God. Our response to temptation will determine whether we honor God or dishonor God. As followers of Jesus Christ, we are not temptation exempt. Living in a fallen world and retaining our sin nature guarantee the presence of temptation. It is not a matter of if we will face temptation, but a matter of when we will face temptation. Even Jesus was tempted.

Temptation is a common feature in this life. Of course, temptation comes in different forms depending on where we are most susceptible. Satan knows what our weaknesses are and what will entice us toward sin.

We are not left alone to fend for ourselves. God is here! God is faithful! We can anchor our faith to the faithfulness of God. He will never leave us. He will not abandon us. In fact, God will not allow us to be tempted beyond what we can bear with Him. Temptation is a constant reminder of our dependency upon God. We need God!

God will also provide an exit strategy. When temptation knocks at our door, we don't have to submit to the temptation. God will always provide a way of escape so that we can stand up under the load and stress of the temptation.

How will you respond when temptation comes your way? Will you seize the opportunity to honor God?

August 15
IN CHRIST ALONE

"I can do everything through him who gives me strength." Phil 4:13 (NIV)

Jesus has saved us to represent Him on the earth. He has instructed us to love our enemies, to pray for those who persecute us, to forgive our debtors, to judge not, to go the extra mile, and to fulfill the Great Commandment and the Great Commission.

- *"Love the Lord your God with all your heart and with all your soul and with all your mind and with all your strength.' The second is this: 'Love your neighbor as yourself.' There is no commandment greater than these." Mark 12:30-31 (NIV)*
- *"Therefore go and make disciples of all nations, baptizing them in the name of the Father and of the Son and of the Holy Spirit, and teaching them to obey everything I have commanded you. And surely I am with you always, to the very end of the age." Matt 28:19-20 (NIV)*

It is impossible to obey Christ's instructions without His power. Jesus does not expect us to obey Him without His enablement. The Christian life is a life of total dependency upon Jesus and His provision.

How did Paul accomplish so much in the Lord's service? Paul lived in full surrender to Christ and in total dependency upon Christ's strength.

Are you relying on Christ's strength? You can do everything Christ calls you to do in the strength He provides. God can accomplish more through your life in six minutes than you can accomplish on your own in sixty years. Will you be found faithful? Rely on the strength Christ provides.

August 16
KNOWING GOD'S WILL

"For this reason, since the day we heard about you, we have not stopped praying for you and asking God to fill you with the knowledge of his will through all spiritual wisdom and understanding." Col 1:9 (NIV)

One of the most profound prayers you can pray for others is for them to know God and to do His will. Knowing and doing God's will is the purpose of life. God has provided the way in Jesus for us to know God personally and to obey His will completely.

The knowledge of God's will comes through spiritual wisdom and understanding. In his letter to the church at Corinth, Paul affirmed, "The man without the Spirit does not accept the things that come from the Spirit of God, for they are foolishness to him, and he cannot understand them, because they are spiritually discerned" (1 Cor 2:14 NIV). Spiritual discernment comes from the Spirit of God living inside of you. At the moment of conversion, you were filled with the Holy Spirit. He lives in you to teach you and to remind you of the things Jesus did and said (John 14:26).

Pray that others might be saturated with the knowledge of God's will. When you pray for others, ask God to give them spiritual wisdom and understanding. As they come to know God's will they will have the opportunity to choose to obey God's will. You will be involved in the process through the avenue of intercessory prayer. What a wise investment of your time!

Are you in the center of God's will? Have you asked God to fill you with the knowledge of His will? Are you willing to ask God for spiritual wisdom and understanding to know His will? Bring honor to God by obeying His will.

August 17
LIVING SACRIFICES

"Therefore, I urge you, brothers, in view of God's mercy, to offer your bodies as living sacrifices, holy and pleasing to God--this is your spiritual act of worship." Romans 12:1 (NIV)

How do we respond to God's mercy? The fact that God pursued us with His redeeming love and did not give us what we deserved engenders a response. Think of where we would be had God's mercy not been applied to our hopeless estate. We were separated from God as a result of our sin. We deserved punishment, alienation, and eternal damnation. In His mercy, God provided the atonement for our sin through the sinless sacrificial death of Jesus on the cross.

In response to His mercy, God is not asking us to die for Him. God wants us to respond to His mercy by living for Him. Instead of being a dead sacrifice, God wants us to be a living sacrifice. Our spiritual act of worship that moves the heart of God is that of being holy and pleasing to Him. To be holy is to work out in practical daily living the holiness of Christ imparted to us at the moment of our salvation. We received the imputed righteousness of Christ which instantly gave us a right standing before our holy God. That event is to be followed by the process of living a holy life that is pleasing to God.

Offer your body as a living sacrifice by loving what God loves and hating what God hates. Live in perpetual dependence upon the power of the Holy Spirit to stay clean while living in this dirty world. Practice His presence throughout the day and be sensitive to His prompting. Confess sin immediately. Choose to stay close and clean.

August 18
RENEW YOUR MIND

"Do not conform any longer to the pattern of this world, but be transformed by the renewing of your mind. Then you will be able to test and approve what God's will is--his good, pleasing and perfect will." Romans 12:2 (NIV)

There is an immense gravitational pull to succumb to the allurements of the world. We combat the pattern of this world, the flaming arrows of the evil one, and the cravings of the flesh. Choosing to conform to the path of worldliness dilutes our spiritual passion and distorts our spiritual focus. We will bypass God's best for us. We will forfeit God's good, pleasing, and perfect will.

God gives us the freedom to choose our path. We do not have to travel down the lane of lust or the highway of hostility or the sidewalk of selfishness. We can choose to be transformed by the renewing of our mind. Floating down the river of culture and allowing the current of compromise to corrode our character is not God's will for us. God did not sacrifice His only Son in order for us to drift into sin.

Renew your mind by replacing sin with Scripture, by replacing falsehood with truth, and by replacing self-centeredness with Christlikeness. Be transformed by renewing your mind. Scrape off the peeling paint of improper thinking and apply the fresh paint of God's Holy Word. Your life is too valuable to allow corrupt thinking to occupy your mind. God's plan for your life is too important to waste another moment allowing toxic thoughts to contaminate your mind.

Unload your mind! Make room for God's Word to take full possession of your mind. Make a commitment to feed on God's Word daily. Seek to memorize a verse each week, internalize that verse, and then align your thinking with that verse.

August 19

Obtain a Proper View

"For by the grace given me I say to every one of you: Do not think of yourself more highly than you ought, but rather think of yourself with sober judgment, in accordance with the measure of faith God has given you." Romans 12:3 (NIV)

Do you have a skewed view of yourself? When you examine your life, what do you see? Perhaps you have a low view of yourself. It may be that you have an inflated view of yourself. Someone has remarked that we view others based on their actions and we view ourselves based on our intentions.

How does God want you to view yourself? The proper way to view yourself is in accordance with the measure of faith God has given you. How do you measure that faith? You need a standard! The wonderful news is that Jesus is our standard. He is the benchmark for our assessment. God wants you to use sober judgment. In other words, you are to measure your life with accuracy. Instead of comparing yourself to others, examine your life in light of Christ.

Assess your current reality using Jesus as your standard. He is the model to follow. Jesus is the example to emulate. Obtain a proper view of yourself. Allow the standard of Christ's life to produce an element of brokenness and humility inside of you. Embrace the desperation and invite Jesus to take you to the place of being more like Him.

Begin to view others through the lens of the journey you are on. Recognize that you haven't arrived. Start viewing others through the perspective of their life fully yielded to Christ. What if they became like Christ? View yourself and others through the measure of faith God has given you. You are in Christ because of God's unconditional love.

August 20
BELONGING TO THE BODY

"Just as each of us has one body with many members, and these members do not all have the same function, so in Christ we who are many form one body, and each member belongs to all the others." Romans 12:4-5 (NIV)

God has placed within us the abiding desire to belong. We were not created to live in isolation. God created us to live in authentic community with other believers. God designed the Body of Christ to function in community. Once you are adopted into God's spiritual family, you immediately belong to every believer on the planet. You are eternally linked with millions of believers.

Now that you are in Christ, you are a member of His global body. You are connected to every believer who has ever lived. Though we are many, we form one body and belong to each other. Being connected to the body of believers has an immediate and local implication. You are to express your spiritual gifts by serving through the local body of believers. That's why it is vital that you connect to a Christ-centered, Bible believing, and soul conscious church.

God wants you to connect with other believers in a local church. Don't try to live the Christian life in isolation. God does not want you to be a closet Christian. God wants you to go public with your faith and He wants you to get connected to a thriving local church so you can worship, grow, and serve.

Your function in the local church is part of God's master plan. Your contribution to the life and ministry of the local church has immediate and eternal implications. God has saved you and adopted you into His forever family so that you can participate with Him in bringing others into His family. Do you long to belong?

August 21
PRIVATE WORSHIP

"God, who has called you into fellowship with his Son Jesus Christ our Lord, is faithful." 1 Cor 1:9 (NIV)

Every believer is called by God and for God. The highest calling on a believer's life is not to become a preacher or an international missionary. The highest calling on a believer's life is to live in unbroken fellowship with Jesus Christ. What we do vocationally and relationally flows out of that calling to perpetually fellowship with Jesus. Being united with Christ and nurturing His life in us is our ongoing assignment.

God is faithful! You can anchor your faith to His faithfulness. God created you for intimacy with His Son and our Savior, Jesus Christ. You have been chosen by God to enter into the most dynamic, meaningful, and purpose driven relationship ever established. The redemptive work of Christ on the cross has given you access to the one relationship that will change your forever. Your life will never operate in the center of God's will until you come into fellowship with Jesus.

Now that you are in Christ, grow in your love relationship with Him. Enjoy daily intimacy with the Lord through having a daily quiet time. Make a standing appointment with the Lord each day. Give Him your undivided attention. Spend unhurried time alone with Him as you read His Word and sit at His feet. Encounter His abiding presence as you pour out your heart in prayer. Share your fears, frustrations, and failures. Express your appreciation for all that Jesus has done to set you free and to empower you to live in victory.

Fellowship with Jesus is not only a specific amount of time carved out to have a daily devotion, but also an ongoing relationship. You can walk with Jesus moment-by-moment in full awareness of His presence. You can talk to Jesus throughout the day. Invite Jesus to live His life through you.

August 22
VERTICAL EXPRESSION

"Worship the LORD with gladness; come before him with joyful songs." Psalm 100:2 (NIV)

What are you passionate about? Perhaps you get excited about engaging in life-giving activities such as playing golf, fishing, shopping, scrap-booking, or painting. Maybe your passion is decorating your home or working in the yard. It would take less than thirty seconds to discover your passion. Whatever you are passionate about will surface rather quickly as you interact with people.

God wants you to bring your passion to public worship. Whenever you assemble with other believers in a corporate setting to worship God, you can choose to engage or to totally disengage. God gives you the freedom to passionately pursue Him in public worship. God desires your passionate worship and God deserves your passionate worship.

It is so easy to direct our passion toward so many other things in life and then bring God the leftovers when we come to a worship service with other believers. We can enter a beautiful worship center filled with fellow believers and drift into a dormant posture for worship. Instead of giving God our best, we can so easily be distracted by the tugs of this life. It it possible to worship our work and fail to work at our worship designed to express our love to God.

Do you worship the Lord with gladness? Is there passion in your expression of worship? Come into His presence with joyful songs. If you have been delivered from the flames of hell and placed on the road that leads to life, then you have a song to sing. If you have been saved by the grace of God and become a citizen of heaven, then you have a song to sing. Bring your passion to worship. Sing with appreciation in your heart for all that God has brought you through. Passionately express your worship to the One who gave you eternal life!

August 23
WITNESS THROUGH WORSHIP

"About midnight Paul and Silas were praying and singing hymns to God, and the other prisoners were listening to them." Acts 16:25 (NIV)

Think about where you sit each Sunday when you attend the worship service at your local church. Maybe you like sitting in the rear of the worship center, or maybe the front, or perhaps on the side. Find your place and think about what you do during that time of worship. This is your weekly experience of joining other believers in public worship of the One who lived, died, and rose again to bring you life eternal.

Your worship is a witness. Did you realize that the way you express your worship to Almighty God is a witness to others. Your worship matters to God and impacts others. Consider your worship the past few Sundays. Were others inspired by your worship? Was it evident to others that Christ is your life? Did you express your love to God in such a way that others nearby where convinced of your devotion?

Paul and Silas were in prison for preaching the gospel. In the middle of the night, they were praying and singing hymns to God. That must have been an unusual sight for the other prisoners to behold. You see, the other prisoners were listening. Paul and Silas' midnight expression of worship was a witness. God showed up in His power and delivered Paul and Silas from their confinement. God also brought salvation to the jailer and his entire household. The prisoners had never seen anything like that before.

What king of witness is your worship to others? The way you focus in worship each week is so important. Expressing your love to God in public worship has the capacity to influence others. Bring your passion to corporate worship this upcoming weekend and be intentional about your worship being a witness.

August 24
Expressing Our Union

"And I tell you that you are Peter, and on this rock I will build my church, and the gates of Hades will not overcome it." Matt 16:18 (NIV)

God ordained marriage and God ordained the church. We are married to Christ and our union is expressed through His Body, the church. Peter confessed that Jesus was the Christ, the Son of the living God. Jesus affirmed that He would build His church on that reality.

In order to become a follower of Jesus Christ and become a member of His Body, the church, a person must confess Jesus as the Christ, the Son of the living God. This profession of our faith is essential to salvation (Rom. 10:9-10). Jesus builds His church by adopting us into His family (Eph. 1:5). Only those who are born again enter into His Kingdom (John 3:3).

Jesus builds His church. Our job is to be the church. Jesus saves people from their sin. Our job is to share the Good News of Jesus so that others can know Jesus personally and eternally. Jesus saves us, not to sit, but to serve. Our role in the Body of Christ, the church, is to empty hell and to populate heaven.

The church is not the physical building. As followers of Jesus Christ, we are the church. We are the church gathered in worship and the church scattered on mission during the week. God wants us to be the church so that the world will have the opportunity to come into a personal relationship with Jesus Christ.

Express your union with Christ. May others be drawn to Christ through your witness. Testify of His redeeming love and share your spiritual story.

August 25
Learning to Wait

"'I am going to send you what my Father has promised; but stay in the city until you have been clothed with power from on high.'" Luke 24:49 (NIV)

Jesus instructed the believers to wait in Jerusalem until they had received what His Father had promised, namely, power from on high. Jesus had to ascend back to the Father so that He could send the Counselor, the promised Holy Spirit (John 16:7). Yet, Jesus did not give them an exact time or date for the Holy Spirit's arrival. They had to wait!

- *"On one occasion, while he was eating with them, he gave them this command: 'Do not leave Jerusalem, but wait for the gift my Father promised, which you have heard me speak about. For John baptized with water, but in a few days you will be baptized with the Holy Spirit.'" Acts 1:4-5 (NIV)*

The 120 believers waited ten days to be clothed with power from on high (Acts 1:15). Have you ever wondered why it took ten days? During that time, they replaced Judas by adding Matthias to the eleven apostles (Acts 1:26). But why did it take ten days? Perhaps the 120 believers had some internal issues to resolve. Maybe they had to confess sin and remove jealously, bitterness, and envy. Maybe it took ten days to come to the place of complete unity as a community of Christ-followers.

Are you currently waiting for God to reveal His next step for your life? Is there anything in your life that God wants you to deal with before He shows you what's next? Ask the Lord to search your heart (Ps. 139:23).

August 26
No Greater Task

"When the day of Pentecost came, they were all together in one place. Suddenly a sound like the blowing of a violent wind came from heaven and filled the whole house where they were sitting. They saw what seemed to be tongues of fire that separated and came to rest on each of them. All of them were filled with the Holy Spirit and began to speak in other tongues as the Spirit enabled them." Acts 2:1-4 (NIV)

God empowers us for participation in His redemptive activity.

We cannot operate in God's kingdom economy without God's kingdom resources. God's agenda can only be fulfilled by God's enabling. Without God's power, we cannot fulfill God's mission. On the day of Pentecost, the Holy Spirit indwelt the believers and enabled them to speak forth the Gospel. Everyone heard the Good News in their own heart language. This miraculous communication of the Gospel was God's demonstration that the Gospel is for everyone!

What is your spiritual story? How did you come to know Christ personally? What has your life been like since being filled with the Holy Spirit? What does God's Word say about how a person can be saved? If you have experienced the Gospel firsthand, then you are now ready to witness to Christ's saving power. You are now ready to share your faith with others. Read Romans 3:23, 5:8, 6:23, 10:9-10, and 10:13.

God has reconciled you to Himself so that you can join God in reconciling others to Himself. Build bridges to those who don't know Jesus so that they can have the saving relationship that you enjoy in Christ. There's no greater task on planet earth!

August 27
FULLY DEVOTED

"Those who accepted his message were baptized, and about three thousand were added to their number that day." Acts 2:41 (NIV)

Wow! On the day of Pentecost, three thousand were adopted into God's family. Three thousand were delivered from the clutches of hell and placed on the path that leads to heaven. Three thousand were saved by God and for God. They became followers of Jesus Christ and were added to His Body, the church. An eternal transaction took place!

What's next? Now that the three thousand are in Christ, how are they to function as a community of Christ-followers? What will be different about their conversation and their conduct? Do they go back to business as usual or do they embrace a new way of living?

> - *"They devoted themselves to the apostles' teaching and to the fellowship, to the breaking of bread and to prayer. Everyone was filled with awe, and many wonders and miraculous signs were done by the apostles." Acts 2:42-43 (NIV)*

Notice how their lifestyle radically changed. On this side of their salvation, the three thousand along with the other 120 believers start doing life together. They begin to operate as a community of believers. They are walking together in unity. Their priorities have shifted and their time allocation reflects the heart of God.

Take a moment to examine your life in light of Acts 2:42-43. Are you devoted to the reading, study, hearing, and application of God's Word? Are you in fellowship with a group of believers you can do life with? Are you consistently embracing the privilege of prayer? Are you in awe of the redemptive activity of God?

August 28
God's Team

"All the believers were together and had everything in common. Selling their possessions and goods, they gave to anyone as he had need. Every day they continued to meet together in the temple courts. They broke bread in their homes and ate together with glad and sincere hearts, praising God and enjoying the favor of all the people. And the Lord added to their number daily those who were being saved." Acts 2:44-47 (NIV)

God's team is made up of those who have been saved by His grace. God's team members wear the Jesus jersey and play for His glory. His team is characterized by unity, community, selflessness, generosity, compassion, loyalty, fellowship, gladness, sincerity, evangelism, and growth.

Doing church first involves being the church. Our doing flows out of our being. It is possible to become so busy doing church that you bypass the relational aspect of being the church. God has called us, the church, to an abiding relationship with Christ.

- *"Consequently, you are no longer foreigners and aliens, but fellow citizens with God's people and members of God's household, built on the foundation of the apostles and prophets, with Christ Jesus himself as the chief cornerstone." Eph 2:19-20 (NIV)*

As a member of God's household, you are called to abide in Christ. Your perpetual connection to Christ and His resources will result in bearing fruit. However, don't focus on bearing fruit. Focus on abiding. As you abide in Christ, fruit will be born. Apart from Christ, you can do nothing. His is your Source and He is your Life! As you abide in Christ, you will instantly add more value to the team, the Body of Christ.

August 29
REDEFINING RETALIATION

"You have heard that it was said, 'Eye for eye, and tooth for tooth.' But I tell you, Do not resist an evil person. If someone strikes you on the right cheek, turn to him the other also." Matt 5:38-39 (NIV)

The religious leaders Jesus confronted during His earthly ministry had perverted the Mosaic Law. They inflamed the law of retaliation, known as the lex talionis, for their personal benefit. The law was intended to control excess and to ensure that the punishment would not exceed the offense (Ex. 21:22-25; Lev. 24:19-20). It was intended to prevent people from employing personal revenge. The religious leaders leveraged the law as a minimum. You would be expected to retaliate by punishing your offender at the same level of their offense to start with and then add to that revenge.

Jesus inverted their perversion by portraying the law of retaliation as a maximum. Revenge and retaliation would not be the proper response for the follower of Jesus Christ. Jesus presented the life-giving response of choosing to see the evil person as an opportunity rather than an obstacle. When someone strikes you on the cheek physically or through verbal assault, the fully yielded follower of Christ is to not retaliate based on his natural proclivity.

Turning the other cheek becomes the choice whereby you respond to the offense in the power of the Holy Spirit rather than reacting in the flesh. Instead of striking back by executing personal revenge, the believer is to respond with the grace and mercy of Christ.

You cannot redefine retaliation without operating in the power of the Holy Spirit. Your natural response will be to unleash revenge. Jesus ushers in a new response that blesses your offender and brings honor to God!

August 30
CALLING FOR PRAYER SUPPORT

"Is any one of you sick? He should call the elders of the church to pray over him and anoint him with oil in the name of the Lord." James 5:14 (NIV)

The Christian life is not a solo flight. God never intended for us to live out our faith in isolation. As followers of Christ, we have Jesus at the right hand of the Father making intercession for us (Rm. 8:34) and we have the Holy Spirit interceding for us with groans that words cannot express (Romans 8:26-27). God has also given us fellow believers who can stand in the gap for us in prayer.

The Apostle Paul asked for the believers in the church at Ephesus to pray that he would fearlessly make known the mystery of the gospel (Eph. 6:19). Paul asked the church at Colossae to pray that God would open a door for his message so that he could proclaim the mystery of Christ (Col. 4:3). Paul asked the church at Thessalonica to pray for he and his ministry partners that the message of the Lord would spread rapidly and be honored and that they would be delivered from evil and wicked men (2 Thes. 3:1-2).

James affirms the need for outside prayer support for our lives. If you are experiencing spiritual weakness or even a physical illness, ask a spiritual leader to pray for you. If you are walking through a challenging situation or combating a difficult season, ask a spiritual leader to pray for you. Surround yourself with prayer warriors who will do warfare praying on your behalf. Don't be afraid to ask for prayer support. God has placed people within your sphere of influence who can stand in the gap for you in prayer.

Do you have someone praying you through?

August 31
He Can Hear You Now

"Is any one of you in trouble? He should pray. Is anyone happy? Let him sing songs of praise." James 5:13 (NIV)

Independence is valued in our society. Being strong and self-sufficient tend to be the marks of success by the world's standards. However, God's economy has a much different value system. It's not about personal strength, but reliance upon God's strength. Self-sufficiency is replaced with dependency upon God and His provision. Success in God's economy is marked by instant obedience and alignment with God's plan.

Part of God's plan includes our relational connection to God through an abiding relationship with Jesus Christ. The love relationship that God has made available to us in Christ is nurtured by our daily communion with God in prayer. The prayer connection flows from God to us and from us to God. God invites us into an intimate prayer connection that radiates from His heart of love and our response of awe and wonder. Imagine being able to share your heart as well as your heartaches with the God of the universe. We have that amazing privilege to bring everything to God in prayer. In Christ, we have been given access to the Creator of the universe.

Are you in trouble? Are you experiencing challenging circumstances or strained relationships? Don't delay! Take your burdens to the Lord in prayer. Empty the contents of your heart before the loving and faithful God that you have come to know by experience. God has provided you with the ultimate communication instrument called prayer. Just pray! Begin to articulate to God whatever is perplexing you and whatever is bothering you. God can handle your hurt. God can make the fog lift. Be still and know that He is God (Ps. 46:10). God's line is never busy and yes, He can hear you now!

September 1
AUTHENTIC FAITH

"I have been reminded of your sincere faith, which first lived in your grandmother Lois and in your mother Eunice and, I am persuaded, now lives in you also." 2 Tim 1:5 (NIV)

What kind of faith has been handed down to you? Maybe you had a godly upbringing where Christ was honored in your home and where the Christian faith was modeled consistently. Perhaps the environment in which you grew up was not characterized by Christian values. When you look into the rear view mirror of your life you may see a perpetual flow of spiritual markers or you may be stunned by the absence of authentic faith.

Paul recognized the sincere faith that was modeled before Timothy by his grandmother and his mother. Timothy had the privilege of being taught the Scriptures from infancy (2 Tim. 3:15). Though his daddy was not a follower of Jesus Christ, Timothy observed the authentic faith exemplified by his grandmother and his mother.

Regardless of your upbringing, the wonderful news is that you can become the conduit through which authentic faith is demonstrated before a watching world. God can use you to model Christ in your conversation and your conduct. You can grow in your faith and allow your sincere, un-hypocritical faith to impact others.

Is your faith the real deal? Have you experienced saving faith in Jesus Christ and given evidence to that faith through practical faith and obedience to God's Word? Genuine faith will draw others to Christ. Repent of those things that neutralize your faith. Identify those attitudes and actions that prevent your faith from being authentic and sincere.

September 2
SEEING THE INVISIBLE

"Now faith is being sure of what we hope for and certain of what we do not see."
Heb 11:1 (NIV)

Are you convinced that you are saved and that you will go to heaven? Are you convinced that God is who He says He is? That's faith! Being confident of your current reality in Christ is the evidence of faith. If you have placed your faith in the completed work of Jesus on the cross, then you are certain of what you do not see.

The Christian life often involves seeing the invisible. You are trusting that what Jesus did two thousand years ago on Calvary makes a difference in your life today and for eternity. You hope for eternal life and heaven and you are certain of that reality because of faith being operative in your life.

God gives you the ability to see the unseen through the eyes of faith. When you view life through your eyes of flesh you will often miss the activity of God and the reality of His abiding presence. Viewing life through the eyes of faith is to view life from God's perspective. Through the eyes of faith, you begin to see the unseen and God enables you to discern His activity. Your faith is anchored in God's Word and your confidence is placed in the character of God.

What are you unsure of right now? In what areas has your confidence been wavering? Your faith will be tested and your dependence upon God will not go unchallenged. Draw near to God and trust His heart during times of uncertainty. God is trustworthy. He knows where you are and He knows what is best for you, even in the midst of your immediate concerns. God will see you through.

September 3
COMMENDED AS ONE WHO PLEASES GOD

"By faith Enoch was taken from this life, so that he did not experience death; he could not be found, because God had taken him away. For before he was taken, he was commended as one who pleased God." Heb 11:5 (NIV)

Two people in the Bible had the distinct privilege of not experiencing death, namely, Enoch and Elijah. Elijah went up into heaven in a whirlwind (2 Kings 2:11). Enoch walked with God and was no more because God took him away (Gen 5:24). Can you imagine walking with God and then bypassing death altogether in order to be instantly ushered into the presence of the Lord?

What kind of life did Enoch live before he was taken up to heaven? The Bible gives us clarity that Enoch lived by faith. He is honored in the Hall of Faith found in Hebrews chapter eleven. Enoch's walk with God gave evidence of a lifestyle devoted to pleasing God. Enoch embraced a consistent lifestyle that brought honor to God. He was an avid God pleaser!

Do you please God? Are you loving what God loves and hating what God hates? Assess your current reality. Examine the motives behind your lifestyle. Consider the spiritual resume that you are building through your walk with God. Think about how your life influences others. Can you be commended as one who pleases God?

If the focus of your life has been pleasing others, repent of that sin. Reorient your life to embrace a lifestyle of pleasing God. Make God's smile the goal of your life. Remember that you will stand before God one day to give an account of how you lived your life on earth. You will not give an account to any of the people you are currently trying to please. Become a God pleaser!

September 4
FAITH AND PLEASING GOD

"And without faith it is impossible to please God, because anyone who comes to him must believe that he exists and that he rewards those who earnestly seek him." Heb 11:6 (NIV)

Pleasing the Creator of the universe seems impossible. God is omnipotent, omniscient, and omnipresent. God is holy, perfect, immutable, and eternal. God is infinite. How can finite man please God?

The vital ingredient to pleasing God is faith. This type of faith is the conviction that God is who He says He is. To live a life pleasing to God, you must operate in faith. The focus of your life becomes God's agenda. You demonstrate belief in God's existence by fearing Him and revering Him through a lifestyle of obedience.

Choose to come to God knowing that He desires intimacy with you. As a child of God, you have the distinct privilege of knowing that God rewards you as you seek Him earnestly. God rewards you with abiding peace, continual fellowship, and eternal hope.

Is your life pleasing to God? Is faith operative in your conversation and your conduct? Portray your conviction about the truth of God's nature and character. God has pursued you with His love. Respond to God's pursuit by living a life of faith that brings pleasure to Him. Determine to please God through behavior that is consistent with His Word.

Ask God to reveal those areas of your life that are out of alignment with His purpose and plan. As God brings those specific areas to your attention, choose to repent and go in a new direction. Remove those things in your life that rob your love relationship with God. Put your faith in action. Remember, without faith it is impossible to please God!

September 5
FAITH AND HOLY FEAR

"By faith Noah, when warned about things not yet seen, in holy fear built an ark to save his family. By his faith he condemned the world and became heir of the righteousness that comes by faith." Heb 11:7 (NIV)

Making decisions about things not seen requires faith. However, faith is not walking in the dark. Faith is taking God at His Word and trusting Him to do what He says He will do. Faith is being confident that God honors obedience. Faith is walking in the light God gives you.

Noah was willing to build a boat even though it had never rained. In the natural, constructing an ark made no sense. To his neighbors, the process of building such a massive floatation vessel was foolish. They did not see the need. Yet, Noah was operating in holy fear. Noah revered God and wanted to do whatever was needed to save his family. Noah's faith in God and his holy fear of God motivated him to embark on a major construction project to demonstrate instant obedience.

What decisions are you praying through right now? Have you patiently waited upon the Lord to hear from Him? Has God given you a clear sense of direction? Obey what God has already revealed to you. Trust God to show you the next step. Maybe God is calling you to do something that, in the natural, makes no sense.

God will never ask you to do anything that He won't equip you to do. God's provision always matches His assignment. Discern what God wants you to do and then activate your faith by obeying what God shows you.

September 6
Taking God at His Word

"By faith Abraham, even though he was past age--and Sarah herself was barren--was enabled to become a father because he considered him faithful who had made the promise." Heb 11:11 (NIV)

Is the level of your faith determined by the intensity and severity of your circumstances or by the One in whom you are placing your faith? Abraham and Sarah's situation was desperate and seemingly impossible. Abraham was 100 years old and Sarah was ninety years old and barren.

Don't miss the blessing behind "even though." Even though Abraham was past age and Sarah was barren, God enabled them to become parents because Abraham considered God faithful. God had already made the promise of blessing Abraham with offspring (Gen. 12:2-3). Abraham believed God!

- *"And so from this one man, and he as good as dead, came descendants as numerous as the stars in the sky and as countless as the sand on the seashore." Heb 11:12 (NIV)*
- *"Cast your cares on the LORD and he will sustain you; he will never let the righteous fall." Psalm 55:22 (NIV)*

Instead of focusing on your circumstances, focus on the faithfulness of God. You can bring your burdens to the Lord with openness and transparency. You can bear your soul before the Lord as you navigate the terrain of a fallen world. God formed you and fashioned you for His glory. Your circumstances will not derail the purposes of God from being fulfilled in your life. Trust God to demonstrate His faithfulness to you. Be sensitive to God's activity today in the midst of your circumstances.

September 7
STILL LIVING BY FAITH

"All these people were still living by faith when they died." Heb 11:13 (NIV)

It's not how you start; it's how you finish. Commit to finish well. When you study the Hall of Faith found in Hebrews chapter eleven, you will discover great men and women who chose to finish well. They were still living by faith when they died.

What are you giving your life to? Have you determined the focus of your life? Living by faith involves allowing Christ to live His life through you. Living by faith includes surrendering your life to God's agenda. Yielding to the Lordship of Christ moment by moment validates the reality of living by faith.

- *"Though you have not seen him, you love him; and even though you do not see him now, you believe in him and are filled with an inexpressible and glorious joy, for you are receiving the goal of your faith, the salvation of your souls."* 1 Peter 1:8-9 (NIV)
- *"Therefore, prepare your minds for action; be self-controlled; set your hope fully on the grace to be given you when Jesus Christ is revealed."* 1 Peter 1:13 (NIV)

Determine to cross the finish line of this life living by faith. Don't let anything or anyone deter you from living a life pleasing to God. Grow in your love relationship with the Lord so that your daily walk will give evidence to a life of faith. Trusting God with the details of your life requires activating your faith. Will you submit to God's authority? Will you obey God's Word and embrace His way? Finish well by demonstrating a life of instant obedience.

September 8
HEARING OF YOUR FAITH AND LOVE

"We always thank God, the Father of our Lord Jesus Christ, when we pray for you, because we have heard of your faith in Christ Jesus and of the love you have for all the saints." Col 1:3-4 (NIV)

What are people hearing about you? Do they hear about your obsession with hobbies? Do they hear about your addiction to technology? Are they hearing about your misplaced priorities? What if they were hearing about your faith and love?

Paul and Timothy were thankful to God in prayer for the church at Colossae because of their visible faith in Christ Jesus and their love for other believers. The church was bearing the fruit of being connected to Christ. Their love relationship with Jesus was producing in them a deep abiding love for other believers. The vertical faith they had in Christ was being demonstrated through a horizontal love for fellow believers. Their faith was expressed through active love for others.

Take inventory of your faith and love. How's your faith in Christ? Are you growing in your faith relationship with Christ? Think about your connection to Christ and assess your devotion to His agenda. Are you loving others the way Christ has loved you? Are you serving others the way Christ has served you?

You can't go horizontal with love until you have gone vertical with faith. Your relationship with Christ will determine your relationship with others. You cannot give what you do not possess. Until you are connected to Christ through an abiding relationship, you will not be able to express His love to others. Make certain of your connection to Christ. Guard your daily intimacy with the Lord. Nurture your relationship with Jesus. Stay connected! Stay close and clean!

September 9
ASKING GOD

"For this reason, since the day we heard about you, we have not stopped praying for you and asking God to fill you with the knowledge of his will through all spiritual wisdom and understanding." Col 1:9 (NIV)

One of the most profound prayers you can pray for others is for them to know God and to do His will. Knowing and doing God's will is the purpose of life. God has provided the way in Jesus for us to know God personally and to obey His will completely.

The knowledge of God's will comes through spiritual wisdom and understanding. In his letter to the church at Corinth, Paul affirmed, "The man without the Spirit does not accept the things that come from the Spirit of God, for they are foolishness to him, and he cannot understand them, because they are spiritually discerned" (1 Cor 2:14 NIV). Spiritual discernment comes from the Spirit of God living inside of you. At the moment of conversion, you were filled with the Holy Spirit. He lives in you to teach you and to remind you of the things Jesus did and said (John 14:26).

Pray that others might be saturated with the knowledge of God's will. When you pray for others, ask God to give them spiritual wisdom and understanding. As they come to know God's will they will have the opportunity to choose to obey God's will. You will be involved in the process through the avenue of intercessory prayer. What a wise investment of your time! You can impact the lives of others through praying specifically for them to know and to do God's will.

Are you in the center of God's will? Have you asked God to fill you with the knowledge of His will? Are you willing to ask God for spiritual wisdom and understanding to know His will? Bring honor to God by obeying His will.

September 10
PLEASING GOD IN EVERY WAY

"And we pray this in order that you may live a life worthy of the Lord and may please him in every way: bearing fruit in every good work, growing in the knowledge of God, being strengthened with all power according to his glorious might so that you may have great endurance and patience, and joyfully giving thanks to the Father, who has qualified you to share in the inheritance of the saints in the kingdom of light." Col 1:10-12 (NIV)

Are you living for the audience of one? God wants you to live a life worthy of the Lord. Consider all that Jesus did to purchase your salvation and to provide for your abiding peace. Think about what Jesus did to take care of your forever. You are saved for all eternity. Heaven is your home!

As you live to please God, He desires for you to bear fruit, grow in your knowledge of Him, be strengthened by His might, and perpetually and joyfully give thanks to Him. God has qualified you to participate in the inheritance of the saints. You are blessed and highly favored of the Lord. You are fruitful, you are growing, you are strengthened, and you are joyful in the Lord. As a child of the living God, you have been lavished with His unconditional love.

Make pleasing God the passion of your life. As you trust God daily to provide the strength for Christian living, you will bring pleasure to Him. God loves you and wants you to please Him in every way. Be conscious of His abiding presence. Be alert to opportunities to bear fruit, as you stay connected to Christ. Allow the life of Christ to be evidenced through your life as you do what Jesus did to love God and to serve others.

September 11
RESCUED AND REDEEMED

"For he has rescued us from the dominion of darkness and brought us into the kingdom of the Son he loves, in whom we have redemption, the forgiveness of sins." Col 1:13-14 (NIV)

Desperate situations call for desperate measures. The extreme nature of our sin and rebellion demanded the extreme nature of complete atonement for our sin. Jesus was willing to endure the scorn and shame of the cross to pay the penalty of our sin in full. Because of His obedience to death on the cross, we are the recipients of God's rescue package known as redemption.

Jesus came to our rescue. He lived a sinless life, died a substitutionary death, and rose victorious over the grave. As Isaiah prophesied, "But he was pierced for our transgressions, he was crushed for our iniquities; the punishment that brought us peace was upon him, and by his wounds we are healed" (Isaiah 53:5 NIV). Jesus rescued us from the kingdom of darkness and brought us into the kingdom of light.

In Jesus, we have redemption. In Jesus, we have the forgiveness of sins. Being rescued from sin and eternal separation from God places us on the path that leads to life. What a joy to live the rescued life!

Now that you have been rescued from darkness, you have a life-changing message to share with others. What Jesus has done for you, He can do for others. What Jesus is doing in you, He can do in others. How will they know unless you are willing to share your rescue experience with them?

September 12
ENCOUNTERING GOD'S GRACE

"I always thank God for you because of his grace given you in Christ Jesus."
1 Cor 1:4 (NIV)

Paul was writing from Ephesus on his third missionary journey a personal letter to the church at Corinth. He acknowledged God's call on them to be holy along with the other believers who were calling on the name of the Lord. Paul gave evidence to the content of his prayer life for the church at Corinth through the theme of grace.

God's grace had been clearly given to the church at Corinth. Paul had spent eighteen months there teaching them the Word of God (Acts 18:11). The grace Paul identified in them was the same grace that had rescued Paul from the path of being a persecutor of the church. Paul had a life-changing encounter with God's grace. Now he is giving thanks to God for the grace they have in Christ Jesus.

When you became a follower of Jesus Christ, you encountered the grace of God firsthand. God gave you what you did not deserve. Because of your sin, you deserved alienation, separation, and eternal damnation. However, God graced you with His abiding peace and lavished you with His unconditional love. If you ever doubt God's grace, just look into the rearview mirror of your life and recall the portraits of grace God has painted throughout the terrain of your past.

In Christ Jesus, you have been given grace. God has blessed you with a new identity in Christ. You are a new creation (2 Cor. 5:17). You have been saved by grace through faith (Eph. 2:8-9). You are God's workmanship (Eph. 2:10). God's grace has been poured out on you abundantly.

September 13
ENRICHED AND EQUIPPED

"For in him you have been enriched in every way--in all your speaking and in all your knowledge--because our testimony about Christ was confirmed in you. Therefore you do not lack any spiritual gift as you eagerly wait for our Lord Jesus Christ to be revealed." 1 Cor 1:5-7 (NIV)

Once you are in Christ, the realities of your eternal relationship come to fruition. In Christ, you are enriched in every way. Your life is no longer your own. You become God's possession and God's masterpiece. He enriches you in every way so that you can know Him personally and make Him known relationally. When you speak on God's behalf, He enriches your speech. When you are pursuing the knowledge of God, He enriches you with knowledge reserved for His children.

Another reality of your eternal relationship is that in Christ, you are equipped with spiritual gifts. At the moment of your conversion, you were filled with the Holy Spirit and you received the impartation of spiritual gifts as determined by God (1 Cor. 12:11). God has placed you in the Body of Christ to fulfill His purpose and mission and you exercise the spiritual gifts He equipped you with.

Are you operating in the enrichment and equipping provided by God? God saved you so that you can invest your life in serving Him and leading others into a growing relationship with Christ. You have been enriched in every way. You have been equipped with spiritual gifts. God has given you everything you need for life and godliness (2 Peter 1:3).

September 14
ENTRUSTED TO HIS CARE

"He will keep you strong to the end, so that you will be blameless on the day of our Lord Jesus Christ." 1 Cor 1:8 (NIV)

What do you base your eternal security on? Are you placing your confidence in your own ability to finish strong? The same grace that saved you is the same grace that will keep you strong to the end.

Jesus sacrificed His life to deliver you out of the kingdom of darkness and to place you in the kingdom of light. Your eternal security is not based on your performance, but rather on the grace of Jesus operative in your life. Once you are in Christ, you are secure for eternity. Your eternal security does not give you a license to sin. Don't presume upon the grace of God.

When you became a follower of Jesus Christ, you received the imputed righteousness of Christ. Your standing before God became that of being blameless. When God sees you, He sees you through the atoning work of Christ applied to your life. God views your life based on the shed blood of Jesus. You are now a saint because of your position in Christ. Jesus will keep you strong to the end. Join Him in that journey of holiness and purity. Participate with Christ by keeping yourself from being polluted by the world (James 1:27).

In Christ, you are entrusted to His care. The caregiver of your soul is the Lord Jesus Christ. You are sealed by the Holy Spirit (Eph. 4:30). Your name is written in the Lamb's book of life (Rev. 21:27). Now walk in the security you have in Christ. Live a life pleasing to God and help others come to know the security they can have in Christ.

September 15
FELLOWSHIP WITH JESUS

"God, who has called you into fellowship with his Son Jesus Christ our Lord, is faithful." 1 Cor 1:9 (NIV)

God formed you for fellowship. In the language of the New Testament, the word fellowship means communion, communication, partnership, or intimacy. Just as God called you into salvation, He also calls you into fellowship with Jesus. You are invited to enjoy unbroken fellowship with the Lord.

God's invitation is rooted in His faithfulness. God is faithful. He is true to His word. You come to know His companionship through an abiding relationship with Christ. Your fellowship with the Lord is enhanced as you enjoy His companionship and embrace His joint partnership in the gospel.

- *"We proclaim to you what we have seen and heard, so that you also may have fellowship with us. And our fellowship is with the Father and with his Son, Jesus Christ." 1 John 1:3 (NIV)*

Fellowship with the King of Kings is realized through the avenue of prayer. As a child of God, you have the privilege of enjoying sacred communication with the Creator of the universe. As you pray, your fellowship with Jesus becomes more intimate. Sharing your heart with the Lord in prayer and responding to His voice are vital components to continual fellowship.

Are you enjoying unbroken fellowship with the Lord? Have you created space in your life for the most important relationship initiated by God? You have to make room for fellowship with the Lord. Spend time communing with the Lord in prayer each day.

September 16
SEEING GOD

"He is the image of the invisible God, the firstborn over all creation." Col 1:15 (NIV)

God has set eternity in your heart (Ecc. 3:11). As a result, there is a longing for humanity to discover their true identity. There is a compulsion to find God. God has revealed Himself through nature (Romans 1:20) and ultimately through Jesus. God chose to robe Himself in flesh and dwell among us (John 1:14).

Over the centuries, individuals have sought to make God in their own image. Tangible and visible gods have been fashioned to help humanity make sense out of the invisible God. God is spirit (John 4:24). Philip had a longing to see God so he asked Jesus to show him the Father. Jesus replied to Philip, "Anyone who has seen me has seen the Father" (John 4:24).

Jesus is the exact representation of God. If you want to know what God is like, just look at Jesus. As you study the life of Christ and seek to emulate Him, you will discover what God is like. God has made Himself known through Jesus.

When you receive the gift of eternal life and allow Jesus to become the Lord of your life, you begin to discover the heart of God. His nature and character become evident because He chooses to live inside of you in the Person of the Holy Spirit. You become the walking tabernacle of the Presence of God. You have Christ in you, the hope of glory (Col. 1:27).

Have you seen God? Walk with Jesus and you will see God. Read and feed on God's Word daily. Become a person of prayer and seek the Lord through the discipline and devotion of unbroken fellowship with Christ. God will reveal His glory to you as you walk in daily intimacy. Don't settle for casual Christianity. Draw near to God and He will draw near to you (James 4:8).

September 17
CREATED ON PURPOSE

"For by him all things were created: things in heaven and on earth, visible and invisible, whether thrones or powers or rulers or authorities; all things were created by him and for him." Col 1:16 (NIV)

God made you. You were His idea. Before God formed you in the womb, He knew you (Jer. 1:5). You are not an accident. God designed you and there is not another person just like you.

Why did God create you? Why are you here? You were created by God and for God. You were made for God's pleasure. His redeeming love was demonstrated through the sacrifice of His one and only Son, Jesus. In Christ, you are God's workmanship. You are God's masterpiece.

All things were created by Christ and for Christ. As a Christian, you have the privilege of entrusting your life to Him. He knows what is best for you because He designed you. You were fashioned for His glory.

Regardless of what you endure throughout the seasons of life, you can anchor your life to the fact that God loves you and will accomplish His purposes through you. Your present circumstances will not stifle the activity of God. Christ will be formed in you in the midst of your challenges. Obstacles become opportunities for Christ to reveal His love and to extend His comfort.

Are you having trouble going to sleep at night due to the situation you face? Don't count sheep, just talk to the Shepherd. Turn to the Shepherd and Overseer of your soul (1 Pt. 2:25). Christ is still the Great Physician.

September 18
Jesus is Supreme

"He is before all things, and in him all things hold together. And he is the head of the body, the church; he is the beginning and the firstborn from among the dead, so that in everything he might have the supremacy." Col 1:17-18 (NIV)

Jesus is supreme! He is eternal and supernal. Jesus is the glue that holds everything together. Without Him, life would not exist. Jesus is also the head of the church. He gave birth to the church and He has empowered the church to represent Him on the earth.

In everything, Jesus reigns supreme. No one else can satisfy the longings of your heart. No one else can deliver you from the clutches of the enemy. No one else can rescue you from eternal damnation and place you on the path that leads to heaven and eternal life.

Jesus is more than enough. He is sufficient to meet all of your needs. Jesus is more than capable to equip you to continue His ministry upon the earth. God did not create you to live out the Christian life on your own strength. You need God's power to accomplish God's mission.

Will you allow Jesus to reign supreme in your life? Will you give Him both prominence and priority in your life? Jesus designed you to operate at your best when He is first in your life. Remove whatever occupies the throne of your life and allow Jesus to be enthroned in His rightful place. Surrender to His leadership and to His Lordship.

September 19
GOD'S INITIATIVE

"For God was pleased to have all his fullness dwell in him, and through him to reconcile to himself all things, whether things on earth or things in heaven, by making peace through his blood, shed on the cross." Col 1:19-20 (NIV)

God was pleased! His unconditional love prompted His pursuit of rescuing us from our depravity. Having all His fullness dwell in Jesus brought God pleasure. God built the ultimate love bridge by becoming like us in Christ. The incarnation is a declaration of the fantastic love of God that transcends our understanding and benefits our forever.

Through Christ, God reconciled us. In our sin, we were separated and alienated from Holy God. Only the depth of God's love could bridge the gulf of our indifference. We were hopeless, helpless, and hell bound. But God acted in history to revolutionize our eternal destiny. God decided what to do for us long before we could do anything with God or for God!

How did God accomplish the reconciliation and restoration of fallen humanity? God provided the ultimate sacrifice to remove our utter sin. Jesus made peace with God on our behalf through shedding His blood on the cross. Jesus did for us that which we could not do for ourselves. We were not qualified to pay the penalty of our own sin. We were not fit to receive the full wrath of God for sin. The iniquity of us all was laid on Jesus (Is. 53:6).

Have you responded to the pleasure of God in Christ? Have you received the wonderful gift of eternal life, which God was pleased to provide to you in Christ? God became like you in Christ, so that you could become like Him in Christ. What is your current reality? You have been reconciled by God and for God. Now invest your life in sharing the message of reconciliation and extending the ministry of reconciliation.

September 20
PRAYING FOR YOUR CHILDREN'S SALVATION

"The Lord is not slow in keeping his promise, as some understand slowness. He is patient with you, not wanting anyone to perish, but everyone to come to repentance." 2 Peter 3:9 (NIV)

Enjoying sacred communication with the Creator of the universe is one of your highest privileges. Praying to God for your children is one of your greatest investments in their future. Pray for their salvation. As you pray for your children's salvation, be sure to join God in His redemptive activity.

Your witness matters to your children. They are watching you. Let them see the evidence of the salvation you have in Christ. Let them observe the fruit of the Spirit exhibited through your life. As you pray for your children's salvation, seek to live out the life of peace and abundance provided to you in Christ.

God does not want anyone to perish. However, everyone has to respond to God's offer of salvation by placing his or her faith in the completed work of Christ on the cross. The atoning work of Jesus on the cross is applied to those who turn from their sin and trust in Jesus alone for salvation. Your children have the freedom to choose Christ or to reject Christ. Pray for them to receive the gift of eternal life.

You can impact your children's forever through the avenue of prayer. Commit to pray for your children's salvation. Commit to pray that they will come to see their need for the Savior. Pray for their heart to be tender toward God and sensitive to the Holy Spirit's prompting.

September 21
PRAYING FOR SPIRITUAL MATURITY

"I keep asking that the God of our Lord Jesus Christ, the glorious Father, may give you the Spirit of wisdom and revelation, so that you may know him better." Eph 1:17 (NIV)

What is your desire for your children, grandchildren, and great grandchildren? What is your desire for those you love so deeply? You want them to receive the gift of eternal life and be saved. You want them to grow spiritually and reach their God given potential. You desire for them to develop spiritual muscles that will demonstrate Christ-likeness.

What are you currently praying on their behalf? If your prayers were transcribed, what would the content of your intercession be? Pray for your children's spiritual maturity. Pray for their spiritual sensitivity. Ask God to give them an appetite for His Word. Ask God to elevate their thirst for His righteousness.

- *"Like newborn babies, crave pure spiritual milk, so that by it you may grow up in your salvation, now that you have tasted that the Lord is good."* 1 Peter 2:2-3 (NIV)
- *"But grow in the grace and knowledge of our Lord and Savior Jesus Christ. To him be glory both now and forever! Amen."* 2 Peter 3:18 (NIV)

Are you living up to the prayers you pray for your children, your grandchildren, and your great grandchildren? Practice daily spiritual disciplines that will help you grow spiritually. As you pray for others to experience spiritual maturity, demonstrate that same pursuit by allocating your time wisely. Invest in growing spiritually. Let others see Jesus in you!

September 22
Participating in Your Children's Future

"He who finds a wife finds what is good and receives favor from the LORD." Prov 18:22 (NIV)

Have you ever thought about participating in your children's future by praying for their future spouse? Even if your children, grandchildren, or great grandchildren are young, you can invest in their future by praying for their future spouse. Just as you pray for your children, your grandchildren, or great grandchildren, you can pray for their future spouse.

What specifically would you pray for? Commit to pray for their salvation. Pray that their future spouse would come to a saving knowledge of Jesus Christ. Ask God to reveal His love to them and to bring them to the place of recognizing their need for salvation. Ask God to bring godly people into their path to help point them to Christ.

You can also pray for their spiritual maturity. Ask God to give them vibrant godly examples to follow. Ask God to steer them to environments that are Christ exalting. Praying for your children's future spouse is a tangible way for you to participate in your children's future.

Think about the value of looking into the eyes of your children's future spouse and being able to say to them, "I've been praying for you since you were a child." Can you imagine the impact that will have on their lives? Your prayer life is important, not only to your own future, but also to your children's future.

September 23
FLOURISHING IN GOD'S HOUSE

"But I am like an olive tree flourishing in the house of God; I trust in God's unfailing love for ever and ever. I will praise you forever for what you have done; in your name I will hope, for your name is good. I will praise you in the presence of your saints." Psalm 52:8-9 (NIV)

Are you flourishing in this life? Are you connected to the source of life and peace? The abundant Christian life is lived from the inside out. You start with your inner life, the private world of your love relationship with the Lord. You are the house of God. You are the temple of the Holy Spirit (1 Cor. 6:19-20). Are you nurturing the life of Christ in you?

You flourish in the house of God when you trust in God's unfailing love. God's love is not conditioned by your response. God's love is not extended to you based on your performance. There is nothing you can do to cause God to love you any more and there is nothing you can do to cause God to love you any less. God's love for you is unfailing and unchanging.

You flourish in the house of God when you praise God for what He has done. Gratitude is the attitude of the child of God. Being grateful for the activity of God in your life is demonstrated through your vertical recognition of God's faithfulness. Begin praising God now for His wonderful acts of compassion and tenderness.

When you hope in His name, you flourish in the house of God. "Some trust in chariots and some in horses, but we trust in the name of the LORD our God" (Psalm 20:7 NIV). Be careful where you land your trust. Anchor your faith to the Master of the sea. Fasten your faith to the Rock of Ages!

September 24
PACING YOURSELF THROUGH PRAYER

"I spread out my hands to you; my soul thirsts for you like a parched land."
Psalm 143:6 (NIV)

One of my mentors, Dr. Adrian Rogers, who is now in heaven, taught me how to PACE myself for each new day. Using the acrostic PACE, I lift my hands each morning and pray, "Lord, I PRAISE You! I accept Your ACCEPTANCE of me! I surrender to Your CONTROL! I EXPECT great things to happen today!"

When you pray, your physical posture can intensify your focus. When you spread out your hands toward heaven, you are demonstrating through your physical posture an attitude of total surrender. You are expressing your dependence upon God and upon His daily provision. You are acknowledging His abundance and your desperation.

Does your soul thirst for God? Have you ever gone through a dry season spiritually? Jesus is the Bread of Life and He provides Living Water for your soul. Jesus is your Shepherd and He restores your soul (Ps. 23:3). As you put your trust in God, He will show you the way you should go (Ps. 143:8).

- *"As the deer pants for streams of water, so my soul pants for you, O God."* Psalm 42:1 (NIV)
- *"Jesus answered, 'Everyone who drinks this water will be thirsty again, but whoever drinks the water I give him will never thirst. Indeed, the water I give him will become in him a spring of water welling up to eternal life.'"* John 4:13-14 (NIV)

Commit to PACE yourself each day. Consider lifting your hands toward heaven as you praise God, as you accept His acceptance of you, as you surrender to His control, and as you expect great things to happen today. God loves you and God is for you! Express your love to Him. PACE yourself through prayer!

September 25
RELEASING ANXIETY

"Humble yourselves, therefore, under God's mighty hand, that he may lift you up in due time. Cast all your anxiety on him because he cares for you." 1 Peter 5:6-7 (NIV)

Is it hard for you to admit when you are anxious about something? Does your pride keep you from acknowledging your anxious thoughts? That's why humility is a vital component to receiving God's comfort. When you humble yourself, you take the initiative to present yourself before God in a proper attitude. In humility, you recognize your dependency upon God.

Living in a fallen world generates anxiety. The uncertainty of the economy fosters an environment of anxiety. The presence of competing agendas creates tension which gives birth to worry.

- *"Therefore do not worry about tomorrow, for tomorrow will worry about itself. Each day has enough trouble of its own." Matt 6:34 (NIV)*
- *"Do not be anxious about anything, but in everything, by prayer and petition, with thanksgiving, present your requests to God." Phil 4:6 (NIV)*

Choose to bring your burdens to the Lord. What are you worrying about? What consumes your thoughts? What is keeping you up at night? Bring every apprehension to the Lord because He cares for you. Receive His compassion and enjoy His comfort.

As you humble yourself before the Lord, He will lift you up. Take off the spirit of heaviness and put on the garment of praise (Is. 61:3). Release every anxious thought and renew your mind with God's Word.

September 26
PERPETUAL INTERCESSION

"In the same way, the Spirit helps us in our weakness. We do not know what we ought to pray for, but the Spirit himself intercedes for us with groans that words cannot express. And he who searches our hearts knows the mind of the Spirit, because the Spirit intercedes for the saints in accordance with God's will."
Romans 8:26-27 (NIV)

Prayer is our privilege and responsibility of engaging in sacred communication with the Creator of the universe. The completed work on the cross has given us access. We can share our heart with God through prayer and deepen our love relationship with Him. Prayer is the avenue through which we maintain a vibrant connection with the One who created us and redeemed us.

Doing life in the rugged terrain of a fallen world often emphasizes our weaknesses and our human frailty. We are susceptible to fear, despair, and apathy. In those times of weakness, the Holy Spirit helps us. The Person of the Holy Spirit lives in us and knows us intimately. He engages in the ministry of intercessory prayer on our behalf.

Have you ever been in a season in which you did not know what to pray? Perhaps you would say that you are in that season now. Be assured that the Holy Spirit living in you is interceding for you in alignment with God's will. Your name and your circumstances are being brought before the Creator of the universe. The Holy Spirit is your constant Companion. He will comfort you. He will guide you. Even when you don't know what to pray for, the Holy Spirit takes your burdens to the Lord through intercession.

September 27
SOLVED MYSTERY

"To them God has chosen to make known among the Gentiles the glorious riches of this mystery, which is Christ in you, the hope of glory." Col 1:27 (NIV)

Is He in you? Do you have Christ living in you? God has unveiled the mystery. You can have Christ in you, the hope of glory. You were alienated from God without Christ and without hope. God chose to make Himself known to you so that you could have union with Christ. By His grace, God has made you fit for habitation by the Spirit of Christ.

- *"Therefore, since we have been justified through faith, we have peace with God through our Lord Jesus Christ, through whom we have gained access by faith into this grace in which we now stand. And we rejoice in the hope of the glory of God." Romans 5:1-2 (NIV)*
- *"You, however, are controlled not by the sinful nature but by the Spirit, if the Spirit of God lives in you. And if anyone does not have the Spirit of Christ, he does not belong to Christ. But if Christ is in you, your body is dead because of sin, yet your spirit is alive because of righteousness." Romans 8:9-10 (NIV)*

In Christ, you are dead to sin, but alive to righteousness. You have been justified through faith. In Christ, you have peace with God. Rejoice in the reality of Christ residing in you. The hope of glory is living in you.

What if your friends and acquaintances had Christ in them? What if those in your workplace or on your campus had Christ in them? Can you imagine the entire population of every continent having Christ in them? Let's be intentional about helping others have the opportunity to experience Christ in them, the hope of glory.

September 28
REFUGE FOR YOUR SOUL

"Have mercy on me, O God, have mercy on me, for in you my soul takes refuge. I will take refuge in the shadow of your wings until the disaster has passed."
Psalm 57:1 (NIV)

Where do you turn when you need refuge? The world offers many choices. You can lose yourself in the stream of entertainment. You can anesthetize your pain with busyness. You can dive into your work and allow your energy to be consumed by that pursuit. Another option is to embrace worldliness and allow the current of the culture to take you places you haven't been.

The only choice that delivers on the promise is the choice to turn to God. When you call out to God, the response is that of mercy. God does not give us what we, in our sin, truly deserve. God lavishes us with His love and provides us with His peace. His mercy is evidenced as your soul takes refuge in Him.

What disaster has come your way? Take refuge in the shadow of His wings. Whenever you go through a season of uncertainty, take refuge in God. When the path is unclear, take refuge in your merciful God. As you wait for the answer to your prayers, take refuge in the God who hears and responds. The enemy will not thwart God's will. Nothing will separate you from the love of God.

As you take refuge in the Lord, thank Him for being merciful in your past, your present, and your future. Give God glory for His consistent measure of comfort during your seasons of desperation. Rely upon God's provision to see you through. God will make a way when there seems to be no way. He is the waymaker!

September 29
Having a Song to Sing

"The LORD is my strength and my song; he has become my salvation." Psalm 118:14 (NIV)

When you contemplate the depth of God's love demonstrated in your salvation, it will create in you a song to sing. When you think about what God has saved you from, it will produce in you a song to sing. God has saved you from hell and for heaven. God has saved you from your sin and for His righteousness. God has saved you from darkness and for the kingdom of light.

The Lord is your salvation. The Lord is your song. Draw strength from Him in your moment of despair. Cling to the Lord and employ His strength for the journey of life. Whenever you are navigating troubled waters, rely on His strength. Whenever your faith is being tested, remember that He is your strength.

- *"God is our refuge and strength, an ever-present help in trouble."* Psalm 46:1 (NIV)
- *"I lift up my eyes to the hills--where does my help come from? My help comes from the LORD, the Maker of heaven and earth."* Psalm 121:1-2 (NIV)

Present your needs before the Lord in prayer. Consider writing down the specific burdens you are bearing. As you pray over each item, begin to claim the promises of God in these verses above. Claim the Lord's strength over every situation. Affirm God's ever-present help in your time of trouble. Remember that God can handle every situation that comes your way. He is the Maker of heaven and earth. There's nothing beyond the scope of God's power. There's nothing beyond the reach of God's Hand. You can know His strength, even in your weakest moment.

September 30
SEEKING GOD

"I seek you with all my heart; do not let me stray from your commands. I have hidden your word in my heart that I might not sin against you." Psalm 119:10-11 (NIV)

What guides your decision making process? What is your moral compass? How do you know if your decisions line up with God's will? As you seek the Lord with all your heart, He will make His will known to you. God is a God of revelation. His desire is for you to know Him personally and to obey Him instantly. Passionately pursue God's agenda. Focus your life on accomplishing His will. Practice moment-by-moment surrender to His Lordship and respond to His prompting.

God has given you His Word. As you read and feed on the Bible, God will unveil His will. You will discover what God loves and what God hates. You will begin to discern what God has for you to join Him in. God invites you to join Him in His activity so that you can experience His love and benefit His kingdom.

Choose to meditate upon God's Word. Read through a few chapters of the Bible and slow down on the verses that speak into your life. Ask God to illuminate His Word as you read. Meditate on what you sense God is saying to you and then apply that truth in practical living. Obey what God shows you.

Seek the Lord with all your heart and demonstrate obedience as you hide God's Word in your heart. Internalize God's Word so that you can live a life of instant obedience. Hide God's Word in your heart and embrace a lifestyle of moral purity. God's way is always the best way!

October 1
LEVELS OF INTIMACY

"Build an altar of acacia wood, three cubits high; it is to be square, five cubits long and five cubits wide. Make a horn at each of the four corners, so that the horns and the altar are of one piece, and overlay the altar with bronze." Ex. 27:1-2 (NIV)

When you think about relationships, there are different levels of intimacy. Some relationships are emotionally distant and surfaced whereas some relationships have the capacity to be more consistent and feature an element of closeness. Then there are those relationships where the interaction is meaningful, transparent, and magnetic.

The Encarta Dictionary defines the word intimacy as a close personal relationship; a detailed knowledge resulting from a close or long association. One of my favorite definitions of intimacy is: "in to me you see."

God desires intimacy with you. In the Old Testament, the portrait of intimacy was the formation and utilization of the Tabernacle. God made a way for His people to experience intimacy with Him through a religious relationship.

As you enter the Tabernacle, the first item you encounter is the altar of burnt offering. The New Testament equivalent is the cross of Jesus Christ. Jesus became the ultimate sacrifice for your sin. As you pray through the Tabernacle, spend some time at the "altar of burnt offering" to praise God for His ultimate love gift and for Jesus being willing to pay the penalty for your sin.

October 2
BRINGING GLORY TO GOD

"After Jesus said this, he looked toward heaven and prayed: 'Father, the time has come. Glorify your Son, that your Son may glorify you.'" John 17:1 (NIV)

Jesus values bringing glory to God.

There are 650 prayers in the Bible and the Gospels record nineteen occasions upon which Jesus prayed. The longest prayer we have of Jesus is found in the twenty-six verses of John 17. Jesus prays for Himself, He prays for the Disciples, and then He prays for future followers, which includes us.

You can discover what is important to people by listening to their prayers. The Disciples had the privilege of overhearing this prayer of Jesus while they were in the Upper Room. As Jesus prayed to His Father in heaven, He requested to be glorified by God so that He in turn could bring glory to God.

As you study the life of Christ in the Gospels, you will discover that Jesus oriented His life around the focus of bringing glory to God. Everything Jesus said and everything Jesus did was to bring glory to God. His message, His miracles, and His personal touch ministry were featured to bring glory to God.

What do you value? What have you been praying? Your prayers indicate what you value. Do you value bringing glory to God? Eliminate motives that are contrary to God's heart. Eradicate the corrosive attitudes that dishonor the Lord. Bring your life to the place of living to bring glory to God. God deserves all of the glory for what He has rescued you from and saved you for.

October 3
REACHING LOST PEOPLE

"For you granted him authority over all people that he might give eternal life to all those you have given him. Now this is eternal life: that they may know you, the only true God, and Jesus Christ, whom you have sent." John 17:2-3 (NIV)

Jesus values reaching lost people.

As Jesus was praying in the Upper Room, the Disciples had the privilege of overhearing the sacred communication. Jesus identified the authority He had been given to give eternal life. Then Jesus defined eternal life as that of knowing God and knowing the One whom God had sent.

Jesus came to seek and to save the lost (Lk 19:10). His mission was to bring salvation to fallen humanity. The entirety of Jesus' life and ministry was centered upon reconciling the world to God. Jesus provided eternal life through His atoning work on the cross.

- *"'Whoever believes in the Son has eternal life, but whoever rejects the Son will not see life, for God's wrath remains on him.'" John 3:36 (NIV)*
- *"And this is the testimony: God has given us eternal life, and this life is in his Son. He who has the Son has life; he who does not have the Son of God does not have life." 1 John 5:11-12 (NIV)*

Do you place the same value on reaching lost people that Jesus did in His earthly ministry? If His life was focused upon bringing people into the kingdom of light, shouldn't that be our mission? Decide to view people through the eyes of Jesus. He established our value and their value on the cross. The price Jesus paid for the penalty and removal of our sins is far too much to calculate. If you ever wonder how much Jesus values reaching lost people, just look to the cross.

October 4
COMPLETING GOD'S MISSION

"I have brought you glory on earth by completing the work you gave me to do."
John 17:4 (NIV)

Jesus values completing God's mission.

How do you bring glory to God? By doing God's work God's way! Jesus brought glory to God by fulfilling God's mission God's way. Jesus was sensitive to the activity of God. Jesus recognized that God was always at work (John 5:17) and that God's invitation to join in would require faith and obedience. Jesus completed the work God gave Him to do.

- *"'My food,' said Jesus, 'is to do the will of him who sent me and to finish his work.'" John 4:34 (NIV)*
- *"'For the very work that the Father has given me to finish, and which I am doing, testifies that the Father has sent me.'" John 5:36 (NIV)*

What has God given you to do? God has a mission for you to fulfill. Do not bypass your love relationship with God in Christ. Being on mission with God will flow out of that abiding relationship you have with Jesus. Stay connected to Jesus through daily nurturing your love relationship through prayer and Bible study.

Seize opportunities to spread the fragrance of Christ. Doing God's work God's way will flow out of being intimately connected to Christ. As you spend uninterrupted time alone with the Lord in solitude, you will hear His voice speaking to you through your Bible reading and prayer time. Focus on being. Focus on becoming the man or woman of God that you were created to be. Draw near to the heart of God and allow Him to reveal His specific plan for your life as you do His work His way in His timing. Start by saying, "Speak, Lord, your servant is listening!"

October 5
LIVING FOR HEAVEN

"And now, Father, glorify me in your presence with the glory I had with you before the world began." John 17:5 (NIV)

Jesus valued returning to heaven.

The Priestly prayer of Jesus in John 17 demonstrated His passion to return to heaven to be glorified in His Father's presence. Jesus served, preached, healed, and prayed with heaven in view. In His pre-existence, Jesus was involved in creation of man. In His incarnation, Jesus provided redemption for fallen man.

- *"Then God said, 'Let us make man in our image, in our likeness, and let them rule over the fish of the sea and the birds of the air, over the livestock, over all the earth, and over all the creatures that move along the ground.'" Gen 1:26 (NIV)*
- *"Your attitude should be the same as that of Christ Jesus: Who, being in very nature God, did not consider equality with God something to be grasped, but made himself nothing, taking the very nature of a servant, being made in human likeness." Phil 2:5-7 (NIV)*

Jesus was willing to leave the glory of heaven in order to become the only appropriate sacrifice for your sin. He endured the agony of the cross to benefit your forever. Once you come to faith in the completed work of Jesus, your life is transformed, your sins are forgiven, and your body becomes the temple of the Holy Spirit. Your name is written in the Lamb's book of life.

Are you ready for heaven? Have you made your reservation by grace alone through faith alone? Jesus has made heaven and eternal life available to all who trust in Him alone for salvation. Once you have solidified your eternal transaction, invest the rest of your life helping others come to faith in Christ.

October 6
COVERED IN PRAYER

"Therefore he is able to save completely those who come to God through him, because he always lives to intercede for them." Heb 7:25 (NIV)

Jesus values intercessory prayer.

You are covered in prayer. There is One who lives to intercede for you. Jesus became like you so that you could become like Him. He knows what you wrestle with. He has experienced your fears and frustrations. Jesus was tempted just as you are, yet without sin (Heb. 4:15). He endured the agony of the cross on your behalf. He took away your sin and imputed His righteousness. Jesus gave you a new name and a new nature to bring glory to God.

The ministry of reconciliation Jesus fulfilled in you has now become your assignment. As you seek to extend the ministry of reconciliation to others, Jesus is fulfilling His ministry of intercession for you. As you serve Him by serving others, Jesus is serving you by interceding for you.

Can you fathom the Son of God and the Savior of the world being that invested in you and that interested in you to level of praying for you perpetually? You are His treasure and valued possession. You are the apple of His eye. Not only did Jesus sacrifice His life for you, but also He now lives to bring your needs before our Heavenly Father. Jesus prays for you based on His all-sufficient knowledge of your circumstances, your dreams, and your obstacles. Jesus prays for you with the full knowledge of God's will for your life.

Jesus completely saved you. Jesus will completely keep you. Cast your cares upon Him. Release your fear to Him. Submit your lips and your life to His control. Rest in His intercession. Walk in the Spirit today and remember that you are covered in prayer.

October 7
GOD IS WORKING

"And we know that in all things God works for the good of those who love him, who have been called according to his purpose." Romans 8:28 (NIV)

God is working in all things for your good and His glory. Nothing can thwart God's will and nothing can circumvent His provision. God is still on His throne and has the final say on every action and interaction. Nothing happens without God's permission. If God allows something to come into your life, He will use it. If God permits it, He will use it.

- *"You intended to harm me, but God intended it for good to accomplish what is now being done, the saving of many lives."* Gen 50:20 (NIV)
- *"For I know that through your prayers and the help given by the Spirit of Jesus Christ, what has happened to me will turn out for my deliverance."* Phil 1:19 (NIV)

Do you love God? Are you called according to His purpose? Then know that God is working in and through your circumstances to accomplish His plan. You may not know what tomorrow holds, but you can know who holds tomorrow. You may not be able to see clearly in your present situation, but God will enable the fog to lift and His path for you will become evident.

Trust in God's perfect timing. He will see you through your dilemma. Your faith will be strengthened. Your experience of God's presence and peace will be elevated. You will come to know God at a deeper level as you walk with Him through your pain. He will provide comfort. God will redeem your pain.

October 8
BECOMING LIKE CHRIST

"For those God foreknew he also predestined to be conformed to the likeness of his Son, that he might be the firstborn among many brothers." Romans 8:29 (NIV)

God saved you to become like Christ. Your sin has been forgiven and your eternal destiny has been secured. In Christ, you are adopted into God's family and sealed by the Holy Spirit. Now you are in the process of becoming who you are in Christ. God predestined that you be conformed to the image of Christ. You get to participate in the process of that transformation.

What are some of the tools God uses to conform us to the likeness of Christ? Sometimes God uses the hammer of adversity and the chisel of suffering to bring us into conformity with the character of Christ. Other times, God may use seasons of silence to test our faith and to prove our devotion. God allows fully yielded and fully devoted followers of Christ to come into our path to model Christ likeness. They give us a portrait of what we can become as we mature in our faith.

Assess your current reality? How is God conforming you to the likeness of Christ? Are you being responsive to His prompting? Allow God to chip off anything in your life that does not bring honor to Christ. Invite the Holy Spirit to reveal any area of your life that distracts from your spiritual progress. Daily surrender to the Lordship of Christ and seek His face in prayer. Embrace the reality of God's will. God desires that you become more and more like Christ each day.

October 9
A PERSONAL QUESTION

"One who was there had been an invalid for thirty-eight years. When Jesus saw him lying there and learned that he had been in this condition for a long time, he asked him, 'Do you want to get well?'" John 5:5-6 (NIV)

We know more than we are doing. We know that we are to eat right, exercise, and get plenty of rest in order to be healthy. We know that we are to give, save, pay bills, and pay taxes. We know that we are to make the most of every moment that God gives us. We know that we are to forgive others, to love others, to pray for others, to be considerate of others, and to serve others. Yet, we don't always do the things we know we are supposed to do.

Jesus asked a thirty-eight year old invalid if he wanted to get well. That question seems out of place. Why wouldn't a lame man want to walk? What would keep a person from wanting to experience healing? It is a matter of want. If you had the "want to" then you would find a "way to" be healed.

Sometimes we can become comfortable with our misery. The question is, "Do you want to get well?" Do you want to continue living like you are living? Do you want to continue to operate in your current reality?

Jesus is the answer to your situation. Are you obeying what you know? Have you responded to what He has already revealed to you?

October 10
CONSIDERING CONTENTMENT

"I am not saying this because I am in need, for I have learned to be content whatever the circumstances. I know what it is to be in need, and I know what it is to have plenty. I have learned the secret of being content in any and every situation, whether well fed or hungry, whether living in plenty or in want." Phil 4:11-12 (NIV)

What are you waiting for? Will it ever be enough? If you have to move one inch to have joy, you will not find it. Happiness is based on happenstance. If the conditions are just right, then you may be happy for a season. However, joy is not connected to circumstances. Joy is the product of living a life of contentment founded upon your relationship with Christ.

Paul experienced the palace and the prison. He knew what it meant to live with much and to live on very little. Paul had experienced popularity and persecution. He knew suffering on a first name basis. Yet, in the midst of shifting circumstances, Paul learned the secret of being content. He did not allow the external realities to rob him of the internal relationship he had with Jesus. Paul had surrendered his life to the Lordship of Christ and yielded to the prompting of the Holy Spirit. Paul's contentment was demonstrated through the experience of peace in the midst of the storms of life.

What is your level of contentment? Have you learned the secret of being content in any and every situation? Are you waiting for ideal circumstances to develop? Are you postponing your joy until a future accomplishment comes to fruition? Don't hesitate! Don't delay your decision to embrace contentment. Stop worrying and fretting over the things you have no control over. Rest in the peace of God and the all-sufficient provision of God.

October 11
KEEPING THE FAITH

"I have fought the good fight, I have finished the race, I have kept the faith. Now there is in store for me the crown of righteousness, which the Lord, the righteous Judge, will award to me on that day--and not only to me, but also to all who have longed for his appearing." 2 Tim 4:7-8 (NIV)

This verse comes to life when you bury someone close to you. There's something about funerals that remind us of the brevity of life and the reality of heaven. Maybe it causes us to move closer to the reality of our mortality. The pace of life on earth can sometimes numb our emotions and keep us from dealing with life beyond the grave. Seeing your loved one in a casket is a stark reminder that we are one breath away from eternity.

Paul was at the end of his life and wrote a final letter to his son in the ministry, Timothy. Paul had truly fought the good fight. Paul had finished the race and kept the faith. He finished strong! Paul reminded Timothy of the crown of righteousness that Jesus would be awarding at the finish line.

Think about your life. How are you doing? When you look into the review mirror of life, do you have any regrets? Remember, it's not how you start; it's how you finish that matters most! Fight the good fight of the faith. Yes! It is a fight because we are in a spiritual battle that has eternal implications.

- *"Timothy, my son, I give you this instruction in keeping with the prophecies once made about you, so that by following them you may fight the good fight, holding on to faith and a good conscience. Some have rejected these and so have shipwrecked their faith." 1 Tim 1:18-19 (NIV)*
- *"Fight the good fight of the faith. Take hold of the eternal life to which you were called when you made your good confession in the presence of many witnesses." 1 Tim 6:12 (NIV)*

Your life has eternity written all over it. Finish strong!

October 12
COURAGE AND STRENGTH FOR THE JOURNEY

"Be strong and courageous, because you will lead these people to inherit the land I swore to their forefathers to give them. Be strong and very courageous. Be careful to obey all the law my servant Moses gave you; do not turn from it to the right or to the left, that you may be successful wherever you go." Josh 1:6-7 (NIV)

Joshua had the privilege of serving under Moses during the wilderness wanderings. Joshua reaped the benefit of seeing his leader in action responding to challenges and seizing opportunities. Moses died and Joshua became God's chosen leader. It was time for Joshua to rise to the occasion and lead the children of Israel to inherit the Promised Land.

God reassured Joshua that He would be with him just as He was with Moses. God affirmed Joshua and gave him the timely message to be strong and courageous. Obedience to God's law was vital for bringing honor to God and for being successful in the journey ahead.

Do you enjoy that kind of relationship with God where you draw daily from God's Word? Do you have a growing relationship with the Lord that enables you to conduct your life with the strength and courage God provides? God will be with you just as He was with Joshua and just as He was with Moses. You are chosen by God to bear His image and to bring His salvation message to the masses. Your life belongs to God for His use and for His glory.

Do you sense God leading you to do something that will require His strength? Are you anticipating an adventure with the Lord that will require being courageous? We are in a spiritual battle, which demands spiritual power to walk in victory.

October 13
PREPARATION FOR GOD'S DEMONSTRATION

"Joshua told the people, 'Consecrate yourselves, for tomorrow the LORD will do amazing things among you.'" Josh 3:5 (NIV)

Have you experienced the thrill of anticipation? When you are anticipating something special, it seems as though time stands still. You live with a sense of urgency and you embrace a sense of expectancy.

Joshua knew that God was up to something special that included his participation and preparation. It was vital for Joshua to have the people consecrate themselves in preparation for what God was going to do in their midst. They were to set themselves apart for God's use. Their sin was to be confessed, their relational strife was to be released, and their motives were to be pure. God wanted the children of Israel to prepare for a demonstration of His power. Joshua declared that the Lord would do amazing things among them.

Are you prepared for a move of God in your life? Have you consecrated yourself before the Lord? Have you confessed known sin and received God's forgiveness? Make sure that your motives are pure and that your focus is on God. God wants to do amazing things among you. However, God wants you to prepare for the demonstration of His power.

Prepare for your daily time alone with God through intensive soul-searching prayer. Invite the Holy Spirit to search your heart and to reveal anything in you that is displeasing to God. Ask Him to reveal any attitudes that are inconsistent with the character of Christ. Ask Him to show you areas of your life that have not been submitted to the Lordship of Christ. Stay close and clean as you walk with God and anticipate His redemptive activity.

October 14
NAVIGATING OBSTACLES

"So when the people broke camp to cross the Jordan, the priests carrying the ark of the covenant went ahead of them." Josh 3:14 (NIV)

Joshua came face to face with an obstacle that prevented entry into the Promised Land. He was in charge of mobilizing the children of Israel to inherit the land flowing with milk and honey. The Jordan River was the obstacle, which became an opportunity for God to do something great to reveal His glory.

We serve a great God who can take any obstacle and turn it into an opportunity for us to experience His power and for us to know His provision. Everyone has a Jordan. We all encounter obstacles along the path of life on this broken planet. Living in a fallen world ensures our confrontation with obstacles.

The challenge is not facing obstacles, but responding to the obstacles we face. Is it possible to turn an obstacle into an opportunity? Is it possible to navigate obstacles and be in the center of God's will? Some of the most meaningful experiences with God are those in which you feel like you are in the fourth quarter with only a few seconds left and God comes through for you.

The priests carrying the ark went ahead of the people in order to confront the obstacle. The Jordan River did not stand a chance on sabotaging God's agenda. God will make a way when there seems to be no way. God will give you just what you need in the moment of your need. God will not leave you hanging. God will not abandon you.

Identify your Jordan. What is keeping you from entering the land flowing with milk and honey? What is keeping you from operating in the center of God's will?

October 15
GOING ANKLE DEEP

"Now the Jordan is at flood stage all during harvest. Yet as soon as the priests who carried the ark reached the Jordan and their feet touched the water's edge, the water from upstream stopped flowing. It piled up in a heap a great distance away, at a town called Adam in the vicinity of Zarethan, while the water flowing down to the Sea of the Arabah (the Salt Sea) was completely cut off. So the people crossed over opposite Jericho." Josh 3:15-16 (NIV)

Get your feet wet and go with God. God invites you to join Him in His activity. Look to see where God is at work and seek to join Him. Sometimes God may ask you to do something that just doesn't make sense at the time. Can you imagine how the priests felt as they carried the Ark of the Covenant to the water's edge? They were willing to get their feet wet in order to go with God. They were willing to take God at His word and watch God demonstrate His power.

As they went ankle deep, the priests carrying the ark noticed the waters of the Jordan River parting. God worked a miracle in their midst. Did God need them to go ankle deep in order to perform His miracle? Of course not! God could have parted the waters without their participation. However, God delights in involving His children in His plans. God is moved when we move into position to obey Him and to trust Him with our lives.

Once you choose to do your part in God's plan, you will notice how God does His part to fulfill His plan. God involves you in the process so that you can experience His presence and to enable you to know his heart.

October 16
SPIRITUAL MARKERS

"So Joshua called together the twelve men he had appointed from the Israelites, one from each tribe, and said to them, 'Go over before the ark of the LORD your God into the middle of the Jordan. Each of you is to take up a stone on his shoulder, according to the number of the tribes of the Israelites, to serve as a sign among you. In the future, when your children ask you, "What do these stones mean?" tell them that the flow of the Jordan was cut off before the ark of the covenant of the LORD. When it crossed the Jordan, the waters of the Jordan were cut off. These stones are to be a memorial to the people of Israel forever.'"
Josh 4:4-7 (NIV)

Don't miss what God is up to in your life. Don't forget what God has done to bring you to the place where you are right now. Take note of all the difficulties God has brought you through. Recognize all the mountaintop experiences God has lavished on you in your lifetime.

Joshua wanted to solidify the crossing of the Jordan River as a spiritual marker for all of Israel. He wanted to ensure that future generations would know what God had done to bring about deliverance to the people of God. Joshua utilized the twelve stones, which were selected from the middle of the Jordan to serve as a memorial.

Solidify your spiritual markers. Think through the activity of God in your life. When did you come to a saving knowledge of Jesus Christ? When did you follow the Lord in believer's baptism? Where were you when God revealed Himself to you during a season of adversity? Identify some God-moments you have experienced in the journey of life. Slow down long enough to pray through those spiritual markers. You may want to list them out specifically so that you can thank God for each one.

October 17
Continuing the Faith Journey

"And the priests came up out of the river carrying the ark of the covenant of the LORD. No sooner had they set their feet on the dry ground than the waters of the Jordan returned to their place and ran at flood stage as before." Josh 4:18 (NIV)

The Christian life is a life of faith. To be a fully devoted follower of Christ, your life with be marked by a journey of faith. Faith is taking God at His Word and entrusting your life to His care. As you walk in daily dependency upon the Lord, you will discover the joy of seeing God at work and seizing opportunities to join God in His activity.

Crossing the Jordan River on dry ground was a tremendous experience of faith for the priests carrying the ark. They remained in the middle of the river while the children of Israel passed through on dry ground. Once the priests came up out of the river carrying the Ark of the Covenant, the waters of the Jordan returned to their place. God had worked a miracle and involved the people in the process!

Continue to walk in faith. Sometimes your journey will be as clear as crystal, but at other times the way may appear foggy. You will experience seasons of high spiritual energy and focus and at other times, you will experience seasons of uncertainty. That's part of the faith journey! The scenery changes and the pace shifts from time to time.

Don't get so fixated on the destination that you miss the God-moments along the way. Enjoy the process of knowing and obeying God. Enjoy the journey. God has some Jordan's for you to cross. He will turn your obstacles into opportunities for you to see His glory and for your faith to be exercised. Obey what you know!

October 18
Living God's Way

"As for God, his way is perfect; the word of the LORD is flawless. He is a shield for all who take refuge in him." Psalm 18:30 (NIV)

God's way is always the best option. Making decisions is a perpetual necessity in this life. You have the freedom to choose to follow God's way or to reject God's way. You have the freedom to honor God or to dishonor God. As you make decisions each day, remember that God's way is always the best way. Why? Because God's way is perfect. God created you for His glory. God made you and He has a plan for your life that involves deciding to go His way.

How do you find God's way? Fortunately, God has given you His roadmap, namely, the Bible. God's Word is flawless. His Word will never lead you down a path that brings dishonor to His name. God's Word unveils God's will for your life. The beauty of the Christian life is that God invites you into a journey of discovery. In relationship, God enables you to know Him personally and to walk with Him progressively. As you obey God's Word, He entrusts you with more.

Living God's way is a threat to the devil. However, you can take refuge in the Lord for He is your shield. God will protect you from the flaming arrows of the evil one. God will give you everything you need to walk in victory. Instead of trying to live the Christian life in your own strength and fight the spiritual battles in your own power, choose to take refuge in the Lord. Let Him become your shield.

October 19
BENEFIT OTHERS

"I rejoice greatly in the Lord that at last you have renewed your concern for me. Indeed, you have been concerned, but you had no opportunity to show it."
Phil 4:10 (NIV)

God chooses to use people to help us. The Christian life is not a solo flight. God saved us to live in union with Christ and in community with other believers. We need each other. We do better together. As a result of being adopted into God's family, we are to communicate and collaborate as fellow followers of Christ. In Christ, we are family!

Paul was imprisoned in Rome when he wrote this personal letter to the church at Philippi. He had a deep abiding love for them and wanted to encourage them in their faith. Paul identified their willingness to put their compassion into action. They sent their gifts to Paul via Epaphroditus (Php. 4:18). Paul acknowledged their gift as a fragrant offering pleasing to God.

Spend a moment thanking God in prayer for the people He has placed in your life over the years to be a blessing to you. Think about the individuals God used to encourage you on your faith journey. You may even want to write a letter or type an email to someone God has used to elevate your faith. People matter to God and He delights in bringing people into our lives to bring us closer to Christ.

Are you available for God's use? Would you be willing to be used of God to encourage someone today? Would you be willing to be used of God to model Christ before a watching world? Remember that God blesses you so that you can be a blessing to others. Who will benefit from your life today?

October 20
UNIVERSITY OF ADVERSITY

"I am not saying this because I am in need, for I have learned to be content whatever the circumstances. I know what it is to be in need, and I know what it is to have plenty. I have learned the secret of being content in any and every situation, whether well fed or hungry, whether living in plenty or in want."
Phil 4:11-12 (NIV)

Paul had experienced life in the palace and in the prison. He knew the extremes of life whether spending a night and a day in the open sea (2 Cor 11:25) or being shown unusual kindness by the islanders on Malta (Acts 28:2). The erratic conditions of life where no match for Paul in that he learned the secret of being content. Circumstances did not dictate Paul's level of joy and peace.

The process God uses to develop us includes the varying conditions we experience on this broken planet. The fallen world we abide in provides us with a fitness center of equipment to build our spiritual muscles and to stretch our faith. God does not waste the resistance we face in this life. In fact, without resistance, there is no growth.

Paul lived with the tension of straining and pressing (Php 3:13-14) in collaboration with the tranquility of contentment. We are to forget what is behind and strain toward what is ahead. We are to press on toward the goal for which Christ took hold of us.

Contentment is best learned in the university of adversity. You learn contentment on the playing field of life. Experiencing real life in the real world of adversity will bring you to the place of learning to be content in any and every situation. If you have to move one inch to find contentment, you will never find it. Are you learning the secret of being content?

October 21
FINDING HIS STRENGTH

"I can do everything through him who gives me strength." Phil 4:13 (NIV)

Jesus is the person God uses to empower us. You can do all things through Christ. He is your strength. He is your sustenance. He is your energy. Your relationship with Jesus is the most vital relationship you will ever have. Your love relationship with Christ is the dynamic link to doing God's work, God's way.

Stay connected to Christ through an abiding relationship (John 15:5). Nourish your soul through continuous communication with the One who died sacrificially and rose supernaturally to bring you life abundant and eternal. As you walk with Jesus, you will be able to do what Jesus did. He will empower you to be on mission with God just as He was on mission during His earthly existence.

God created you to continue the ministry of Jesus on the earth. However, you cannot do what Jesus did without the strength He provides. Even on your best day, you are not fit for kingdom work without kingdom power. Your energy level will not suffice for the agenda God has for you to fulfill. To do the supernatural work of God, you will need the supernatural strength Jesus provides.

Through Christ, you can do anything! Through Christ, you will experience the strength to keep you in the center of God's will and to keep you on mission with God. As you obey His Word, Jesus will empower you to touch lives for eternity. Your investment of time and energy in serving the purposes of God in your generation will be rewarded one day. Keep serving! Keep operating in the strength Jesus provides! Fight the good fight, finish the race, and keep the faith (2 Tim. 4:7).

October 22
Expressing Your New Identity

"Since, then, you have been raised with Christ, set your hearts on things above, where Christ is seated at the right hand of God. Set your minds on things above, not on earthly things." Col 3:1-2 (NIV)

When you placed your faith in the completed work of Christ on the cross, your identity changed. You received a new name and a new nature. Your name was written in the Lamb's book of life and you were adopted into God's family. You were raised with Christ. Through faith in Christ, you identified with the death and resurrection of Christ. You became a child of God!

Your new identity in Christ mandates a new expression of your life on this fallen planet. Since you have been raised with Christ, you are to focus your ambition and your drive to things above. You are no longer living for this world and the aptitudes of fallen humanity. Your life is now fixated on the reality of Christ being seated at the right hand of God. The heavenly reality becomes your earthly normality. Set your heart and mind on things above.

The gravitational pull of earthly things will continue to seek to pull your practical living away from your new identity in Christ. The necessity of setting your heart and mind on things above increases as you walk with God in purity and devotion.

Choose to live your life with your heavenly status in mind. You have been saved and set apart to represent Christ on the earth. Jesus is at the right hand of God interceding for you as you continue His ministry upon the earth. Don't compromise your convictions. Don't maneuver into mediocrity. Stay vertical!

October 23
Unleashing the Life of Christ

"For you died, and your life is now hidden with Christ in God. When Christ, who is your life, appears, then you also will appear with him in glory." Col 3:3-4 (NIV)

Dying to self unleashes the life God has for you. Once you die to self and allow Christ to take over your life, the great adventure begins. From the moment of your conversion, your life is hidden with Christ in God. You are no longer your own, you belong to Christ. Because of your profession in faith, you become His possession. When God sees you, He views you through the shed blood of Jesus. You are made holy and fit for eternity.

Christ is your life. Wow! That means that everything around you and everything above you takes second place. Your number one devotion is Christ. You died to self and now Christ lives His life in you and through you to bring glory to God. You are the chosen vessel that God has made holy for the habitation of the Spirit of Christ. You belong to Jesus!

Because Christ is your life, you will appear with Him in glory. One day you will stand before the King! One day you will be rewarded for what you have done with the life God has given you. One day you will give an account to God for what you have done with the time, energy, and resources God provided you with. Every moment of your life matters to God. Make every moment count!

What does the hidden life look like? It looks like Jesus! He must increase and you must decrease. The focus of your life is not to put yourself on display, but to put Christ on display for a watching world to see. You don't have to convince others of the reality of Christ in your life. Just let Christ have His way in your life and His light will shine brightly through your conversation and your conduct.

October 24
STARVING THE SINFUL NATURE

"Put to death, therefore, whatever belongs to your earthly nature: sexual immorality, impurity, lust, evil desires and greed, which is idolatry." Col 3:5 (NIV)

People, power, pleasure, and prestige can become idols. Idolatry is worshipping created things rather than the Creator (Romans 1:25). Anything that comes between you and God is an idol. Idolatry is the sin of the mind against God. The first two commandments of the Ten Commandments confront our propensity to have other gods and to worship idols

God created us for worship. We are created to worship the One true living God. God is seeking the kind of worshipers who worship Him in spirit and truth (Jn 4:23-24). Worship is in our DNA. We will worship! However, we must decide the focus of our worship. We choose who or what we worship.

- *"Therefore, my dear friends, flee from idolatry."* 1 Cor 10:14 (NIV)
- *"Those controlled by the sinful nature cannot please God."* Romans 8:8 (NIV)

We are to mortify that which belongs to our sinful nature. The cravings of our sinful nature seek to pull us back into the lifestyle God delivered us from. Upon salvation, we received the imputed righteousness of Christ. We became a new creation (2 Cor 5:17). Yet, we still live in this body of flesh, which craves sin.

Starve the flesh. Eliminate sexual immorality, impurity, lust, evil desires, and greed. Run from sin and run to Christ. Surrender to the complete control of the Spirit. Yield to the prompting of the Holy Spirit. Do not think about how to gratify the cravings of the sinful nature (Rm 13:14). Confess sin specifically and receive God's forgiveness completely.

October 25
STAYING CLEAN IN A DIRTY WORLD

"But now you must rid yourselves of all such things as these: anger, rage, malice, slander, and filthy language from your lips." Col 3:8 (NIV)

Is it possible to stay clean while living in a dirty world? Every possibility for contaminating our lives is available to us. Sin is rampant. We face trials from without and temptation from within. The cultural current is moving in the opposite direction of the Christ honoring flow. We must make a conscious and continuous decision to walk in purity.

- *"Since we have these promises, dear friends, let us purify ourselves from everything that contaminates body and spirit, perfecting holiness out of reverence for God." 2 Cor 7:1 (NIV)*
- *"Come near to God and he will come near to you. Wash your hands, you sinners, and purify your hearts, you double-minded." James 4:8 (NIV)*

Purify yourself and perfect holiness. Purify your heart and set an example for the believers in purity. In Christ, you are positionally pure. In Christ, you are a new creation. In Christ, you are adopted into God's family. Now live out practically what you are positionally in Christ. The only way to reign in this life is to allow Christ to reign in your life. Submit to His authority in your life. Allow Jesus to live His life through you.

Staying clean while living in a dirty world is only possible in the strength Christ provides. Jesus has already set the example. Jesus has demonstrated the life of purity in a sin-polluted culture. Jesus lived a sinless life and died a sacrificial death so that you can walk in victory.

October 26
LIVING BY THE SPIRIT

"So I say, live by the Spirit, and you will not gratify the desires of the sinful nature. For the sinful nature desires what is contrary to the Spirit, and the Spirit what is contrary to the sinful nature. They are in conflict with each other, so that you do not do what you want." Gal 5:16-17 (NIV)

Every believer is living in two worlds: the world of the Spirit or the world of the sinful nature. Light and darkness abound. They are in conflict with each other. As a result, the believer has to combat the gravitational pull of the sinful nature. At salvation, a believer receives the Holy Spirit and is made fit for heaven. However, the believer retains the sinful nature and must daily crucify the sinful nature with its passions and desires.

Have you been combating the cravings of the flesh? Have you noticed that your sinful nature is addicted to sin? However, you must daily crucify the flesh. "Those who belong to Christ Jesus have crucified the sinful nature with its passions and desires" (Gal 5:24 NIV). In Christ, you must starve the flesh. Whatever you feed grows and whatever you starve dies. Feed the Spirit living in you and starve the cravings of your sinful nature. Do not be a slave to sin. Choose to be a slave to righteousness.

Pray with me: Father, thank You for redeeming me from my sin. You have rescued me from this body of death. You have brought me out of the kingdom of darkness and placed me in the kingdom of Light. Help me to crucify the sinful nature and to live by the Spirit. Enable me to live the Christ-centered life in the power of Your Holy Spirit. Protect me from the flaming arrows of the evil one. Help me to finish strong for Your glory. In Jesus' Name, Amen.

October 27
RETURNING TO YOUR FIRST LOVE

"Yet I hold this against you: You have forsaken your first love. Remember the height from which you have fallen! Repent and do the things you did at first. If you do not repent, I will come to you and remove your lampstand from its place." Rev 2:4-5 (NIV)

The church at Ephesus had a lot going for them. They were strong in deeds, hardworking, and known for their perseverance. They sought purity of doctrine, endured hardship, and served diligently. Yet, they bypassed their love relationship with God. The church had forsaken their first love.

There are so many things vying for your affection and devotion. You can give your life to an endless array of commitments and neglect the most important relationship. It is possible to give a little bit of yourself to everything and have nothing left for the most vital relationship. Keeping you fragmented is one of Satan's goals to keep you from nurturing the life-giving relationship that Christ provides. As long as you are distracted from that which is eternal, Satan knows that your effectiveness in the Kingdom of God will be stifled.

Do you remember when your love relationship with Christ was your top priority? Measure how far you have drifted from that passionate intimate relationship you had with Christ. Repent! Choose to go a new direction by forsaking those things that hinder your love relationship with Christ. Give your full devotion to the One who died sacrificially so that you could live abundantly and eternally. Return to guarding your love relationship with Christ. Give the best of your life each day to the One who deserves first place in your life. Make a standing appointment with the Lord each morning to spend time with Him. Yield your life to the One who gave you life!

October 28
Exhibiting the Character of Christ

"Therefore, as God's chosen people, holy and dearly loved, clothe yourselves with compassion, kindness, humility, gentleness and patience." Col 3:12 (NIV)

What are you displaying for a watching world to see? You are chosen, holy, and dearly loved by God. Display the garments you have been given in Christ. As a child of the Living God, you have a spiritual wardrobe that must be put on each day. God places you in the display window of life to give evidence of the reality of Jesus living His life through you.

Are you exhibiting the character of Christ? Put on the garment of compassion. Let others see your compassion in action. Put on the garment of kindness. Be gracious and kind toward others by placing their needs before your own. Put on the garment of humility. Don't think less of yourself; just think of yourself less. Consider others better than yourself (Php 2:3). Be sure to put on the garment of gentleness. Show the tenderness of Christ as you interact with others today. Are you a patient person? Put on the garment of patience and trust God's timing.

Who you are in Christ on the inside needs to be evident on the outside. As you build meaningful relationships with others, demonstrate the character of Christ. As you navigate the difficult places in life, exhibit the character of Christ. God will use the tests you face in life to help build your testimony. When you are squeezed by the circumstances of life, what is on the inside of you will come out. Clothe yourself with compassion, kindness, humility, gentleness, and patience. Let these garments become the fabric of your life.

October 29
TAKING CARE OF OTHERS

"But a Samaritan, as he traveled, came where the man was; and when he saw him, he took pity on him. He went to him and bandaged his wounds, pouring on oil and wine. Then he put the man on his own donkey, took him to an inn and took care of him." Luke 10:33-34 (NIV)

Hurting people saturate the landscape of life. Living in a fallen world generates pain, suffering, and sorrow. People are shouldering harmful habits, hurts, and hang-ups. Detours and disappointments frequent our daily existence. The reality of living on a broken planet necessitates a deep abiding compassion for others.

The Good Samaritan was willing to see the needs of an unnamed individual and to seize the opportunity to meet his needs. The Good Samaritan was willing to put his compassion in action by getting personally involved in the solution to this wounded man's unfortunate situation. He had been left for dead.

The Priest and the Levite were too preoccupied with themselves to care about someone else in need. If we are not careful, that can be our tendency. We get so caught up in our own lives and consumed with what we want to accomplish in a given day, that we can neglect those God brings into our path. Busyness and selfishness blur our vision to the reality of pressing needs around us. We might even begin seeing people in need as an interruption rather than an opportunity to display the compassion of Christ.

What is keeping you from putting your compassion in action? Have you lost your love for people? Has your heart become numb toward the individuals in need who come across your path? Slow down and allow the compassion of Christ to flow through you to a world in need. Continue the ministry of Jesus on the earth. View others as sheep without a shepherd. You are the shepherd! Go help some sheep!

October 30
RELEASING UNFORGIVENESS

"Bear with each other and forgive whatever grievances you may have against one another. Forgive as the Lord forgave you." Col 3:13 (NIV)

Motion causes friction. Doing life with real people can generate feelings of irritability and agitation. Real people in real life can get on your nerves at times. Our self-absorbed society elevates relational strife. Our proclivity toward selfishness accelerates the relational turmoil.

The Body of Christ is not exempt from relational challenges. Every church family experiences tension, jealousy, and relational drift. We combat the world, the flesh, and the devil. We combat the tendency to turn inward and neglect relationships. Self-preservation prevents us from experiencing the depth of meaningful relationships God has for us.

Perpetual forgiveness and bearing with each other are required for maintaining unity in the Body of Christ. If you have a grievance against someone, release it! If you have been fertilizing a spirit of un-forgiveness, renounce it! Forgive others just as the Lord Jesus has forgiven you.

Don't forget about the forgiveness you have received in your lifetime. Calculate the grace, mercy, and compassion that Christ has lavished on you. Think about where you would be without His abundant forgiveness. Your sin has been placed as far as the east is from the west. Your sin has been placed in the sea of forgetfulness. You are totally forgiven. You have been set free! Now, choose to forgive others as the Lord has chosen to forgive you. Let others experience your forgiveness in the same degree upon which you have experienced the forgiveness of Christ.

In prayer, visit the scene of the cross. Picture for a moment the Lord Jesus on the cross paying the penalty for your sin. Consider the weight of taking on the full wrath of God for your sin. Jesus did that for you. Would you be willing to extend forgiveness to others in response to the forgiveness Jesus extended to you?

October 31
God's Unfailing Love

"May your unfailing love be my comfort, according to your promise to your servant." Psalm 119:76 (NIV)

We are made for love. Loving God, loving people, and being loved by God is our privilege and responsibility. God's love sustains us through seasons of uncertainty. God's love preserves us in the storms of life. The fluctuation of our circumstances cannot disrupt, nor hinder the love of God. Nothing can separate us from God's love (Romans 8:38-39).

God's love is unfailing. God's love does not ebb and flow. The love of God is not conditioned by our performance. God loves us unconditionally. There is nothing we can do to cause God to love us more. There is nothing we can do to cause God to love us any less. God's love is perfect!

- *"The thief comes only to steal and kill and destroy; I have come that they may have life, and have it to the full." John 10:10 (NIV)*
- *"This is love: not that we loved God, but that he loved us and sent his Son as an atoning sacrifice for our sins." 1 John 4:10 (NIV)*

We must combat the enemy and his attempt to distort God's love for us. The enemy cannot attack God, so he attacks God's children. Remember, Jesus came to give us life abundant and complete. Jesus came to enable us to experience God's love personally and eternally. God demonstrated His love for us by sending Jesus to be the atoning sacrifice for our sin.

Receive comfort today through God's unfailing love. Even when you fail, God's love never fails. God will love you through your pain. God will love you through your valley and mountaintop experiences. God will love you when you have nothing to give and when your cup is overflowing. May His unfailing love be your comfort!

November 1
PREPARE FOR ACTION

"Therefore, prepare your minds for action; be self-controlled; set your hope fully on the grace to be given you when Jesus Christ is revealed." 1 Peter 1:13 (NIV)

We are at war. As followers of Jesus Christ, we have to confront the reality of spiritual warfare. The kingdom of light and the kingdom of darkness are in opposition. As children of the light, we must combat the forces of evil. God's agenda is our agenda. God's mission is our mission. Loyalty to Christ will produce opposition from Satan and his demonic forces.

Be proactive by preparing your mind for action. Fill your mind with the Word of God and choose to claim God's promises. God has revealed His plan and provided His spiritual armor for the spiritual battle. Prepare your mind for the warfare of combating temptation, sin, and compromise.

Be self-controlled. This is no time for apathy or lethargy. Don't drift into complacency. Submit to the control of the Holy Spirit and allow Him to bear the fruit of self-control in you. Yield to the Spirit's prompting for perpetual victory over sin and Satan.

Where have you anchored your hope? Your life in Christ is established on the basis of God's grace. The grace that saved you is the grace that keeps you secure in the midst of opposition. God's grace will sustain you whether you are in the valley of intense spiritual warfare or on the mountain of heavenly bliss.

November 2
UNLIMITED SUPPLY

"So do not worry, saying, 'What shall we eat?' or 'What shall we drink?' or 'What shall we wear?' For the pagans run after all these things, and your heavenly Father knows that you need them." Matt 6:31-32 (NIV)

How do you overcome anxiety? How do you win the war against worry? These questions remind me of a story about a man who offered to pay another man an annual salary of $200,000 to do his worrying for him. On the first day at work the hired man asked, "Boss, how are you going to get $200,000 to pay me?" The response came quickly, "That's your worry!"

Worry is like rocking in a rocking chair, it will keep you busy, but you don't get anywhere. Our English word, worry, comes from an old German word, which means "to strangle" or "to choke." As you may know by experience, worry can strangle the life out of you and choke the flow of joy in your life. Worry produces unhealthy side-effects such as: ulcers, backaches, headaches, and insomnia.

Invert worry by trusting in God's unlimited supply. You are more valuable to God than the birds of the air and He feeds them. You are more valuable to God than the lilies of the field and He causes them to grow. Worrying won't lengthen your life. Worrying won't benefit your future. Worry is practical atheism. When we worry, we are saying, "We don't believe God will do what He says He will do."

Your heavenly Father knows what you need. He created you and has a plan for your life. God will provide you with everything you need to accomplish His will on the earth. No need to worry about your circumstances or to fear the unknown. Your heavenly Father knows right where you are and He knows exactly what you need to operate in the center of His will.

November 3
Obvious Faith

"What good is it, my brothers, if a man claims to have faith but has no deeds? Can such faith save him?" James 2:14 (NIV)

You can profess Christ and not possess Christ. What does it take for a person to be saved? Is it possible to have saving faith without deeds? Will my faith be demonstrated by my deeds? So many have embraced an "easy believism" theology which can produce a false sense of security. You can spend your entire life on the earth thinking that you are saved and in reality, be lost.

- *"'Not everyone who says to me, "Lord, Lord," will enter the kingdom of heaven, but only he who does the will of my Father who is in heaven.'" Matt 7:21 (NIV)*
- *"Therefore, my brothers, be all the more eager to make your calling and election sure. For if you do these things, you will never fall, and you will receive a rich welcome into the eternal kingdom of our Lord and Savior Jesus Christ." 2 Peter 1:10-11 (NIV)*

Your eternal destiny is determined by how you respond to God's offer of salvation found in Christ alone. Knowing about Christ is not sufficient for salvation. You must know Christ personally through faith in the completed work of Jesus on the cross.

Take inventory of your spiritual condition. Don't rely on feelings. Trace your steps and identify the moment you had a life-changing experience. Clarify your conversion experience. When did you come to realize your sin and your need for God's forgiveness? When you did acknowledge that Jesus is God's Son and the only way to heaven? When did you receive God's gift of eternal life?

November 4
CONVINCING FAITH

"Suppose a brother or sister is without clothes and daily food. If one of you says to him, 'Go, I wish you well; keep warm and well fed,' but does nothing about his physical needs, what good is it? In the same way, faith by itself, if it is not accompanied by action, is dead." James 2:15-17 (NIV)

If you have been born from above, adopted into God's family, and filled with the Holy Spirit, shouldn't the reality of your salvation be evidenced? If you have experienced transformation on the inside, shouldn't that show up on the outside? Faith void of action is dead. Your faith is to be demonstrated by action.

- "In the same way, let your light shine before men, that they may see your good deeds and praise your Father in heaven." Matt 5:16 (NIV)
- "The Lord's message rang out from you not only in Macedonia and Achaia--your faith in God has become known everywhere. Therefore we do not need to say anything about it, for they themselves report what kind of reception you gave us. They tell how you turned to God from idols to serve the living and true God, and to wait for his Son from heaven, whom he raised from the dead--Jesus, who rescues us from the coming wrath." 1 Thes 1:8-10 (NIV)

God has put you in the display window of life to demonstrate your faith in practical ways. Find a need and meet it. Shine the light of Jesus and share the love of Jesus. Pray continually, give sacrificially, and worship passionately. May those who know you but don't know Jesus, come to know Jesus because they know you. May your faith be that convincing! May your faith be activated and demonstrated to a watching world!

November 5
DIVINE TRANSACTION

"You believe that there is one God. Good! Even the demons believe that--and shudder." James 2:19 (NIV)

Believing in God will not get you to heaven. God has revealed Himself generally through nature and specifically through the incarnate Word, Jesus. To say that you believe in God is not sufficient for salvation. James asserts that even the demons believe there is one God. Their monotheism is not enough. Judaism, Islam, and Christianity embrace monotheism. However, believing in one God does not produce salvation.

- *"For since the creation of the world God's invisible qualities--his eternal power and divine nature--have been clearly seen, being understood from what has been made, so that men are without excuse." Romans 1:20 (NIV)*
- *"'Salvation is found in no one else, for there is no other name under heaven given to men by which we must be saved.'" Acts 4:12 (NIV)*

God has revealed Himself to us in the Person of Jesus Christ. The question is: What will you do with Jesus? The atoning work of Jesus on the cross is sufficient to save anyone, but effective only for those who trust in Christ alone for salvation. The gift of eternal life doesn't become a gift to you until you personally receive it.

Do you believe that Jesus is God's Son? Do you believe that Jesus died to pay your sin debt in full? Do you believe that Jesus is the only way to heaven? Have you received the gift of eternal life?

Trace the spiritual markers in your life. Spend a moment reflecting on the most important spiritual marker that changed your forever. Revisit the moment you experienced the divine transaction of transferring your trust from yourself to Jesus alone for salvation.

November 6
SALVATION THAT WORKS

"You foolish man, do you want evidence that faith without deeds is useless? Was not our ancestor Abraham considered righteous for what he did when he offered his son Isaac on the altar? You see that his faith and his actions were working together, and his faith was made complete by what he did." James 2:20-22 (NIV)

Your good works will not produce salvation. If only you could work your way to heaven! Then the challenge would be knowing how much work would be required by God for you to deserve entrance into heaven. How would you know if you have done enough to get there? What if you almost made it, but fell short by one good deed? Fortunately, God does not base your salvation on your works.

The Bible does not present a works salvation, but a salvation that works. You cannot work for your salvation, but your salvation will be evidenced by good works. In response to God's gracious gift of salvation, you will want to express your appreciation to God through deeds of righteousness. Your deeds will not produce righteousness, but your righteousness in Christ will produce righteous deeds. Your "want to" changes as a result of your salvation.

- *"God made him who had no sin to be sin for us, so that in him we might become the righteousness of God." 2 Cor 5:21 (NIV)*
- *"Those who obey his commands live in him, and he in them. And this is how we know that he lives in us: We know it by the Spirit he gave us." 1 John 3:24 (NIV)*

Your salvation is a gift from God and is marked by a life of obedience.

November 7
THE FACT OF FAITH

"And without faith it is impossible to please God, because anyone who comes to him must believe that he exists and that he rewards those who earnestly seek him." Hebrews 11:6 (NIV)

How does faith work? Faith works for you. God is always at work to bring us to the point of recognizing our need for a saving relationship with Jesus. The Holy Spirit convicts us of sin and convinces us of our need for salvation. God enables us through faith to respond to His gift of eternal life. In faith we choose to receive God's provision of forgiveness made available through the sacrifice of Jesus on the cross.

- *"'For God so loved the world that he gave his one and only Son, that whoever believes in him shall not perish but have eternal life.'" John 3:16 (NIV)*
- *"That if you confess with your mouth, 'Jesus is Lord,' and believe in your heart that God raised him from the dead, you will be saved. For it is with your heart that you believe and are justified, and it is with your mouth that you confess and are saved." Romans 10:9-10 (NIV)*

Have you experienced faith working for you? God took the initiative to bring you into a right relationship with Himself. Jesus paid the ultimate price for the forgiveness of your sins. At salvation, you became the temple of the Holy Spirit. Faith is not a feeling. Faith is a fact of God's activity in your life.

November 8
PRAYER AND FAITH

"At the time of sacrifice, the prophet Elijah stepped forward and prayed: 'O LORD, God of Abraham, Isaac and Israel, let it be known today that you are God in Israel and that I am your servant and have done all these things at your command. Answer me, O LORD, answer me, so these people will know that you, O LORD, are God, and that you are turning their hearts back again.'" 1 Kings 18:36-37 (NIV)

Elijah prayed a bold prayer and experienced the power of God. He had challenged the four hundred and fifty prophets of Baal and the four hundred prophets of Asherah to a showdown on Mount Carmel. The prophets called on the name of Baal from morning till noon and received no response. However, Elijah had the sacrifice drenched in water and then he stepped forward to call on God. The power of God fell and consumed the sacrifice, the wood, the stones, the soil, and the water in the trench.

Elijah prayed to God in faith and experienced a demonstration of God's power. The people saw this and fell prostrate to the ground and exclaimed, "The Lord, he is God!" This was truly a mountaintop experience that portrayed the effectiveness of praying in faith. God answers prayer!

What are you currently combating? What is perplexing you? Have you considered taking that burden to the Lord in prayer? You know that God is able to consume a water-soaked sacrifice. You know that God can cause fire to fall at a moment's notice. There's nothing beyond God's reach.

Do you believe that God will do what He says He will do? Do you believe that God is able to deliver you through your circumstances? God is waiting for you to take Him at His Word and to entrust your life to His care. You will never face anything that God cannot handle. God will work everything together for your good and for His glory!

November 9
UNLOAD YOUR ANXIETY

"Cast all your anxiety on him because he cares for you." 1 Peter 5:7 (NIV)

Anxiety has the potential to cause us to lose perspective. When we are anxious, butterflies become helicopters. When we are anxious, grasshoppers become giants. Anxiety demands emotional fuel that depletes our passion and distorts our vision. The confetti of anxiety is applied with the spray paint of unrealistic expectations, overcommitment, and lack of margin. Where do you go when you are drowning in the liquid of anxiety?

Our tendency is to subdue our anxiety by covering up our pain with a cascade of calories or sprinting into the fast lane of excessive busyness. We seek to divert the pain by suppressing our current reality with the blanket of escape. There is a much better option! God's way is always the best way!

God did not create you to be a wagon of worry. Unload your anxiety. Choose to run to God in prayer. Decide to unpack the heavy load you are bearing. Release your regrets. Dump your doubts and disappointments. Cry out to God in prayer in brokenness and humility and acknowledge your desperate need to cast all your anxiety on Him. God cares for you and cares about every intricate detail of your life. He intimately knows the burdens you are bearing and the concerns you are carrying.

Write on a sheet of paper or type on your computer or cell phone a list of the specific items consuming your emotional energy. It helps me to see in print what is generating anxiety in my life. Once I bring these items into the light, they lose their bite. Then I unload each item out of the cargo area of my life and place them at the feet of Jesus in prayer.

What do you need to unload? What do you need to release? As Dr. Johnny Hunt says, "Anything over your head is beneath His feet."

November 10
GUARD YOUR TOP PRIORITY

"But seek first his kingdom and his righteousness, and all these things will be given to you as well.'" Matt 6:33 (NIV)

What are you giving your life to? There's only so much of you to give away. God has given you a certain amount of time, energy, and resources to accomplish His will each day.

Take a look at your priorities and assess your life. Detect where you are allocating your time, energy, and resources. One of Satan's most effective tools to diffuse a believer's focus is busyness. Your life becomes consumed with keeping too many plates spinning. Before you know it, you have over-committed and over-scheduled your life. Jesus has the answer.

Jesus offers a promise that is activated upon your obedience. To seek first the kingdom of God is to align your life with God's agenda. To seek first His kingdom is to embrace God's priorities. Jesus includes the pursuit of His righteousness. When a person is born again, that person receives the imputed righteousness of Christ. The believer's position is that of being in Christ. In order to seek His righteousness, you allow the righteousness on the inside of you to be worked out. It is the process of working out what God has worked in.

Make it your priority to seek His kingdom and His righteousness. All the other things that you need will be provided to you as well. Before seeking things, seek God's agenda. Seek to love what He loves and to hate what He hates.

What has first place in your life? Who gets the most of you? Remove the competing objects of your affection. Make your daily pursuit of His kingdom and His righteousness your top priority.

November 11
PRESENT YOUR REQUESTS

"Do not be anxious about anything, but in everything, by prayer and petition, with thanksgiving, present your requests to God. And the peace of God, which transcends all understanding, will guard your hearts and your minds in Christ Jesus." Phil 4:6-7 (NIV)

Why do we worry about stuff instead of praying to God about the stuff we worry about? Anxiety evaporates our joy and constricts our passion. The things we worry about become fixated in our minds and consume our emotional reserves. This is not the life God has for us.

When all else fails, we then choose to pray. Why is that? What keeps us from turning to God in prayer the moment worry appears? Our first response to anxiety should be to pray. Maybe we feel that we just don't have time to pray. We always have plenty of time to worry. Let's make time to pray.

Instead of being anxious about anything, in everything, let's choose to present our requests to God by prayer and petition. Prayer is our unbroken communion with God through heartfelt communication. When we present our requests to God through petition, we are praying specifically about those things that produce anxiety in us.

The more specific your prayer life becomes, the more dynamic the results will be. Move beyond generic prayers and ambiguous requests. Get specific about each detail that keeps you from walking in the victory and the freedom that has been purchased for you by Christ.

Be thankful in your circumstances. Express your gratitude to God in prayer by specifically articulating all the things you are thankful for. It is possible to miss the rose by focusing on the thorns. What are you thankful for right now? Express that to God. Thank Him for your salvation. Thank Him for allowing you to have this day to experience His presence and to know His peace.

November 12
FOCUS ON TODAY

"Therefore do not worry about tomorrow, for tomorrow will worry about itself. Each day has enough trouble of its own." Matt 6:34 (NIV)

Aren't you thankful that there are 365 days in a year, 24 hours in a day, sixty minutes in an hour, and sixty seconds in each minute? Jesus does not want us to worry about tomorrow. Don't be anxious about the next installment of 24 hours. That's why Jesus did not teach us to pray, "Give us this month our monthly bread." Rather, Jesus taught us to pray, "Give us this day our daily bread."

Instead of worrying about tomorrow, focus on today. To worry is to be drawn in multiple directions. Worry causes you to feel fragmented and overwhelmed. Someone has said, "Today is the tomorrow you worried about yesterday." Where does worry take you? Worry takes you to an unhealthy place!

God gives you the grace you need for today. God gives you the provision you need for today. Focus on today. Release the fear and anxiety related to tomorrow. Jesus made it clear that tomorrow will worry about itself and each day has enough trouble of its own.

Instead of worrying about tomorrow, choose to focus on what God wants to do in you and through you today. God is building you and developing you to fulfill His will for today. This is the day God has for you to operate in His strength and to continue to shine His light and to share His love. Don't waste one moment today. Every moment matters to God so make every moment count for God's glory.

I remember memorizing a poem when I was sixteen that has meant so much to me over the years: "Today whatever may annoy, the word for me is joy, just simply joy. Whatever there be of sorrow, I'll put off until tomorrow. And when tomorrow comes, it will be today, and joy again."

November 13
Gain Clarity

"After Paul had seen the vision, we got ready at once to leave for Macedonia, concluding that God had called us to preach the gospel to them." Acts 16:10 (NIV)

Fog has the capacity to limit visibility and to stall progress. If you have ever driven in fog you know firsthand the challenge it creates. Living life in a fallen world can be like trying to drive in the fog. The path God wants you to take may not be crystal clear.

Paul and his traveling companions experienced the canopy of fog when they sought to preach the word in the province of Asia. The Holy Spirit prevented them from moving in that direction. When they tried to enter the border of Bithynia, the Spirit of Jesus would not allow them to. Their path was foggy until Paul had a vision during the night of a man from Macedonia standing and begging him, "Come over to Macedonia and help us."

Sometimes the fog doesn't lift until God has prepared you for your next assignment. Even when your path doesn't seem clear, know that God is working to develop you and to prepare the circumstances in your future for the life He has for you. Wait patiently before the Lord and trust in His impeccable timing to reveal to you the step He wants you to take.

Keep yielding to His authority and control in your life. Keep drawing near to God and grow in your daily intimacy with Him. God is passionate about developing the character of Christ in you so that you will be more like Jesus whether the path is foggy or radiantly clear.

Paul did not know it, but God was preparing him for some divine appointments that were positioned just beyond the fog. God sees where you are and He knows exactly where He wants you to be. The fog will lift and you will gain clarity.

November 14
DIVINE APPOINTMENTS

"After Paul and Silas came out of the prison, they went to Lydia's house, where they met with the brothers and encouraged them. Then they left." Acts 16:40 (NIV)

Have you ever been tempted to question God? Maybe you have gone through a season that did not make sense to you and appeared to divert you from God's will. Paul had delivered a fortune-teller from her demon possession. As you can imagine, her owners where not happy with the cessation of their flow of income. As a result, Paul and Silas were thrown in prison for obeying God's will.

Just before that encounter, Paul and Silas met Lydia at a place of prayer by the river in Philippi. The Lord opened her heart to respond to Paul's message and she and her family had a life changing experience and were baptized. She invited Paul and his companions to her home. Lydia's home became an oasis.

After Paul and Silas were thrown into prison, they were praying and singing hymns to God when the foundations of the prison were shaken by an earthquake. Chains were loosed and the prison doors flew open. The jailer was about to take his own life until Paul declared that all the prisoners where still there. The jailer fell trembling before Paul and Silas and asked, "Sirs, what must I do to be saved?"

Immediately the jailer and his family were baptized. Paul and Silas went to Lydia's house and met with the believers and encouraged them. God birthed the church of Philippi out of adverse circumstances. Lydia's home became the church of Philippi.

Don't underestimate what God wants to do in the midst of your circumstances. God orchestrates divine appointments throughout the terrain of turbulence.

November 15
ASK THE RIGHT QUESTION

"Now I want you to know, brothers, that what has happened to me has really served to advance the gospel." Philippians 1:12 (NIV)

God had transformed Paul from a persecutor of the church to a preacher of the gospel. Later in his journey, the Apostle Paul was instrumental in the birth of the church at Philippi. Paul was fully yielded to the Lordship of Christ and fully surrendered to God's will. He sought to maintain the posture of living on mission with God and joining God in His redemptive activity.

Sometimes obedience to God's will leads to imprisonment. Paul was imprisoned in Rome and chained to two Roman soldiers rotating shifts every eight hours. Can you imagine being chained to the Apostle Paul for eight hours? God used the very chains that bound Paul to unleash the gospel of grace to throughout the whole palace guard.

When you look into the rear view mirror of your life, maybe you can quickly remember a season of adversity that made no sense at the time. Now, looking back you see how God used that season in your life to build your faith and to bless others. Hindsight gives you a view of clarity that provides comfort.

Our tendency is to ask God, "Why?" We like knowing the reason behind the season of adversity. We find comfort in clarifying the unknown and resolving the mystery of our circumstances. For some reason, we just passionately want to know why God allows certain things into our lives. We convince ourselves, that if we knew why, then we would be able to accept the reality of our circumstances.

Instead of asking why, consider asking what! Start asking, "God, what would you like to accomplish in me and through me in the midst of this season of adversity?" Remember, if God allows it, He will use it to build your faith and to bless others.

November 16
AUTHENTIC CHRISTIANITY

"I was personally unknown to the churches of Judea that are in Christ. They only heard the report: 'The man who formerly persecuted us is now preaching the faith he once tried to destroy.' And they praised God because of me." Galatians 1:22-24 (NIV)

Think about someone you are acquainted with that would be characterized as being far from God. When you think of this person, maybe you wonder if he or she could ever change. Perhaps their perpetual behavior has made you consider them unreachable and indifferent to the grace of God.

Paul would have been considered someone like this. He was far from God and far from operating in the center of God's will. Paul was deeply passionate, but his passion was misdirected and brought immeasurable harm to the followers of Jesus. Paul, known as Saul before his conversion, was steeped in legalism and sought to strip believers of their identity in Christ.

God revealed His grace through a powerful transformation of Paul's life. Instead of persecuting the church, Paul began preaching the faith he once sought to destroy. Can you imagine the followers of Jesus contemplating the transformation of such an avid opponent to the movement of God such as Paul.

The churches of Judea praised God because of Paul. Though they did not know him personally, they praised God for the report of the life change Paul experienced. He became a portrait of God's grace.

There's no one beyond the reach of God's grace. Even the vilest sinner can be radically saved and transformed by the power of God. The grace of God is sufficient to produce an authentic Christian out of anyone, including those far from God. What if you heard a report that gave testimony to the revolutionary transformation of the person you deem farthest from God?

November 17
HUMAN INSTRUMENTALITY

"For God, who was at work in Peter as an apostle to the Jews, was also at work in me as an apostle to the Gentiles." Galatians 2:8 (NIV)

God still uses human instrumentality in the redemptive process. God chooses to use us in unique ways to shine His light and to share His love. You were created by God to know Him personally by grace alone through faith alone in Jesus. God sought you, bought you, redeemed you, forgave you, adopted you, included you, filled you, and sealed you so that you could be an instrument of His redeeming love.

Peter was uniquely gifted by God to be an apostle to the Jews. God transformed Paul from a persecutor of the church to be a preacher of the gospel as an apostle to the Gentiles. Of course Peter was to be an irresistible influence for the Lord to everyone he came in contact with. Yet, God was at work through Peter to specifically bring the saving news of Jesus to the Jews. Paul had an assignment from God to spread the aroma of Christ to every person who did not have a saving relationship with Jesus. However, God was strategically at work in Paul to build a bridge of hope to the Gentiles.

Your life is to be lived in such a way as to demonstrate and communicate the redemptive love of God. Your conversation and conduct are to point people to Jesus so they can know Him personally and eternally just as you do. Maximize the moments God gives you to make Jesus known. Capture the opportunities to ask spiritual questions that take your conversations vertical. Feature the grace of God by sharing with others how they can come into a personal relationship with Jesus Christ.

November 18
LOVE OTHERS AS YOURSELF

"'Love the Lord your God with all your heart and with all your soul and with all your mind and with all your strength.' The second is this: 'Love your neighbor as yourself.' There is no commandment greater than these." Mark 12:30-31 (NIV)

We are by nature self-absorbed, self-centered, and self-focused. When anything happens around us our first question is: How will this affect me? In many ways, we act as though the earth really does rotate around us. The reality of our fallen nature pops up from time to time like a ground hog trying to catch a glimpse of daylight.

Jesus acknowledges the presence of our self-love. We truly love ourselves. As one of my colleagues would often say, "Sometimes you just have to be good to yourself!" We have no problem being good to ourselves do we? We value comfort. We value pleasure. We value looking good and feeling good and sleeping good.

As we begin viewing others from God's perspective, we will begin to value others the way God values them. The resulting choice will be to love others as we love ourselves. In other words, we will begin to treat others the way we want to be treated. We will love others with the same kind of love that we desire to receive.

James identifies that we are doing right when we love others as we love ourselves. Longing to do right is not enough. Putting our faith in action by loving others brings honor to God (James 2:17).

Do you love others as much as you love yourself? Ouch! That's a painful question.

November 19
LIVING IN TWO WORLDS

"So I say, live by the Spirit, and you will not gratify the desires of the sinful nature. For the sinful nature desires what is contrary to the Spirit, and the Spirit what is contrary to the sinful nature. They are in conflict with each other, so that you do not do what you want." Gal 5:16-17 (NIV)

Every believer is living in two worlds: the world of the Spirit or the world of the sinful nature. Light and darkness abound. They are in conflict with each other. As a result, the believer has to combat the gravitational pull of the sinful nature. At salvation, a believer receives the Holy Spirit and is made fit for heaven. However, the believer retains the sinful nature and must daily crucify the sinful nature with its passions and desires.

Have you been combating the cravings of the flesh? Have you noticed that your sinful nature is addicted to sin? However, you must daily crucify the flesh. "Those who belong to Christ Jesus have crucified the sinful nature with its passions and desires" (Gal 5:24 NIV). In Christ, you must starve the flesh. Whatever you feed grows and whatever you starve dies. Feed the Spirit living in you and starve the cravings of your sinful nature. Do not be a slave to sin. Choose to be a slave to righteousness.

Pray with me: Father, thank You for redeeming me from my sin. You have rescued me from this body of death. You have brought me out of the kingdom of darkness and placed me in the kingdom of Light. Help me to crucify the sinful nature and to live by the Spirit. Enable me to live the Christ-centered life in the power of Your Holy Spirit. Protect me from the flaming arrows of the evil one. Help me to finish strong for Your glory. In Jesus' Name, Amen.

November 20
First Love

"Yet I hold this against you: You have forsaken your first love. Remember the height from which you have fallen! Repent and do the things you did at first. If you do not repent, I will come to you and remove your lampstand from its place." Rev 2:4-5 (NIV)

The church at Ephesus had a lot going for them. They were strong in deeds, hardworking, and known for their perseverance. They sought purity of doctrine, endured hardship, and served diligently. Yet, they bypassed their love relationship with God. The church had forsaken their first love.

There are so many things vying for your affection and devotion. You can give your life to an endless array of commitments and neglect the most important relationship. It is possible to give a little bit of yourself to everything and have nothing left for the most vital relationship. Keeping you fragmented is one of Satan's goals to keep you from nurturing the life-giving relationship that Christ provides. As long as you are distracted from that which is eternal, Satan knows that your effectiveness in the Kingdom of God will be stifled.

Do you remember when your love relationship with Christ was your top priority? Measure how far you have drifted from that passionate intimate relationship you had with Christ. Repent! Choose to go a new direction by forsaking those things that hinder your love relationship with Christ. Give your full devotion to the One who died sacrificially so that you could live abundantly and eternally.

Return to guarding your love relationship with Christ. Give the best of your life each day to the One who deserves first place in your life. Make a standing appointment with the Lord each morning to spend time with Him. Yield your life to the One who gave you life!

November 21
SPIRITUAL WARDROBE

"Therefore, as God's chosen people, holy and dearly loved, clothe yourselves with compassion, kindness, humility, gentleness and patience." Col 3:12 (NIV)

What are you displaying for a watching world to see? You are chosen, holy, and dearly loved by God. Display the garments you have been given in Christ. As a child of the Living God, you have a spiritual wardrobe that must be put on each day. God places you in the display window of life to give evidence of the reality of Jesus living His life through you.

Are you exhibiting the character of Christ? Put on the garment of compassion. Let others see your compassion in action. Put on the garment of kindness. Be gracious and kind toward others by placing their needs before your own. Put on the garment of humility. Don't think less of yourself; just think of yourself less. Consider others better than yourself (Php 2:3). Be sure to put on the garment of gentleness. Show the tenderness of Christ as you interact with others today. Are you a patient person? Put on the garment of patience and trust God's timing.

Who you are in Christ on the inside needs to be evident on the outside. As you build meaningful relationships with others, demonstrate the character of Christ. As you navigate the difficult places in life, exhibit the character of Christ. God will use the tests you face in life to help build your testimony. When you are squeezed by the circumstances of life, what is on the inside of you will come out. Clothe yourself with compassion, kindness, humility, gentleness, and patience. Let these garments become the fabric of your life.

November 22
DISPLAY COMPASSION

"But a Samaritan, as he traveled, came where the man was; and when he saw him, he took pity on him. He went to him and bandaged his wounds, pouring on oil and wine. Then he put the man on his own donkey, took him to an inn and took care of him." Luke 10:33-34 (NIV)

Hurting people saturate the landscape of life. Living in a fallen world generates pain, suffering, and sorrow. People are shouldering harmful habits, hurts, and hang-ups. Detours and disappointments frequent our daily existence. The reality of living on a broken planet necessitates a deep abiding compassion for others.

The Good Samaritan was willing to see the needs of an unnamed individual and to seize the opportunity to meet his needs. The Good Samaritan was willing to put his compassion in action by getting personally involved in the solution to this wounded man's unfortunate situation. He had been left for dead.

The Priest and the Levite were too preoccupied with themselves to care about someone else in need. If we are not careful, that can be our tendency. We get so caught up in our own lives and consumed with what we want to accomplish in a given day, that we can neglect those God brings into our path. Busyness and selfishness blur our vision to the reality of pressing needs around us. We might even begin seeing people in need as an interruption rather than an opportunity to display the compassion of Christ.

What is keeping you from putting your compassion in action? Have you lost your love for people? Has your heart become numb toward the individuals in need who come across your path? Slow down and allow the compassion of Christ to flow through you to a world in need. Continue the ministry of Jesus on the earth. View others as sheep without a shepherd. You are the shepherd! Go help some sheep!

November 23
FORGIVEN TO FORGIVE

"Bear with each other and forgive whatever grievances you may have against one another. Forgive as the Lord forgave you." Col 3:13 (NIV)

Motion causes friction. Doing life with real people can generate feelings of irritability and agitation. Real people in real life can get on your nerves at times. Our self-absorbed society elevates relational strife. Our proclivity toward selfishness accelerates the relational turmoil.

The Body of Christ is not exempt from relational challenges. Every church family experiences tension, jealousy, and relational drift. We combat the world, the flesh, and the devil. We combat the tendency to turn inward and neglect relationships. Self-preservation prevents us from experiencing the depth of meaningful relationships God has for us.

Perpetual forgiveness and bearing with each other are required for maintaining unity in the Body of Christ. If you have a grievance against someone, release it! If you have been fertilizing a spirit of un-forgiveness, renounce it! Forgive others just as the Lord Jesus has forgiven you.

Don't forget about the forgiveness you have received in your lifetime. Calculate the grace, mercy, and compassion that Christ has lavished on you. Think about where you would be without His abundant forgiveness. Your sin has been placed as far as the east is from the west. Your sin has been placed in the sea of forgetfulness. You are totally forgiven. You have been set free! Now, choose to forgive others as the Lord has chosen to forgive you. Let others experience your forgiveness in the same degree upon which you have experienced the forgiveness of Christ.

In prayer, visit the scene of the cross. Picture for a moment the Lord Jesus on the cross paying the penalty for your sin. Consider the weight of taking on the full wrath of God for your sin. Jesus did that for you. Would you be willing to extend forgiveness to others in response to the forgiveness Jesus extended to you?

November 24
CALLED TO PEACE

"Let the peace of Christ rule in your hearts, since as members of one body you were called to peace. And be thankful." Col 3:15 (NIV)

God created us to be relational, not robotic. He designed us for relationship. Sin damaged our relationship with God and He took the initiative to provide for our reconciliation and restoration. In Christ, we have been positioned as righteous before God. Now that our relationship with God has been restored, we are to ensure right relationships with others.

- *"Therefore, since we have been justified through faith, we have peace with God through our Lord Jesus Christ, through whom we have gained access by faith into this grace in which we now stand. And we rejoice in the hope of the glory of God." Romans 5:1-2 (NIV)*
- *"Make every effort to live in peace with all men and to be holy; without holiness no one will see the Lord." Heb 12:14 (NIV)*

Our lives have a vertical and horizontal dimension. We are to have a right relationship with God and with others. We cannot have a right relationship with God unless we have a right relationship with others. Also, we cannot have a right relationship with others unless we have a right relationship with God.

Once you have received the peace of God by being justified through faith, seek to live at peace with others. Let others see Jesus in you. Love others the way Jesus loves you.

Gossip is when you say something about someone you would not say to his or her face. Flattery is when you say something to someone's face that you would not say behind his or her back. Let the peace of Christ find lodging in your heart and be evident in your conversation and your conduct.

November 25
FEEDING ON GOD'S WORD

"Let the word of Christ dwell in you richly as you teach and admonish one another with all wisdom, and as you sing psalms, hymns and spiritual songs with gratitude in your hearts to God." Col 3:16 (NIV)

Is God's Word at home in your heart? Are you reading and feeding on God's Word? Your daily intake of God's Word will help you grow spiritually and develop relationally. God's Word will help you know the nature and character of God and His plan.

Henry Blackaby shared in a message at the Gideon Convention the following insight: "God is the center of His own activity and He invites us to join Him in His activity." As you read God's Word, you come to learn how to detect the activity of God. Constant intake of God's Word increases your awareness of His activity and heightens your sensitivity to His redemptive activity.

- *"Your word is a lamp to my feet and a light for my path." Psalm 119:105 (NIV)*
- *"All Scripture is God-breathed and is useful for teaching, rebuking, correcting and training in righteousness, so that the man of God may be thoroughly equipped for every good work." 2 Tim 3:16-17 (NIV)*

Do you have room for God's Word? You must place a high value on spending time in God's Word. Don't rush your daily reading. Slow down and meditate on God's Word. Be discipline to journal what God is saying to you through His Word. Seek to write down specific application steps that you will incorporate in your day. Align your life with God's Word and embrace His agenda. Make room for God's Word to take root and to bear fruit through your life and your lips.

November 26
MOTIVE BEHIND MINISTRY

"And whatever you do, whether in word or deed, do it all in the name of the Lord Jesus, giving thanks to God the Father through him." Col 3:17 (NIV)

Everything matters to God! Everything you say and everything you do and everything you think, matters to God. Nothing is hidden from God's sight. Even when others may overlook your contribution, God never misses a moment of your life. God is omniscient, omnipotent, and omnipresent. Nothing slips through His comprehensive view.

So whatever you do, whether speaking words that build others up or extending a helping hand, do it all under the authority of Jesus. You are saved and filled with the Holy Spirit to continue the ministry of Jesus upon the earth. Your conversation is vital to fulfilling the Great Commission. Your conduct is of utmost importance in living out the Great Commandment. As you share Christ with others and express His love to others, you will be doing God's work God's way.

The motive behind your ministry to others is just as important as the benefits that your ministry produces. What compels you to put others first? What propels you to place the needs of others before your own? Are you motives pure?

Speak and serve as a representative of Jesus Christ. You may be the only Jesus others see in their lifetime. Your conversation will either point people to Christ or repel them from Christ. Your conduct will either give evidence that Jesus is Lord of your life or demonstrate that He is not enthroned.

Be sure to give thanks to God the Father as you serve Him by serving others. May your life be a portrait of gratitude for all that God has done and continues to do in you and through you.

November 27
EXPAND YOUR VISION

"After this I looked and there before me was a great multitude that no one could count, from every nation, tribe, people and language, standing before the throne and in front of the Lamb. They were wearing white robes and were holding palm branches in their hands." Rev 7:9 (NIV)

God loves variety. When you observe His creation, it doesn't take long to comprehend the variety that God infused into everything He made. God delights to display His glory through the variety of His creation.

People matter to God. Currently, there are just over 12,500 people groups within the 6.8 billion people on planet earth. Every person in each of the people groups is a unique creation of Almighty God. Every individual has an eternal destiny. God's desire is for every person to spend eternity with Him in heaven. However, God will not allow sin into heaven. The only cure for the cancer of sin is Jesus. We must bring God's plan of salvation to every person on this broken planet so that each one will have an opportunity to receive the gift of eternal life.

Pray selflessly. Pray beyond your skin. Begin to pray for those who aren't just like you. Pray for those who do not have a personal love relationship with Jesus. Pray for those who do not have the same background as yours. Pray for those who do not have the same skin color as yours.

Embrace God's vision of having a great multitude from every nation, tribe, people, and language standing before the throne in heaven. Pray to become a participant in making God's vision a reality. You can pray for the salvation of other people groups. You can go on short-term mission trip to engage an unreached people group. You can give so that others can go. Pray for Africa, Asia, Australia, Europe, North America, and South America.

November 28
UNDERSTANDING TO KNOW HIM

"We know that we are children of God, and that the whole world is under the control of the evil one. We know also that the Son of God has come and has given us understanding, so that we may know him who is true. And we are in him who is true--even in his Son Jesus Christ. He is the true God and eternal life."
1 John 5:19-20 (NIV)

What if the content of your prayers this week were transcribed and put into book form and placed on the end table in a doctor's office waiting room for others to read? What would your prayer life reveal to others? What would the content of your prayers reveal about your walk with God?

Choose to pray specifically. Instead of articulating generic requests and ambiguous petitions, begin to pray with specificity. For example, begin pray for others to know and enjoy the personal presence of Jesus. Pray for lost people by name. Write their names down and pray specifically for these individuals to become children of God.

If the whole world is under the control of the evil one, then who will rescue the perishing? Who will do spiritual battle in prayer for the lost souls on this planet? Pray evangelistically and be willing to be used of God in the process of bringing others to Christ.

Jesus has given us understanding so that we can know Him personally and make Him known intentionally. Jesus is the true God! There is no other! Jesus is eternal life! Jesus is the hope of the world. Jesus has saved us so that we can continue His ministry on the earth of bringing others into His kingdom. As a kingdom citizen, you have a kingdom assignment. Pray specifically for the salvation of individuals by name. Pray expectantly by making yourself available for God's use in His redemptive activity.

November 29
Pray Around the World

"The LORD has made his salvation known and revealed his righteousness to the nations." Psalm 98:2 (NIV)

You may not have the opportunity to travel to every continent on the planet, but you can touch every continent through prayer. Choose to pray strategically by employing a weekly prayer plan for the continents. Pray for Africa on Monday, Asia on Tuesday, Australia and Oceania on Wednesday, and Europe on Thursday. Pray for North America on Friday, South America on Saturday, and then pray for the church you are connected to on Sunday.

Our natural proclivity is to be individualistic in our praying. We get so self-absorbed and self-centered that we bypass the joy and delight of praying for those outside of our sphere of influence. Go global with your prayer life.

- *"Salvation is found in no one else, for there is no other name under heaven given to men by which we must be saved." Acts 4:12 (NIV)*
- *"The Lord is not slow in keeping his promise, as some understand slowness. He is patient with you, not wanting anyone to perish, but everyone to come to repentance." 2 Peter 3:9 (NIV)*

Embrace God's heart for the nations of the earth. God loves every people group and provides salvation by grace alone through faith alone in Jesus. You can participate in God's redemptive activity through the powerful avenue of prayer. Pray for the softening of the hearts of the people throughout the earth. Allocate some time each day to pray for one of the continents.

Would you be willing to go on a short-term mission trip to one of the continents that you pray for? God has saved you so that you can invest your life in bringing others to Christ. It all begins with praying for those not connected to Christ. Yes! You can change the world through prayer.

November 30
The Bridge Called Death

"'The kingdom of heaven is like treasure hidden in a field. When a man found it, he hid it again, and then in his joy went and sold all he had and bought that field.'" Matt 13:44 (NIV)

When I stood behind the pulpit to speak at the funeral of the surgeon who saved my life, it was as though time stood still. He had been our family doctor during my childhood and teenage years. He was a devoted husband, father, and deacon at my home church. Every scar on my body bears his workmanship from stitching up deeps cuts to performing emergency surgery following my Jet Ski accident during my junior year in High School. He was a godly man my family treasured.

There's something about death that makes us measure the value of life. When someone dear to us dies, we experience the agony of their loss and the joy of their gain. Knowing that we will see them again in heaven brings such comfort. Knowing that they are in the Presence of God beholding the face of Jesus and walking on streets of gold generates the affirmation of our faith.

Jesus shared a parable that helps us understand what the kingdom of heaven is like. When a man found treasure hidden in the field, he hid it again, and then in his joy went and sold all that he had and bought that field. The kingdom of heaven is to be treasured. The kingdom of heaven is worth being treasured.

Your most valued possession is the gift of eternal life that you received at the moment of your conversion. When Jesus became the Lord of your life, you became secure for eternity. You became a kingdom citizen. Death is not a wall to climb, but a bridge to cross. Jesus has made a way for you to face death with certainty and clarity.

December 1
REMOVING THE PLANK

"Why do you look at the speck of sawdust in your brother's eye and pay no attention to the plank in your own eye? How can you say to your brother, 'Let me take the speck out of your eye,' when all the time there is a plank in your own eye? You hypocrite, first take the plank out of your own eye, and then you will see clearly to remove the speck from your brother's eye." Matt 7:3-5 (NIV)

Jesus exposed the sin of self-righteousness. He identified our tendency to embrace a higher standard when evaluating others. We become preoccupied with judging others extensively to the neglect of examining our own lives accurately. While bearing a plank in our own eye, we seek to isolate the speck of sawdust in the eye of someone else. We fail to come to grips with the truth of our current reality.

Self-righteousness erodes our relationship with others and with God. Self-righteousness is a byproduct of an inflamed pride and arrogance. We forget where we were when Jesus came to our rescue. We begin to think of ourselves more highly than we ought.

The antidote to self-righteousness is humility. The first step toward humility is embracing a proper view of yourself. Begin to view your life in light of the holiness of God. Ask the Lord to search your heart (Ps. 139:23). As God reveals the presence of self-righteousness in your life, confess it as an offense to Him. Acknowledge your sin before God and receive His provision of forgiveness. Confess sin immediately and specifically.

Now ask God to help you love the person you have been judging. Ask God to remind you of that person's value in God's eyes. Pray for God to give you the capacity to see that person the way God does.

It's time to yank the plank.

December 2
LONGING FOR HEAVEN

"All these people were still living by faith when they died. They did not receive the things promised; they only saw them and welcomed them from a distance. And they admitted that they were aliens and strangers on earth." Heb 11:13 (NIV)

Are you living by faith and longing for heaven? God created you for eternity. Your life on earth is just a short stay in light of eternity. Yet, God has a purpose for your life and a mission for you to fulfill during your earthly existence. Your life is ordained by God and for God.

The Hall of Faith in Hebrews chapter eleven captures the lives of Abel, Enoch, Noah, Isaac, Jacob, Joseph, Moses, and a host of others. They were still living by faith when they died. They were longing for a better country a heavenly one (Heb. 11:16). They lived their lives as aliens and strangers on earth.

Don't get too attached to this life on planet earth. You were not designed to live here forever. God created you with eternity in mind. Your eternal destination in heaven is determined by your faith alone in Christ alone by God's grace alone. Once you turn your life over to Christ, eternal life in heaven becomes your reality.

Until you get to heaven, God wants you to continue the ministry of Jesus on the earth. Shine the light of Jesus and share the love of Jesus with others. Bloom where God has planted you and allow Him to use you to bring others into relationship with Jesus.

Living by faith involves trusting God to accomplish His plan through your life. Yield to His Lordship and to His leadership and enjoy the journey of being on mission with God. Live by faith and long for heaven. One day you will cross over from this life into the next.

December 3
Irresistible

"Dear friends, I urge you, as aliens and strangers in the world, to abstain from sinful desires, which war against your soul. Live such good lives among the pagans that, though they accuse you of doing wrong, they may see your good deeds and glorify God on the day he visits us." 1 Peter 2:11-12 (NIV)

As followers of Jesus Christ, we are in the world, but not of the world. We are considered aliens and strangers in the world. God has saved us from our sin and called us to Himself. We are His workmanship (Eph 2:10) and His ambassadors (2 Cor 5:20). God has done a gracious work in us so that He can do a redemptive work through us.

God wants us to be an irresistible influence in our world. Living with eternity in mind will help us to protect our priorities and to reflect what God values. Our testimony will be strengthened by our devotion to living a life of moral purity. Sinful desires war against our soul. Sin infects us and affects our effectiveness in influencing a lost and dying world toward Christ.

Let's commit to stay close and clean. Our purity paves the way for connectivity with a fallen world. God wants us to stay clean and live such good lives among lost people that will cause them to glorify God.

Is there anyone following Jesus as a result of following you? Have you become an irresistible influence for Christ right where you are? Are others being drawn to Christ because of your conversation and your conduct?

Consider the people God has brought in your path over the past few weeks. How has your life impacted their lives? Was the life of Christ in you evident to them? Portray Christ in a real way to a real world in real need. You may be the only Jesus others see.

December 4
BLESSED TO BLESS

"The LORD bless you and keep you; the LORD make his face shine upon you and be gracious to you; the LORD turn his face toward you and give you peace." Num 6:24-26 (NIV)

Did you know that we are blessed by God to be a blessing to others? We are blessed to bless. God made us into relational beings so that we can relate to Him and relate to others. God placed us here to be a blessing.

Moses instructed Aaron and his sons to articulate this priestly blessing over the Israelites. Nearly two million Israelites were wandering in the wilderness and weary from the journey. They were in need of a touch from God. God was ready to put His name on them and bless them (Num. 6:27). Aaron and his sons were to be the instruments of relaying the blessing from God.

Would you be willing to pray this blessing over someone? As an individual comes to mind, simply pray this blessing over him or her. For example, if you were praying for an uncle, you would say, "Lord, bless my uncle and keep him. Lord, make Your face shine upon him and be gracious to him. Lord, turn Your face toward him and give him peace." You can bless someone in prayer in this very moment.

Think about people God has brought into your life as a blessing. Consider how blessed you have been by their time, their friendship, their generosity, and their kindness. Your life has been enriched by their presence in your life. They have blessed you. Now, you can be a blessing to them by praying for them and giving God thanks for them. Life would be so empty without meaningful relationships.

Who will you bless today? Remember, you are blessed to bless!

December 5
COMPASSION FATIGUE

"The LORD said to Moses: 'Bring me seventy of Israel's elders who are known to you as leaders and officials among the people. Have them come to the Tent of Meeting, that they may stand there with you. I will come down and speak with you there, and I will take of the Spirit that is on you and put the Spirit on them. They will help you carry the burden of the people so that you will not have to carry it alone.'" Num 11:16-17 (NIV)

Compassion fatigue is a reality in this life. When you love and care for people, you will experience fatigue. Life has a way of draining your energy and depleting your emotional reserves. Relationships can be refreshing and wonderful, yet some can be taxing and demanding. You can become weary to the point of total exhaustion.

Moses hit a low point after caring for nearly two million Israelites. The journey of wandering in the wilderness had taken its toll. The Israelites were irritable and ungrateful for all that God had done and wanted to go back to Egypt. Moses felt the weight of their complaints. His emotional reserves were empty.

God responded to the desperation Moses was experiencing by providing some much needed help. Moses could not bear this burden alone. God instructed Moses to bring a select group of Israel's elders to the Tent of Meeting. God put His Spirit on them and empowered them to help Moses carry the burden of the people.

Are you overwhelmed by life? Have you experienced compassion fatigue? Maybe you are emotionally depleted and physically exhausted. Perhaps your load has exceeded your limit and you have no margin in your life. Ask God to bring some godly people into your life to help you carry the load. Ask God to show you what you need to stop doing, what you need to continue doing, and what you need to start doing. God will come to your rescue!

December 6
SELECTING YOUR VIEW

"Then Caleb silenced the people before Moses and said, 'We should go up and take possession of the land, for we can certainly do it.'" Num 13:30 (NIV)

Are you facing something beyond your reach? Have you been agonizing over anything lately? Your situation may be relational, familial, financial, or physical. Whatever you view as your greatest obstacle just might be the greatest opportunity for God to reveal His glory.

After twelve of the Israelites returned from spying out the land of Canaan, they returned with a mixed report. Ten of the twelve indicated that the land was filled with giants and could not be conquered. Yet, Joshua and Caleb had a much different report. Instead of focusing on the giants, they focused on God and His ability to bring them into the land flowing with milk and honey. Caleb boldly proclaimed to the people that possession of the land was attainable.

Which voices are you listening to? Are you listening to the voices of doubt and fear or to the voice of God? God knows where you are and the specifics of what you are facing. Remember, nothing is hidden from God. Nothing catches God by surprise. Our limited perspective does not limit God.

God has a plan for you that factors in your circumstances. God will remove the obstacle or He will help you overcome the obstacle. God will eliminate the giant before you or elevate your faith to persevere in light of the giant you face. Nothing will thwart God's will. Take possession of the land God is giving you. Nothing is impossible with God.

Will you focus on the giant or focus on God? Will you view your circumstances from your perspective or from God's perspective? If God has allowed this situation, He will use it for your good and His glory.

December 7
Giving God's Way

"'So when you give to the needy, do not announce it with trumpets, as the hypocrites do in the synagogues and on the streets, to be honored by men. I tell you the truth, they have received their reward in full. But when you give to the needy, do not let your left hand know what your right hand is doing, so that your giving may be in secret. Then your Father, who sees what is done in secret, will reward you.'" Matt 6:2-4 (NIV)

What are you currently doing to benefit others? What resources has God made available to you? Are you using what God gives you to benefit others? You are blessed by God to be a blessing to others.

Give secretly and God will reward you. It is not only what you give but how you give that moves the heart of God. God sees everything you do and everything you don't do. God sees and knows. If you give to be seen of men, then that is the extent of your reward. However, when your giving is done in secret, God rewards you.

- "For we must all appear before the judgment seat of Christ, that each one may receive what is due him for the things done while in the body, whether good or bad." 2 Cor 5:10 (NIV)
- "But just as you excel in everything--in faith, in speech, in knowledge, in complete earnestness and in your love for us --see that you also excel in this grace of giving." 2 Cor 8:7 (NIV)

Motive matters! God sees how much you give and God sees how you give.

December 8
PRAYING GOD'S WAY

"But when you pray, go into your room, close the door and pray to your Father, who is unseen. Then your Father, who sees what is done in secret, will reward you." Matt 6:6 (NIV)

Do you have a special place where you go to spend unhurried time alone with God in prayer? Have you found a location that is conducive to meaningful conversation with the Creator of the universe? We live in such a fast paced and noisy world that sometimes it is a challenge to find a place of solitude.

Praying requires focused attention on God. Seek to eliminate distractions and secure a place where you can enjoy unbroken fellowship with God in prayer. Jesus affirms the need for that special place. He reminds us that when we enter that room, we are to pray in secret and know that God sees the unseen.

It takes discipline to spend time in prayer. Prayer is hard work because the enemy combats your desire to pray. The enemy does not want you to draw near to God. That's one reason why having a special place for prayer helps you to focus and to diffuse the enemy's attacks.

Your prayer life doesn't need to be a public display for public attention and affirmation. God rewards your prayer life. He knows how much time you are carving out for communication with Him. God knows the intensity of your pursuit and He rewards your obedience. He will reward you for praying His way. God's way is always best for you.

If you have been neglecting your prayer life, simply commit to find a place of prayer. Try to go there the same time each day and spend time in meaningful conversation with God. Listen for His voice of truth and clarity. God will reward your devotion and your diligence.

December 9
BEFORE YOU PRAY

"And when you pray, do not keep on babbling like pagans, for they think they will be heard because of their many words. Do not be like them, for your Father knows what you need before you ask him.'" Matt 6:7-8 (NIV)

Before you pray, consider the One you are praying to. God has invited you into the most amazing conversation you will ever have. Prayer is having face-time with the One who designed you. God thought of you long before you thought of Him. You are privileged with the communication that will continue for eternity. Your love relationship with God is continual, perpetual, and eternal.

God does not respond to your prayer based on the number of words you articulate. Unleashing a barrage of words does not give you favor with God. The prayer relationship God invites you into does not depend on excessive verbiage, but rather on the sufficiency of God's omniscience. God knows everything about you and every detail of every situation surrounding your life. God is fully aware of your current reality. He knows where you have been, where you are, and where you are going. God knows your inmost fears and frustrations.

Don't be like the pagan who thinks he will be heard because of his catalogue of words. God knows exactly what you need before you ask Him. Prayer is not bringing God up on your circumstances, but bringing you up on God and His sovereignty over your circumstances.

When you pray, be mindful of God's activity in your life. Be alert to the awesome nature and character of God. The reality of prayer is an abiding comfort in that your lifeline to God is always connected. You have direct access to the One who gave His one and only Son to grant that access. What will you do with the honor and privilege of prayer?

December 10
FASTING GOD'S WAY

"But when you fast, put oil on your head and wash your face, so that it will not be obvious to men that you are fasting, but only to your Father, who is unseen; and your Father, who sees what is done in secret, will reward you.'" Matt 6:17-18 (NIV)

Giving and praying are commanded in God's Word. In the Old Testament, the Israelites were commanded to fast in preparation for the Day of Atonement. Nowhere else in the Bible is fasting commanded. Jesus completed His atoning work on the cross to provide the removal of our sin and the restoration of our relationship with God. Fasting is voluntary.

Jesus made it clear that fasting should be a normal spiritual discipline in the life of a believer. Just as giving and praying flow out of our love relationship with Christ, so fasting is to be a normal practice in the life of every child of God. We are not to fast in order to be praised by others, but rather to concentrate on our relationship with the Lord.

The hypocrites in Jesus' day would fast to be seen of men. They fed their approval addiction by fasting publicly on Monday and Thursdays when the market was overflowing with the masses. They received their reward, namely, the praise of men, but bypassed the reward of God. They got what they were looking for!

There is no need to put your spiritual discipline of fasting on display for others to see. John Piper has identified that there is a difference between fasting to be seen and being seen fasting. Fasting is to be done in secret to allow you to pursue God and to deepen your love relationship with Him. When you fast, it is proper to let your family members know so they will understand your reason behind not participating with them during mealtime. Also, they can pray for you specifically during your fast. God will reward what is done in secret.

December 11
THE NORMAL FAST

"Jesus, full of the Holy Spirit, returned from the Jordan and was led by the Spirit in the desert, where for forty days he was tempted by the devil. He ate nothing during those days, and at the end of them he was hungry." Luke 4:1-2 (NIV)

God has blessed us with an appetite for food. Food fuels our body so that we cannot only survive, but thrive in this life God has for us. We crave food because our bodies need the nutrients food provides. We hunger for food and thirst for water. Our appetite drives us to eat and drink.

Jesus had an appetite for food. He ate and drank to provide His body with the nutrients necessary to sustain life. Yet, Jesus was led by the Spirit to go on a forty day fast in the wilderness. During this time, Jesus did not eat anything. This type of fasting is considered the normal type of fasting in the Bible. Fasting for forty days is not normal, but abstaining from food for a season is normal for the follower of Jesus Christ.

Have you ever gone on a fast? What was your experience like? What was the purpose behind the fast? God will call you to a fast so that you can draw near to Him. You choose to forego your desire for food in order to spend that time concentrating on praying, reading the Bible, and consecrating your life before the Lord. Instead of hungering for food, you re-direct your appetite to feasting on God. As you fast, you deliberately pursue God's presence and yield to His prompting.

If you sense God calling you to a normal fast, be sure to drink lots of water and consider a consistent intake of pure juices. Abstaining from food will challenge your self-control and test your faith. Rely on God's strength to enable you to fast and to seek His face.

December 12
THE ABSOLUTE FAST

"Then Esther sent this reply to Mordecai: 'Go, gather together all the Jews who are in Susa, and fast for me. Do not eat or drink for three days, night or day. I and my maids will fast as you do. When this is done, I will go to the king, even though it is against the law. And if I perish, I perish.'" Esth 4:15-16 (NIV)

There are times when God will lead you into an absolute fast. This type of fast is characterized by abstaining from food and drink for a set amount of time. You have to be very careful with this kind of fast and make certain that God has called you to it. Going any extended length of time without water can be detrimental to your health. Be certain that God has called you into this type fast.

Esther sensed the heaviness of the reality of her circumstances and was willing to invite her people to fast for her. She committed to a three day absolute fast along with them in preparation for standing before the king. Esther was willing to put her life at risk by standing before the king. Her boldness was fueled by the abiding connection she had with God through the spiritual discipline of fasting.

Whenever you are facing a major decision or going through a season of uncertainty, consider inviting a few godly people to fast for you and to seek God on your behalf. Fasting and prayer go together. You can pray and not fast, but you cannot fast without praying if it is to be a biblical fast. God calls you to a fast so that you can passionately pursue Him and place your dependency upon Him.

Do you need to hear from God concerning a situation you are facing? Are you in need of God's wisdom and guidance? God may call you to an absolute fast to remove your dependency upon other things and to enable you to focus your attention on His provision.

December 13
PARTIAL FAST

"At that time I, Daniel, mourned for three weeks. I ate no choice food; no meat or wine touched my lips; and I used no lotions at all until the three weeks were over." Dan 10:2-3 (NIV)

The most common fast among believers is the partial fast. You choose to eliminate certain foods from your diet for a specific time in order to draw near to God. You can choose to give up all types of meat and only eat vegetables for a season. When you participate in a partial fast, you continue to drink fluids and you may also choose to eat certain foods.

A partial fast could include suspending the consumption of coffee for a specified period of time. It could be a choice to abstain from desserts and other sweets for a season in order to seek God.

Daniel chose to go on a partial fast for twenty-one days. God honored his commitment and gave Daniel a special revelation. Daniel was known for drawing near to God and seeking God's agenda. The Lord honored Daniel's obedience and devotion.

You may want to consider embracing a partial fast where you eat the evening meal and then drink only water and juice until the following evening meal twenty-four hours later. You can spend breakfast and lunch praying and reading the Bible. Instead of feasting on food during those two meals, you can maximize that time by feasting on God's Word.

As you fast, consider journaling your journey with God. Write down or type what God shows you during the fast. Be sensitive to God's activity and take note of what you are sensing from God. He may give you a specific verse from the Bible to meditate on. God may identify a relationship in your life that needs attention.

December 14
THE SEED OF DOUBT

"Now the serpent was more crafty than any of the wild animals the LORD God had made. He said to the woman, 'Did God really say, You must not eat from any tree in the garden?'" Gen 3:1 (NIV)

We combat three enemies in this life: Satan, the world, and the flesh. In his pride and rebellion, Lucifer sought to dethrone God (Isaiah 14:12-14). In response, God de-heavened Lucifer and one-third of the angels fell with him (Rev. 12:4). He showed up in the garden in the form of a serpent to tempt Eve. Through temptation, the enemy sought to get Eve to meet a legitimate need in an illegitimate way. The serpent caused Eve to doubt God's Word. Instead of doing life God's way and obeying God's Word, Eve yielded to the promptings of the enemy and disobeyed God.

Satan is still active in our world today. Through temptation, he seeks to get believers to meet their legitimate needs in illegitimate ways. The enemy tries to get children of God to take short cuts and to doubt God's Word. God's way is always the best way, yet the enemy will put seeds of doubt into the minds of believers.

The seed of doubt will cause you to question God's Word and to be suspect of God's plan. You do not have to sacrifice your devotion to the Lord by watering the seeds the devil has sown. Your protection from the attacks of the enemy is the sword of the Spirit, which is the Word of God. Your lifeline is God's holy Word. You do not have to live in defeat. You do not have to operate in the erosive terrain of doubt.

Fix your eyes on Jesus. Look to Him and put your confidence in His completed work on the cross. You are a child of the King! Your victory has been won by the death, burial, and resurrection of Jesus. Replace those seeds of doubt with faith!

December 15
THE FALL OF MAN

"When the woman saw that the fruit of the tree was good for food and pleasing to the eye, and also desirable for gaining wisdom, she took some and ate it. She also gave some to her husband, who was with her, and he ate it. Then the eyes of both of them were opened, and they realized they were naked; so they sewed fig leaves together and made coverings for themselves." Gen 3:6-7 (NIV)

Sin has consequences. When Eve chose to doubt God's Word and to succumb to the temptation presented by the serpent, she fell from her position of being right with God. For a moment, Eve was in her fallen state and Adam was not. Yet, when Eve gave Adam the fruit of the tree to eat, he ate it without reservation. Adam knew better. God had already communicated with Adam personally about the forbidden fruit (Gen. 2:16-17). Adam failed to protect himself and Eve from the devastation produced by their disobedience. It makes you wonder if Adam made God's revelation clear to Eve.

Adam and Eve recognized their nakedness and sought to cover up their shame. Their relationship with God and their relationship with each other shifted into the reality of their fallen state. Their sin had immediate and direct consequences that affected not only them, but also every generation since their fall.

You can trace the root of your sin throughout your family tree all the way back to Adam and Eve. The sin nature you combat today is a direct result of the sin nature you inherited from Adam and Eve. Their struggle is now your struggle. Their battle is now your battle.

Attempting to cover your own shame and sin would be considered futile. In and of yourself, you do not have the capacity to provide the covering and cleansing necessary to be in right standing with God. Praise God that He was willing to come to our rescue!

December 16
WHERE ARE YOU?

"Then the man and his wife heard the sound of the LORD God as he was walking in the garden in the cool of the day, and they hid from the LORD God among the trees of the garden. But the LORD God called to the man, 'Where are you?'" Gen 3:8-9 (NIV)

God cares about you personally and He cares about where you are spiritually. Your condition matters to Him. Throughout the Bible, the thread of God's redeeming love can be traced. His love for you has no limits. God created you so that you can know Him personally and make His love known globally.

Adam and Eve rebelled against God and received immediate consequences. Their eyes were opened to recognize their nakedness and their fellowship with God was inhibited. Their sin hindered their unbroken communion with God. The poison of sin had tainted their spiritual condition.

Our God is compassionate. The depth of His love is evidenced as He pursues Adam with a personal question, "Where are you?" Of course, God knew where Adam was both physically and spiritually. His question was not to aid in locating Adam's whereabouts in the garden. God asked the probing question to get Adam to assess his personal spiritual condition. God's question was a question of compassion.

God could have left Adam and Eve to their own demise. God could have given them an extended silent treatment. Yet, God made the first move toward reconciliation. God went first to restore the fractured relationship.

Where are you? How is your love relationship with the Lord? Have you drifted in your daily devotion and intimacy with Jesus? Assess your current spiritual condition. Repent of anything that has hindered your fellowship with the Lord and return to your first love. Enjoy unbroken fellowship with the One who died to give you life eternal and complete.

December 17
THE RIGHTEOUSNESS OF CHRIST

"Consequently, just as the result of one trespass was condemnation for all men, so also the result of one act of righteousness was justification that brings life for all men. For just as through the disobedience of the one man the many were made sinners, so also through the obedience of the one man the many will be made righteous." Romans 5:18-19 (NIV)

How would God reverse the curse sin produced? What would God do to restore fallen humanity? The most incredible display of unconditional love became God's response to man's sin. God provided for the removal of our sin through the sacrifice of His only Son. God allowed Jesus to pay our sin debt in full and to purchase our salvation. The shedding of blood was essential for the forgiveness of our sin.

God chose to sacrifice an animal to provide garments of skin for Adam and Eve after their fall (Gen. 3:21). God took the initiative to reconcile and to restore them through the shedding of blood. Adam and Eve still had to face the natural consequences of their sin. They were still banished from the garden and Adam had to work the ground (Gen. 3:23).

Through Adam's sin, condemnation came to us all. As a result, we are born in sin and inherit the sin nature. However, through the obedience of Jesus on the cross, we are made righteous. Upon our trusting in Jesus alone for salvation, we receive the imputed righteousness of Christ. We are justified through faith, receive peace from God, and gain access into His grace (Rom. 5:1-2). The righteousness of Christ is deposited into our account. We are reconciled to God through the completed work of Jesus on the cross. Jesus paid it all!

December 18
PRAYING IN FAITH

"At the time of sacrifice, the prophet Elijah stepped forward and prayed: 'O LORD, God of Abraham, Isaac and Israel, let it be known today that you are God in Israel and that I am your servant and have done all these things at your command. Answer me, O LORD, answer me, so these people will know that you, O LORD, are God, and that you are turning their hearts back again.'" 1 Kings 18:36-37 (NIV)

Elijah prayed a bold prayer and experienced the power of God. He had challenged the four hundred and fifty prophets of Baal and the four hundred prophets of Asherah to a showdown on Mount Carmel. The prophets called on the name of Baal from morning till noon and received no response. However, Elijah had the sacrifice drenched in water and then he stepped forward to call on God. The power of God fell and consumed the sacrifice, the wood, the stones, the soil, and the water in the trench.

Elijah prayed to God in faith and experienced a demonstration of God's power. The people saw this and fell prostrate to the ground and exclaimed, "The Lord, he is God!" This was truly a mountaintop experience that portrayed the effectiveness of praying in faith. God answers prayer!

What are you currently combating? What is perplexing you? Have you considered taking that burden to the Lord in prayer? You know that God is able to consume a water-soaked sacrifice. You know that God can cause fire to fall at a moment's notice. There's nothing beyond God's reach.

Do you believe that God will do what He says He will do? Do you believe that God is able to deliver you through your circumstances? God is waiting for you to take Him at His Word and to entrust your life to His care. You will never face anything that God cannot handle. God will work everything together for your good and for His glory!

December 19
JOINING GOD'S JOURNEY

"The angel of the LORD came back a second time and touched him and said, 'Get up and eat, for the journey is too much for you.' So he got up and ate and drank. Strengthened by that food, he traveled forty days and forty nights until he reached Horeb, the mountain of God." 1 Kings 19:7-8 (NIV)

Elijah had experienced the power of God on Mount Carmel and now he is running for his life from the pursuit of wicked Jezebel. Elijah was emotionally and physically exhausted and reached a low point personally. He was so desperate that he prayed that he might die. Elijah was so low that he felt that death was his only source of relief.

God met Elijah at his point of need and provided rest and refreshment. Elijah was strengthened by the provision of God and traveled forty days and forty nights. God was positioning Elijah for a blessing on Horeb, the mountain of God.

The journey God has for you is too much for you. God never intended for you to fulfill His will in your own strength. God always builds your character to match His assignment and God always supplies everything you need for the journey. You cannot accomplish the mission God has for you without God's enablement. Your personal energy will not suffice.

Don't get so focused on the destination that you miss what God wants to do along the journey He has for you. Rest and refreshment are vital components in His journey. Every moment matters!

Slow down. Reflect on what God has done to bring you this far in the journey. God is not through with you. Your life is not over. God has more in store for you. Enjoy His rest and be refreshed by His presence. Spend some time in prayer acknowledging your dependency upon God. Allow Him to meet you at your point of need.

December 20
MORE THAN LISTENING

"Do not merely listen to the word, and so deceive yourselves. Do what it says." James 1:22 (NIV)

God's will involves listening. God speaks to us through the Bible. As you read the Bible, you read God's revelation. God's will is that you obey His Word. God also speaks through prayer. As you connect with God through prayer, He reveals His will to you. In order to hear God's voice, you must listen with expectation and anticipation of God's revelation. You learn to recognize God's voice as you walk with God.

- *"When he has brought out all his own, he goes on ahead of them, and his sheep follow him because they know his voice."* John 10:4 (NIV)
- *"My sheep listen to my voice; I know them, and they follow me."* John 10:27 (NIV)

Listening to God's Word is not enough. You must do what it says. Put God's Word into practice by obeying what God reveals to you. Sometimes God will wait for you to obey what He has already revealed to you before unveiling His next layer of revelation. Are you obeying what God has already revealed to you?

Obey what you know. As you obey, God will show you more and more of His way.

December 21
THE ULTIMATE GIFT

"For God so loved the world that he gave his one and only Son, that whoever believes in him shall not perish but have eternal life." John 3:16 (NIV)

Travel down memory lane with me for a moment. Think about your Christmas experiences as a child. What do you remember as the most meaningful gift you received? Can you still feel the excitement of the anticipation of the gift? That experience is locked in your memory because it was special to you.

The ultimate gift in this life is the gift of eternal life. There is no greater gift and there is no greater demonstration of God's love. The moment you recognized your sin and accepted God's provision for your forgiveness through your faith in Jesus, you received the ultimate gift. Let me ask you a question. Do you know that God is for you?

- *"But God demonstrates his own love for us in this: While we were still sinners, Christ died for us." Romans 5:8 (NIV)*
- *"For the wages of sin is death, but the gift of God is eternal life in Christ Jesus our Lord." Romans 6:23 (NIV)*

Consider the individuals currently in your sphere of influence. Have they received the ultimate gift? Have you shared your salvation story with them? Are you willing to be used of God to make Jesus known to those God places in your path? God still uses human instrumentality in the redemptive process. Once you have received the ultimate gift, you can share that gift with others.

December 22
THE GOD FACTOR

"But the angel said to her, 'Do not be afraid, Mary, you have found favor with God. You will be with child and give birth to a son, and you are to give him the name Jesus.'" Luke 1:30-31 (NIV)

God chooses ordinary people to accomplish the extraordinary. Mary was just a teenager when she encountered the angel of the Lord. You can imagine the fear that gripped her when she had this special visitation. The angel comforted Mary and assured her that she had found favor with God. Then he announced that she would be with child and give birth to a son. Mary was instructed that she was to give him the name Jesus.

Her response was very practical. Mary wanted to know how this could possibly be a reality since she was a virgin. She was thinking in practical and human terms. This conception would not be possible without the God factor.

When you factor in the work of God and the will of God, you come to recognize that nothing is impossible with God. The angel let Mary know that the Holy Spirit would come upon her (Luke 1:35). Mary was soon found to be with child through the Holy Spirit (Mt. 1:18).

What is the God factor? The activity of God through ordinary people to accomplish the extraordinary is the God factor. God will accomplish His will in His timing regardless of the obstacles that seem to surface. God is not limited by our limitations. God is not stifled by our deficiencies. God's agenda will prevail. Will you participate with God in His activity? Are you willing to consider the God factor when assessing your current circumstances?

Don't underestimate the power of God. There is nothing beyond God's reach and there is nothing impossible with God.

December 23
Available for God's Use

"'I am the Lord's servant,' Mary answered. 'May it be to me as you have said.' Then the angel left her." Luke 1:38 (NIV)

Why did God choose Mary to give birth to the Son of God? In His perfect wisdom, God chose Mary because He knew she would willingly make herself available for His use. Mary affirmed her availability by saying, "I am the Lord's servant." She honored God by her posture of availability and humility. She demonstrated such a beautiful portrait of being receptive and responsive to God's will. Mary declared, "May it be to me as you have said." In other words, she was acknowledging that she belonged to God for His glory.

God uses people who are available. What is your level of availability for God's use? Often our lives become so cluttered and overextended, that there's little room for availability. Can you relate? God wants to use you. God is more concerned about your availability than your ability. In humility, make yourself available for God's use. Remember that you were made by God to accomplish His plan. God's plan includes you and your willingness to be His instrument.

What needs to change in your life? Surrender everything in your life to the Lord's control. Give Him free reign in your life. Make the necessary adjustments in your daily schedule to make room for God. Embrace a posture of humility to allow God to have His way in your life. Be receptive to God's agenda and respond to God's invitation to join Him. He loves you so much.

Your availability matters to God. Would you be willing to say, "Lord, I'm Yours?"

December 24
CELEBRATING GOD'S FAITHFULNESS

"And Mary said: 'My soul glorifies the Lord and my spirit rejoices in God my Savior, for he has been mindful of the humble state of his servant. From now on all generations will call me blessed, for the Mighty One has done great things for me--holy is his name.'" Luke 1:46-49 (NIV)

Life moves so quickly that it is sometimes a challenge to slow down long enough to count our blessings. God has lavished us with His love and unleashed His bounty of blessings in our lives. We are so fortunate to be alive and reconciled to God through Christ. Our new identity in Christ is eternally secure. We have instant access to the throne room of God through prayer. The Holy Spirit is living inside of us and Jesus is at the right hand of the Father interceding for us. We have been given every spiritual blessing in Christ. Jesus has given us eternal life and life to the full.

Mary was so overwhelmed by the favor of God in being chosen to bear the Son of God. She celebrated God's faithfulness by glorifying the Lord and rejoicing in God as her Savior. Mary affirmed God's attentiveness to her humble state and praised God for the blessings He bestowed upon her. With deep gratitude, Mary expressed her appreciation to God through song. She acknowledged the great things the Mighty One had done for her.

Have you had that kind of experience where you began singing praise to God for all that He has done for you? You may want to carve out a few moments to write or type a response of praise to God for all that He has done for you. Express your gratitude to God for His faithfulness in your life. He will continue to see you through. Remember, you are the apple of His eye!

December 25
MIRACLE IN THE MANGER

"While they were there, the time came for the baby to be born, and she gave birth to her firstborn, a son. She wrapped him in cloths and placed him in a manger, because there was no room for them in the inn." Luke 2:6-7 (NIV)

What does Christmas mean to you? What will you experience on this special day? Perhaps this will be a busy day for you as you make your rounds to connect with family. Or maybe for you it is a quiet day with minimal activity. Whether the pace is intense or tranquil, there is a miracle in the manger.

When you contemplate the vastness of God's love, you have to consider the decision God made to take on human form and to dwell among us. Mary wrapped the Son of God in cloths and placed Him in a manger. Can you imagine the Creator of the universe being place in a feeding trough? The One who could have created a castle for that moment, chose to be placed in a manger.

The miracle of the manger is that God chose to come to our rescue. God was willing to become like us so that we could become like Him. God orchestrated our reconciliation. Our transformation was initiated and implemented by God and for God.

Will you make room for Jesus in your life? Will you allow Him to be evident in your life as your Savior and Lord? He saved you so that you can present the miracle of the manger to those who are not yet connected to Christ. Jesus provided the miracle of your transformation so that you can join Him in providing that miracle to a dark and decaying world.

December 26
POSITIONING FOR THE FUTURE

"When Joseph and Mary had done everything required by the Law of the Lord, they returned to Galilee to their own town of Nazareth. And the child grew and became strong; he was filled with wisdom, and the grace of God was upon him." Luke 2:39-40 (NIV)

Can you name the people God used to position you for the future you are now in? Think about their investment in your life. Weigh their deposits of encouragement, feedback, and godly counsel. You are a product of the decisions you have made over your lifetime and a product of God's grace through others in your life.

God chose to use Joseph and Mary to position Jesus for the future God had for Him. They obeyed the law and they obeyed God. They returned to their own town and were faithful in parenting Jesus. Jesus grew, became strong, and was filled with wisdom. God's grace was upon Him. God could have positioned Jesus for the future without Joseph and Mary, yet He chose to use human instrumentality.

Just as God has brought people into your life to position you for the future, God wants to use you to help others. Are you available to be used of God to position others for the future? God wants to touch others through your life. Your personal testimony of God's faithfulness and your daily walk with Jesus are vital components for being used of God to impact the lives of others.

You can make an immediate difference as well as an eternal difference in the lives of those God brings into your path. God has blessed you with every spiritual blessing in Christ so that you can be a blessing to others. Will you make yourself available for God's use?

December 27
MY FATHER'S BUSINESS

"'Why were you searching for me?' he asked. 'Didn't you know I had to be in my Father's house?'" Luke 2:49 (NIV)

Diffused light does not have much power to impact the environment it is placed in, but focused light can cut steel. Your life is most powerful when it is most focused. Our proclivity is to drift into a fragmented lifestyle where we are trying to divert our energy into too many tasks. It is so easy to dilute our impact by seeking to keep too many plates spinning at a given time. We become generalist instead of specialists.

Jesus lived a focused life. He was laser focused on being about His Father's business. God's agenda was Jesus' top priority. Even at age twelve Jesus affirmed His devotion to God's will. Nothing was more important to Jesus than operating every moment in the center of God's will. Jesus was committed to fulfilling God's plan. Shortly after His baptism at age thirty, Jesus declared that He had come down from heaven not to do His will but to do the will of His Father.

Have you oriented your life to the Father's will? Have you made necessary adjustments in your life to focus on living in the center of God's will? You will have competing agendas, countless opportunities to drift, and a persistent gravitational pull from the enemy to downplay the urgency of God's agenda. The world, the flesh, and the Devil will seek to capture your devotion. Your life will be tugged from various directions in order to get you off mission.

Don't give in to the temptation to become fragmented. Don't dilute your devotion. Renew your commitment to serve God and to obey His Word. God's will is for you to be fully yielded and fully surrendered to His prompting.

December 28
PASSION FOR HIS PRESENCE

"Seek the LORD while he may be found; call on him while he is near." Isaiah 55:6 (NIV)

What kind of person does God use? What are the characteristics that are evident in the person God uses? God uses the person who has a passion for His presence. One of the characteristics evident in the person God uses is passion. Passion is more than a feeling. Passion is the divine energy from God to accomplish His will His way.

What are you passionate about? What makes you come alive? You may be passionate about your career, your car, your family, or your finances. You may be passionate about your position, prestige, pleasure, or possessions. You can be passionately devoted to things that are good and yet miss God's best for you. God has a plan for your life and you will need His passion to accomplish His plan.

God uses the person who is passionate in the pursuit of God's presence. God wants you to seek Him diligently and passionately. God wants you to call on Him while He is near. Don't allow your passion for temporal things to rob your passion for that which is eternal.

- *"So we fix our eyes not on what is seen, but on what is unseen. For what is seen is temporary, but what is unseen is eternal."* 2 Cor 4:18 (NIV)
- *"Since, then, you have been raised with Christ, set your hearts on things above, where Christ is seated at the right hand of God. Set your minds on things above, not on earthly things. For you died, and your life is now hidden with Christ in God."* Col 3:1-3 (NIV)

God wants to be sought. Draw near to God and He will draw near to you (James 4:8). Ask God to restore your passion for His presence. Confess anything in your life that has diluted your devotion. Return to your first love!

December 29
DEEP CRAVING TO REACH THE LOST

"I pray that you may be active in sharing your faith, so that you will have a full understanding of every good thing we have in Christ." Philem 1:6 (NIV)

God uses the person who embodies a deep craving for the lost. It is possible to live your life each day and become so consumed with your own life that you totally bypass the reality of lost people. You can become so fixated on meeting your own needs that you overlook the glaring reality that lost people go to hell.

Only those who have a saving relationship with Jesus Christ will go to heaven. Hell is real and the path leading there is broad. Heaven is real and the path that leads there is very narrow. As a child of God, you know the way for a person to get to heaven and have eternal life. You know that Jesus is the only way (John 14:6).

Now that you know Jesus personally, be active in sharing your faith with others. You may be the only Jesus others see. You may be their only hope. Don't conceal what God has done for you by providing you with the gift of eternal life by His grace and through faith in Jesus. Reveal the Good News of Jesus to the world beginning with the next person God brings into your path.

Be sensitive to opportunities that God presents you with today. Seize the moment to make Jesus known. Actively share your faith so that those who know you, but don't know Christ, will come to know Christ because they know you!

December 30
DOWN-TO-EARTH HUMILITY

"Do nothing out of selfish ambition or vain conceit, but in humility consider others better than yourselves." Phil 2:3 (NIV)

How do you view yourself? Your answer to that question provides insight into your understanding of humility. It is possible to have an inflated view of yourself. Paul addressed this concept by writing, "For by the grace given me I say to every one of you: Do not think of yourself more highly than you ought, but rather think of yourself with sober judgment, in accordance with the measure of faith God has given you" (Romans 12:3 NIV). To use sober judgment is to view yourself accurately. Begin to see yourself as God sees you. In humility, embrace your dependency upon God and your new identity in Christ.

How do you view others? When you examine the life of Jesus, you will notice that His life was about others. Jesus honored God by serving others. Jesus did not neglect Himself, but He put the needs of others before His own. He lived to benefit others. Jesus valued people and loved them unconditionally. His atoning work on the cross is the ultimate demonstration of the value He placed on others

Exhibit down-to-earth humility by embracing a proper view of yourself in light of what God says about you. Display a lifestyle of placing the same value on others that Jesus does. Begin to view others through the lens of the finished work of Christ on the cross. Jesus has established your value and the value of others through His redeeming love. In humility, reciprocate that same value and that same love to those God brings into your path.

December 31
BROKENNESS

"You do not delight in sacrifice, or I would bring it; you do not take pleasure in burnt offerings. The sacrifices of God are a broken spirit; a broken and contrite heart, O God, you will not despise." Psalm 51:16-17 (NIV)

On the final day of the year, let's explore what moves the heart of God. You have had 365 days to allow God to use you for His glory. You have experienced the ups and downs of living in a fallen world. Each day was filled with challenges and opportunities. Each day presented you with decisions to make and answers to seek. The year may have tested your faith and strengthened your resolve. What did you learn about moving the heart of God?

David clarifies how God desires for His children to respond to Him. Sacrifice and burnt offerings are insufficient. External religion will not move the heart of God. God delights in His children exhibiting genuine brokenness. When we come before God broken over our sin and desperate for His approval, we move His heart. God desires that we seek Him in humility and brokenness. We do not impress God with our external righteousness and religion. God examines the heart to test our motives. God is moved when we acknowledge our dependency upon Him.

Have you been broken before the Lord lately? Have you had a contrite heart? David poured out his soul in anguish before God over the sin in his own life. Personal responsibility for our personal sin will be evidenced by our personal brokenness before the Lord. God's compassion will be unleashed as you pour out your soul before Him in prayer. Pray that God will keep you broken before Him as you live in this fallen world. We need Him every minute of every hour of every day. Confess all known sin and allow God to prepare you for this New Year. Release the past and embrace the future God has for you!

NOTES

NOTES

NOTES

NOTES

NOTES

NOTES

NOTES

NOTES

NOTES